Isabel Allende

Twayne's World Authors Series

TWAS 893

ISABEL ALLENDE
William C. Gordon

Isabel Allende

Linda Gould Levine

Montclair State University

Twayne Publishers
New York

Twayne's World Authors Series No. 893

Isabel Allende
Linda Gould Levine

Twayne Publishers
300 Park Avenue South
New York, NY 10010

Library of Congress Cataloging-in-Publication Data

Levine, Linda Gould.
    Isabel Allende / Linda Gould Levine.
      p.   cm. — (Twayne's world authors series ; TWAS 893)
    Includes bibliographical references and index.
    ISBN 0-8057-1689-0 (alk. paper)
      1. Allende, Isabel—Criticism and interpretation.I. Title.
II. Series.
PQ8098.1.L54 Z72 2002
863'.64—dc21   2001008661

This paper meets the requirements of ANSI/NISO Z3948-1992 (Permanence of Paper).

10 9 8 7 6 5

Printed in the United States of America

*For my mother, Edna Gould, my own Scheherazade,
who told me wonderful stories while I was growing up.*

Contents

Preface

Isabel Allende is the most acclaimed woman writer of Latin America. She has such a large readership that her fame rivals that of Nobel Prize Laureate Gabriel García Márquez. To label her exclusively as a Latin American woman writer, however, is to encase her in a category that her life and work far surpass. She is read throughout the world, and her books have been best sellers in the United States, Latin America, Europe, and Australia. She has resided in the United States since 1988, and her fiction reflects her deep interest in both North and South American culture. A full-length study of her work in the Twayne World Authors Series bears proper tribute to a writer whose contributions to both contemporary Latin American literature and world literature have resulted in countless international prizes and accolades. While some critics have consistently maintained that quality writing and mass appeal are incompatible, this volume demonstrates the contrary; it pays particular attention to Allende's tremendous skill in writing well-crafted fiction that entertains her public while informing them about important historical events and suggesting an agenda of social and political change.

The process of reading and interpreting Isabel Allende for this volume has posed numerous challenges and delights. Because Allende makes no apologies for being a feminist and for infusing her novels with a feminist agenda, my analyses have necessarily—and happily—relied on feminist literary criticism. This approach informs much of my discussion of such aspects as sexuality, the configuration of gendered identity, narrative voice, literary genre, and literary models. However, it is impossible to read Allende and use only one method of criticism. Allende's fiction continually combines such diverse genres as the historical novel, the picaresque novel, the bildungsroman or novel of development, testimonial fiction, historical romance, and the adventure story, creating in the process a hybrid genre. Thus, an analysis of her fiction also requires attention to this particular narrative blend and its relation to the ideological content of her writing.

Allende is an extensive and exhaustive researcher. From her first novel to her last one, her plots are enriched with solid historical data and countless sociological insights that are the product of her careful investigation. I have diligently followed her trail and read the background material that I suspected she herself had read while researching her novels. In this way, the process of analyzing Allende converts the literary critic into an amateur sociologist, historian, and cultural critic, as topics as diverse as Chilean history of the nineteenth and twentieth centuries, the guerrilla movement in Venezuela, the Vietnam War, Latin American popular culture, the California gold rush, the Chinese prostitution trade in nineteenth-century America, the culture of romance, and the creation of myths form an intricate part of her novels. My approach has consistently been to examine the way in which Allende weaves these diverse topics into her narrative world and blends fictional events with historical, cultural, or mythical frames of reference, thus breaking down the barriers that separate different disciplines.

While I have borrowed extensively from critics who have written about Allende, the most significant body of research on her writing is devoted to her early novels. I have found of particular value a collection of interviews published in 1999 and edited by John Rodden, *Conversations with Isabel Allende*. This book contains more than 30 interviews that span a 10-year period and provide innumerable insights into Allende the writer and Allende the person. The penetrating questions asked by her interviewers bring forth the full range of Allende's concerns and are a continual point of reference in my analysis of her fiction. While the majority of these interviews were previously published in journals and magazines, I have cited exclusively from Rodden's edition to provide easy access for the reader. Celia Correas Zapata's excellent book of combined literary analysis and conversations with the author—*Isabel Allende: vida y espíritus* (Isabel Allende: Life and Spirits)—has also been an invaluable guide. At present, there is no book available in English that covers the full range of Allende's fiction; to this degree, the Twayne volume expands the current body of scholarship on this major international writer.

Allende's works are all readily available in English translation. While *The House of the Spirits* was translated by Magda Bogin and published in English three years after the publication of the novel in Spanish, every one of Allende's works since then has been translated by Margaret Sayers Peden and is usually published within two years of the original Spanish version. Peden's translations are graceful and eloquent and have been a pleasure to use in this volume. There exist numerous editions of Allende's translations; I list in the bibliography the edition of the original translation as well as the editions that I cite in this study.

In accordance with the Twayne format, this volume includes an introductory biographical chapter and separate chapters devoted to Allende's major works of fiction and to her memoir, *Paula*. I also include an interview that I conducted with the author in August 2000. During the course of our telephone exchange, and with my manuscript only weeks away from completion, Allende informed me that she had just finished writing *Portrait in Sepia*. While I initially shuddered contemplating that my book was out of date before it was even published, Allende, with characteristic generosity and speed, sent me a copy of the novel so I could frame some comments about it in this volume. If chapter 9 seems brief and inconclusive, I ask the reader's indulgence; time did not allow for a more extensive analysis of this delightful and important novel. While my interview with the author has that special Allende flavor of flowing easily between the personal and the literary, its emphasis on her 1999 novel, *Daughter of Fortune,* as well as the insights she provides about *Portrait in Sepia* and her future writing projects, make it a particularly original contribution to the extensive body of Isabel Allende interviews.

Finally, I hope this volume contributes in some small measure to the reader's understanding of a complex, serious, funny, and thoughtful writer whose concerns are universal and whose narrative style combines an emphasis on the rich plots typical of the nineteenth century and the sense of ambiguity more characteristic of twentieth-century fiction. I know that literary criticism can often be counterproductive; instead of helping the reader appreciate the subtleties of the text, it can kill the text. I hope that my analyses do not detract from the sheer pleasure of reading Isabel Allende, but instead enrich the reader's experience of entering her narrative world.

Acknowledgment

When David William Foster of Arizona State University wrote me a letter some four years ago asking me to write the Twayne volume on Isabel Allende, I was delighted. I first met Isabel Allende shortly after the publication of the Spanish version of *The House of the Spirits* and was greatly impressed by her commitment to social justice and her wonderfully rich narrative style. In the spring of 1985, JoAnne Engelbert and I invited her to be a visiting professor at Montclair State University, and she generously accepted. Watching Isabel Allende teach her course on Latin American culture and her own fiction was like watching a master magician at work. She used every creative device possible to provide students with access to the complex world of literature, even asking them to act out scenes from her novel. The results were not only hilarious, but also a fascinating learning experience for all of us who were there, especially my dear friend and colleague, JoAnne Engelbert, who played the part of Clara's dog, Barrabás. My involvement with Allende's fiction has been a constant since that time, and I am grateful to David Foster for giving me the opportunity to write this book in the Twayne series. I am also greatly indebted to Isabel Allende herself for her continual and always rapid assistance, generosity, and good humor in helping me complete this project. Her assistant, Martha Gutiérrez, deserves a special note of thanks for all her acts of kindness and her invaluable help.

On the home front, there are so many people I want to thank who have helped me during the last four years. They are my version of Allende's spirits who bring inspiration. My colleagues, JoAnne Engelbert, David Gies, Lynn McGovern-Waite, Jean Modig, Gisela Norat, and Helga Barkemeyer were extremely helpful in providing me with bibliographies, addresses, and early insights into Allende. My former students, Yonsoo Kim and Susan Polise, were thorough research assistants who knew just where to go on the internet to find the information I needed. Susan deserves an extra thanks for all her tremendous support during the final weeks. Carmen Alverio, my colleague and delightful friend, was a meticulous reader of the early chapters of the manuscript. Rogelio Zapata, the walking encyclopedia of the Spanish/Italian Department at Montclair State and my literary soul mate, was consistently there to answer all questions, suggest books and references, read the manuscript, and add countless insights. Roger Tovar, my former student, deserves a very special thanks for being the first reader of this manuscript. His very thoughtful comments on each chapter helped me clarify confusing points, obliged me to rethink difficult concepts, and made me believe that my words were indeed readable.

I could not have finished this book without the caring of my special friends who continually cheered me on throughout and especially during the last few months when I needed it the most—Susan Brim, Jan Jaffe, Susan O'Neil, and Marisa Catalina Casey. I especially want to thank Alice Freed for her early morning e-mails of love and support that brightened my day and for her innumerable practical suggestions that always made things seem easier than I thought; Gloria Feiman Waldman for her boundless devotion and invaluable suggestions about translations, interview questions, and all kinds of related anxieties; Joanne Rosen for her constant generosity of spirit; and Ellen Engelson Marson for always reminding me about how happy I would be when I finished the book.

My family deserves my biggest thanks because they lived through this process with me at every step. My sons, Daniel and Andrew, voracious readers and generous souls, were a terrific sounding board. They read parts of my analyses, listened to all my Allende stories, only moaned slightly when I quoted her in every single conversation, and encouraged me from near and far. My mother, Edna Gould, to whom this book is dedicated, has been an incredible friend. Her daily phone calls to inquire about my progress and her interest in reading every Allende novel have made me feel infinitely loved. My husband, Barry, deserves the most special thanks of all. Without him, I suspect my forwarding address would be a rest home for the "literarily" deranged. He not only helped me with a whole range of technological aspects, but more importantly kept me sane by making me laugh, suggesting ways to simplify impossibly convoluted sentences, giving me the space to finish the book, always believing that I would indeed get it done and be normal again, and being the generous and loving person he is.

Finally, I am grateful to Montclair State University for having granted me released time from teaching as well as a sabbatical leave to research and write this book. I am particularly indebted to the staff of Sprague Library and the interlibrary loan department for all their help throughout the years in facilitating my requests.

Chronology

with his left-wing coalition, Unidad Popular (Popular Unity Party).

1970–1975 Works in Chilean television where her humorous programs make her a minor celebrity.

1971 Performance in Santiago of Allende's play, "El embajador."

1973 Miltary coup overthrows Salvador Allende on 11 September. Death of Allende in the presidential palace. Death of Nobel Prize Laureate Pablo Neruda on 23 September. Military junta, under leadership of General Augusto Pinochet, dissolves Congress and suspends civil liberties.

1974 Publishes *Civilice a su troglodita,* a compilation of articles written for *Paula.* Loses her job at *Paula* on political grounds.

1974–1975 Engages in underground political activities to assist victims of persecution.

1975 Frightened by death threats, Allende leaves Chile and goes to live in Caracas, Venezuela. Her family joins her several weeks later.

1975–1984 Writes for the Venezuelan newspaper, *El Nacional.*

1975–1987 Lives in Caracas.

1979–1982 Works as an administrator in a secondary school in Caracas, Colegio Marroco.

1981 On 8 January, begins to write a good-bye letter to her dying grandfather in Santiago. The letter becomes her first novel, *La casa de los espíritus.*

1982 *La casa de los espíritus* is published in Spain.

1983 Receives Best Novel of the Year award in Chile.

1984 Publishes juvenile book, *La gorda de la porcelana.* Publishes *De amor y de sombra.* Receives award for French edition of *La casa de los espíritus.* Receives Author of the Year Award in Germany.

1985 Publication of *The House of the Spirits;* selected for Book-of-the-Month Club. Visiting Professor at Montclair State University, New Jersey (formerly Montclair State College). Receives literary awards in Belgium and Mexico.

1986   Visiting Professor at the University of Virginia. Receives Premio Literario Colima in Mexico. Receives Author of the Year Award in Germany.

1987   Divorces Miguel Frías. Publishes *Eva Luna* and *Of Love and Shadows*. While on a book tour in California, meets San Francisco attorney William Gordon. Moves to San Rafael, California, in December. Receives literary awards in Italy, Portugal, Chile, and Switzerland.

1988   Marries William Gordon and becomes a U.S. resident. Publication of English translation of *Eva Luna*. Returns to Chile to vote in plebiscite. Receives Library Journal's Best Book Award and Before Columbus Foundation Award (USA).

1989   Publication of *Los cuentos de Eva Luna*. Visiting Professor of creative writing at University of California, Berkeley. Named to the Chilean Academy of Letters.

1991   Receives Freedom to Write Pen Club Award. Publication of *The Stories of Eva Luna* and *El plan infinito*. Allende's daughter, Paula, is taken to a Madrid hospital suffering from porphyria and slips into a coma.

1992   Paula dies in Allende's home in California.

1993   Publication of *The Infinite Plan*. World premiere of movie, *The House of the Spirits*. Awarded literary prizes in Italy and England. Receives Brandeis University Major Book Collection Award.

1994   Publication of *Paula* in Spain. Film version of *Of Love and Shadows*. Receives Chile's highest cultural honor, the Condecoración Gabriela Mistral Award.

1995   Publication of English translation, *Paula*. "Listen, Paula," based on Allende's memoir, is broadcast in England.

1996   Named Author of the Year in Los Angeles. Receives Harold Washington Literary Award. Establishes the Isabel Allende Foundation.

1997   Publication of *Afrodita: Cuentos, recetas y otros afrodisíacos*.

1998   Publication of *Aphrodite: A Memoir of the Senses*. Receives literary awards in Italy. Receives the Dorothy and Lillian Gish Award, and the Sara Lee Frontrunner Award (USA).

Chapter One

Weaving Life into Fiction

Isabel Allende's life and fiction form an inextricable bond, woven together with textured strands of love, violence, politics, adventure, and death. Rarely has a contemporary author been so personal and revealing about her life and her creative process; her many interviews, public speaking engagements, and best-selling memoir *Paula* (1994) provide countless insights into a complex writer who has been called the "Latin Scheherazade."[1] Allende relishes nothing more than a good tale; whether the subject is Latin American politics, feminism, aphrodisiacs, or herself and her writing, her stories cast a spell on her reader and audience. A passionate "story-giver" whose lines for book signings—and sometimes napkin signings—wrap around university corridors and bookstores, Allende is also a consummate "story junkie" who continually views life as full of tales waiting to be deciphered and told.[2]

Allende's interviewers are often so seduced by her personal charms that their descriptions of her zany sense of humor, her lack of inhibition, and her exuberance, generosity, and ability to navigate with equal grace the political and the personal create a persona as memorable as those who populate her novels and short stories. In fact, it is not easy to distinguish between Allende and her characters. Her penchant for adventure and risk-taking, her feminist convictions, her belief in the power of the word, and her spiritual view of death evoke familiar shades of her most endearing female characters. Allende herself confesses that reality and fiction are often so merged in her work that she doesn't know where one ends and the other begins. Her unbridled imagination and sense of dramatic exaggeration continually refashion real-life experiences and events, even her own, perhaps because like her character, Eva Luna, she tries to live her life as she "would like it to be, as in a novel."[3] Apparently, many of her readers are equally confused about the dividing line between fact and fiction; when Allende was featured in a book fair in Frankfurt, several people scrutinized her to see if her hair had tinges of green or if she had a finger missing, both of which would have confirmed that she were, indeed, Alba Trueba of *The House of the Spirits*. Despite this blurring

1

between art and life, a formidable portrait of her life emerges from numerous texts that invite the reader on a journey that began in Peru in 1942, when Allende was born.

It is somewhat ironic that Allende's life and last name should be so marked by a father, Tomás Allende, who disappeared from his daughter's life when she was three years old. Her mother, Francisca (Panchita) Llona Barros, raised in a sheltered upper-middle-class Chilean environment, was captivated by the intelligent and worldly Tomás, whose cousin, Salvador Allende, founded Chile's Socialist Party in 1933. Following their marriage, they moved to Lima, where Tomás was secretary of the Chilean embassy. Irascible, extravagant, and shady in his personal dealings, Tomás Allende proved to be a disastrous husband, leading his young wife—the mother of their three small children—to abandon him and return home to Chile. With the assistance of Ramón Huidobro, the consul of Chile in Peru, who would later become her life-long companion and Allende's surrogate father (affectionately called Tío Ramón), Panchita and her children returned in 1945 to her parents' home in Santiago, where they spent the next eight years.

These were formative years in Allende's life, constituting a rich storehouse of memories, experiences, and relationships that are fictionalized in her best-selling first novel, *La casa de los espíritus* (1982) (*The House of the Spirits,* 1985). Her grandmother, Isabel Barros Moreira—the model for Clara in this novel—was an extraordinary woman who inhabited a space between dreams and reality. She practiced spiritism around a three-legged table and moved small objects through telekinesis, and she also inspired her young namesake with her commitment to justice and truth. Today, more than half a century after her death, she is a marked presence in Allende's life and work, as well as a continually reinvented one, because as the author herself admits, "we all need a grandmother."[4] Allende's grandfather, Agustín Llona Cuevas—the model for Esteban Trueba in *The House of the Spirits*—was a fiercely conservative but tender patriarch who inspired both adoration and a touch of fear in his granddaughter, as well as a deep sense of independence and perfectionism. The house itself was an unusual one, filled with countless books, eccentric uncles, and a basement containing old love letters, photos, and a skeleton from a relative's medical career. In that house, Allende formed a close and insoluble bond with her mother, who has been her trustworthy unofficial editor since she began to publish in 1982.

The years Allende lived in her grandparents' house were a period of intense intellectual and creative development. By her own account, it was not a happy childhood, although she did enjoy "vast intellectual freedom."[5] A solitary child and a voracious reader, she devoured everything from the complete works of Shakespeare to Freud to the Marquis de Sade. Being acutely aware of social injustices from an early age and perceiving herself as an "outcast," (P, 50), she rebelled against her Catholic religious education and nurtured the seeds of an incipient feminism when, at age five, she was first subject to codes for growing up female. Reflecting in 1997 on the four dictates that marked her formative years—"sit with your legs together, stand up straight, don't offer your opinion, and eat like a lady"—Allende humorously concludes that the only one that has been of any value is to stand up straight.[6] The little girl, however, lacking such perspective, felt only rage and anger, feelings that would accompany Isabel Allende throughout much of her adult life as she contemplated the double standard for women and men in her native Chile.

With such a heightened sensitivity and love of books, it is not surprising that from an early age, Allende declared her desire to be a writer—Agatha Christie style—and invented dramatic tales that she told to her terrified brothers, her first audience. Like many of her female characters in future years, she also wrote down the record of her life in a notebook, which became her trusted companion during her adolescence. Her independent nature and willingness to explore beyond the boundaries that circumscribed young girls frequently placed her in difficult situations in school and in social settings. Most notably, when she was eight years old, she was the victim of child seduction, an experience that she banished from her mind until her daughter's illness in 1991 took her on a journey through her past and her memory. While this incident will be examined extensively in chapter 7, it is important to note that flashes of child seduction appear in Allende's early fiction, well before she grappled with the topic on a conscious level.

Allende's adolescence was marked by several moves that were the beginning of the "relentless farewell" that has characterized much of her adult life.[7] When she was 11 years old, her mother decided to join Huidobro in his diplomatic missions as Chilean consul. Following a year in Bolivia, Isabel and her family spent three years in Beirut, Lebanon. There, enrolled in an English school for girls, she "learned the English language and stoicism in the face of adversity" (P, 64) and awakened to the sensuality of the world contained in Tío Ramón's hidden copy of the *Thousand and One Nights.* This text not only spoke to Allende's delight in the senses, but also further nourished her incipient belief in the power of the story and the magical quality of the word, a leitmotiv in all her writings that accounts for much of her acclaim as a first-rate narrator and storyteller. Upon the outbreak of the Suez Canal crisis in June 1958 and with the suspension of classes, Panchita sent her children back to Chile to live with their grandfather while she and Ramón were transferred to Turkey. This separation proved crucial for the future author; on the plane ride home, she wrote her first letter to her mother, a daily practice she still maintains—although now by fax—and that she credits as essential in her formation as a writer.

Allende's return to Chile ushered her into an early adulthood. With the help of extensive tutoring from her grandfather to fill in the gaps of a chaotic education, she graduated from high school with superior grades, enveloped herself in the reading of science fiction, and decided that it was more important to earn a living and be independent than to continue her schooling in the university. Expecting to get married and have children, as was ordained for young women of her social class, further education, with the exception of an aborted secretarial course, seemed superfluous. The many anecdotes she has told and written concerning her first job are now part of the rich Allende folklore. In fact, they could easily form part of a picaresque novel. When she applied for a secretarial position at the United Nations Food and Agricultural Organization, the 17-year-old Allende not only pretended to know the boss to get an interview, but also "composed a letter of love and despair" instead of a business letter when asked to demonstrate job-related skills (*P,* 97). Through her wits and her family connections, she landed the job. Thus began a series of opportunities that, following a successful 15-minute slot on television replacing an ailing commentator, eventually led Allende to a career in journalism and television, and even—just to get the exclusive story—a brief stint as a chorus girl clad in ostrich feathers. Married to engineer Miguel Frías and with a first child by the time she was 21, but also employed full-time, Allende both fulfilled and defied social expectations for women of her class, thus defining her ability to be inside and outside the system at the same time.

During the late 1960s and early 1970s Allende worked on the "periphery of literature" (*P,* 275), simultaneously writing for the woman's magazine *Paula,* whose daring social format allowed her to cast pointed barbs at Chilean machismo; directing the children's magazine *Mapato;* publishing two books for children; authoring two musical comedies, "La balada del medio pelo" (1973 [The parvenu's ballad]) and "Los siete espejos" (1974 [The seven mirrors]), and a play called "El embajador" (1970 [The ambassador]), which enjoyed a successful run in Chilean theaters; and interviewing such eminent figures as the poet, Pablo Neruda, as well as murderers, quasi-saints, prostitutes, and seers. Having injected into her horoscope and lovelorn columns in the 1960s and 1970s so much dramatic improvisation that one of her editors even accused her of "making up [her] interviews, without ever leaving the house" (*P,* 172), Allende still relishes Neruda's pointed advice that she switch from journalism to literature where her innate tendency to fabricate would be an advantage and not a liability. Allende's involvement in journalism and the theater, together with her daily letters to her mother—a form of "private writing"[8] important to the development of many women writers—provided her with a rich background and a fascinating storehouse of human experience that proved invaluable when she began to write her first novel in 1981.

In the early 1970s, Allende also voraciously read feminist texts that were circulating in Chile. Proud to belong to the first generation of women in Chile who were part of the women's liberation movement, Allende has spoken passionately about the influence of feminists Germaine Greer and Simone de Beauvoir on her life and most notably her discovery of Greer's 1970 landmark work, *The Female Eunuch:* "I am a different person since I read Germaine Greer's *The Female Eunuch* because she expressed what I felt with a great deal of humor. All my life I had experienced feelings of anger, impotence, and injustice without knowing why. Suddenly I felt someone understood me and I could finally cope with my emotions. That marked not only my writing but my life" (Allende, 1989, 137). Significantly, while the question of a married woman's right to retain her maiden name resonates more in North American circles than in Latin America, Allende's decision to use her maiden name after marriage greatly contributed in later years to her mystique as an Allende.

During these hectic years when Allende transformed her anger against machismo into humor and was known in Chile as a magazine and television celebrity whose satirical articles in *Paula* on male troglodytes were not taken seriously enough to be considered threatening, her country was in the throes of a vast political and social revolution led by her father's cousin, Salvador Allende, whom Isabel considered an uncle. Allende herself has indicated that she has never belonged to a political party and that she spent many years oblivious to politics. Continually amazed at the highly politicized conversations in her uncle's house during Sunday dinners, her awakening was slow and painful. By her own account, few, in fact, were prepared for the events that would radically transform Chilean life in 1973.

Long considered the Switzerland of Latin America because of its democratic traditions and relative lack of military intervention in affairs of state,[9] Chile's political climate in the decade preceding the 1973 military coup was polarized around two crucial issues: control of the Chilean copper industry—the source of the nation's most valuable export—and agrarian reform. While Christian Democrats under the leadership of Eduardo Frei consistently proposed a platform of reform as a means of dealing with these issues, an alliance of socialists and communists led by the experienced politician and medical doctor, Salvador Allende, ran in the 1964 elections on a revolutionary platform that denounced capitalist and imperialist practices. Although Frei won 56 percent of the vote to Allende's 39 percent, the stage was set for a dramatic three-way election in 1970 that gave a majority vote of 36.3 percent to Salvador Allende, whose combined coalition of communists and socialists constituted the Unidad Popular (Popular Unity Party).

As countless historians have documented, Allende's three-year government, which never enjoyed majority rule but was the first leftist coalition ever elected in Chile, was beset by monumental problems from the start. As a response to the Chilean nationalization of U.S. copper interests and of corporations such as International Telephone and Telegraph (ITT), President Nixon initiated an "invisible blockade" of international magnitude against Chile (Skidmore and Smith, 136). In fact, shortly after Salvador Allende's victory in 1970, President Nixon earmarked $10 million to help terminate Allende's regime.[10] The president of ITT contributed one million dollars alone for the same end (Galeano, 209). Within Chile itself, the Agrarian Reform Institute, charged with providing services to both state-controlled cooperatives and peasants who owned small plots of land, was unable to navigate problematic demands by disgruntled landowners and leftist radicals. Lack of congressional support for legislative reforms, together with sabotage by producers, landowners, and merchants, further created a political and economic climate of divisiveness and soaring inflation by 1973. Nonetheless, Allende's supporters, including most significantly the urban working class, demonstrated their approval in the midterm congressional elections of 1973 that gave the Popular Unity Party 43 percent of the vote. The opposition's failure to produce a substantial enough vote to initiate an impeachment process only served to fuel rightist antigovernment plots that had been brewing since Allende's 1970 victory.

By September 1973—the date Allende set for a national plebiscite on his government—political divisions had become extreme. Several factors intervened, setting the stage for a violent overthrow: a renewed strike of truck owners in July 1973 that impeded food from being delivered to the population; a series of strikes by middle-class professionals; the refusal of Christian Democrats to negotiate with Allende to ameliorate the growing conflicts; the destabilizing tactics of U.S. foreign policy designed to overthrow the Allende government; the intense class divisions that impeded coalitions between the workers movement and other sectors of Chilean society; the lack of significant impact on the Chilean economy from new credits supplied by countries of western Europe and the socialist bloc; conflicts within the Popular Unity Party itself between the more radical revolutionary left and the moderates; and the increased participation of the military in the government, a policy supported by Allende himself to create immediate stability. This policy proved to be a fatal mistake that greatly facilitated the brutal CIA-backed military coup of 11 September 1973, "the most violent military coup in twentieth-century South American history" (Skidmore and Smith, 141). The bombing of the presidential palace and the death of Salvador Allende, followed by the military junta's dissolution of Congress and brutal persecution of students, activists, and the urban working class, overturned Chile's democratic traditions within 24 hours.[11] These traditions were replaced by the iron rule of the army commander-in-chief and minister of defense, General Augusto Pinochet, a former professor of geopolitics, trained in the infamous School of the Americas in Panama.

By her own account, Isabel Allende's life has been definitely marked by the events of 11 September 1973. "I think I have divided my life [into] before and after that day," she has stated. "In that moment, I realized that everything was possible—that violence was a dimension that was always around you."[12] The week before the coup, she had enjoyed lunch with her uncle, who had a "beautiful dream" for Chile, and whom she deeply admired.[13] He was steadfast in his intent not to leave the presidential palace unless the people demanded it. He remained faithful to this pledge up to the end, and, from the palace, he broadcast a final radio message to all Chileans that urged them not to lose "faith in Chile and in its destiny" (*P*, 194). His niece, a journalist, who was aware of the rumors circulating prior to the coup and who did not believe that such an uprising would be possible in Chile, listened to his last words while huddled with a friend in a local school. Thirteen days later, she marched through the streets of Santiago holding red carnations and accompanying Pablo Neruda's casket to its final resting place, shouting with others, "Pablo Neruda! Present, now and forever! . . . *Compañero* Salvador Allende . . . Present, now and forever!" (*P*, 214).

Allende soon became involved in a variety of underground political activities to help the persecuted and their families. Recognizing that "the reign of terror [had] started" and that she could not be "indifferent to [her] surroundings,"[14] she joined the efforts of church-sponsored programs that responded to the crisis by providing food and aid to the needy. She cajoled money out of the president of her husband's company to feed hungry children. She spent hours gathering testimonies of families of the disappeared, taping and interviewing victims, and assisting in the efforts to publicize information in Germany about the disappeared and tortured. She housed the persecuted and transported them to safe asylums in her Citroën with the brightly painted flowers. She listened to stories about children being tortured in front of their parents and carefully documented the horrendous acts of cruelty and the inspirational deeds of courage that she would later summon from memory when she began to write *The House of the Spirits*.

Allende eventually lost her job as director of the children's magazine, and along with others, was fired from *Paula* in 1974, marking the demise of this remarkable magazine and its transformation into "another of the many publications for 'young ladies'."[15] She continued broadcasting her television program until she realized that both she and her last name were being utilized by the military to cultivate the false image of a tolerant regime. She resigned from her position and continued her political work until slowly fear started seizing hold of her. As she herself has recounted, "I left because I could no longer stand the fear. I felt a visceral terror in Chile. It is difficult to talk about that. It is difficult to understand fear when you have not lived it. It is something that transforms us, that takes over completely."[16] Unable to sleep at night, broken out in hives, and terrified by a death threat she received in 1975, she and her husband left Chile in 1975 and moved to Venezuela with their two children, Paula and Nicolás. Taking with her a copy of the complete works of Pablo Neruda—whom she attributes with marking her vision of the world—a handful of dirt, and a forget-me-not to transplant in the tropical climate of her newly adopted land, Allende recalls her exile from Chile as one of tremendous loss, "When I left Chile, after the military coup, I lost in one instant my family, my past, my home."[17]

In later years, Allende would reflect on the danger and risk involved in her clandestine political activities of the 1970s, concluding that she was moved not only by a sense of "compassion for such desperate people," but also by "the irresistible attraction of adventure" (P, 218). While this statement may appear at best brutally honest or at worst overly romanticized, it strikes at the core of Allende's life and fiction. Guided by deep emotions that invite dangerous and impulsive actions of a political and personal nature, Allende has delivered a package handed to her by an unknown individual during the military regime; she has swum with piranhas in the Rio Negro of the Amazon and witnessed the death of a man at her feet;[18] and she has accompanied her daughter, Paula, through a painful year of illness and then death. Her many female protagonists—Alba Trueba, Irene Beltrán, Eva Luna, Carmen Morales, Eliza Sommers, and Aurora del Valle—similarly believe that life is a risky business requiring a daring and adventurous spirit and that individual actions can make a difference.

Allende's early years in exile contained little of that sense of daring. Although her initial sense of isolation and paralysis were gradually replaced by a strong feeling of liberation from the strictures of conservative Chilean society and an intense assimilation of the sensuality and warmth of the Venezuelan people and landscape, her life was radically different from the one she had lived in Chile and certainly much more conventional. Working two shifts as a school administrator in Caracas because she was unable to find a full-time job as a journalist, cut off from her roots and her "personal history,"[19] separated from her extended family, and in the midst of a difficult marital crisis that was only temporarily resolved, she was obliged to put her creativity on the back burner for several years. But the distance and pain of separation from Chile provided fertile terrain for the germination of her first novel, *The House of the Spirits,* which flourished from a letter to her dying grandfather in Chile into a 365-page novel that captures the life of the Trueba–del Valle family from the 1920s to the Chilean military coup in 1973.

Allende has often spoken about her years of exile in Venezuela and their relationship to both her personal growth and the genesis of her first novel. She observes, "If there had been no exile, no pain, no rage built up over all those years far from my country, most likely I would not have written this book, but another" (Allende, 1984, 39). The publication of *The House of the Spirits,* made possible by the Spanish literary agent, Carmen Balcells, launched Allende on a path of stellar success. The prominence of Latin American literature in the early 1980s, the resonance attached to the name "Allende," and the author's skill in telling a story of universal proportions accounted for much of the immediate popularity of this work. The writing of this novel unleashed Allende's creative muse; in the space of the next five years, she published two more novels, *De amor y de sombra* (1984) (*Of Love and Shadows*, 1987), which similarly draws on events that transpired during the Chilean military regime, and *Eva Luna* (1987) (*Eva Luna*, 1988), a novel that pays particular tribute to the author's love of storytelling.

Allende has stated repeatedly that she feels as if she has lived several lives. The events in her life almost exceed the dramatic experiences lived by her characters and stretch the limits of reality, or at least, conventional reality. In 1987, following a divorce from Miguel Frías and while on a two month lecture tour concluding in northern California, Allende met San Francisco lawyer William Gordon, who had received a copy of *Of Love and Shadows* for a fiftieth birthday present. As she has humorously related, she was immediately attracted to this "last heterosexual bachelor in San Francisco" (*P*, 299) and to his extraordinary tale of growing up Anglo in an east Los Angeles barrio; she was also somewhat horrified by his chaotic existence as the single father of a dysfunctional family. After spending several evenings alone with him and deciding, with characteristic resolve, daring, and heightened romanticism, to once again uproot herself, she issued him, express mail from Venezuela, a lengthy contract for living together. He accepted, and they were wed. As she humorously tells it, she "fell in lust" and married the story,[20] and since 1988 Allende has lived in San Rafael, California, where she has written all her other works. These include many of the stories included in *Los cuentos de Eva Luna* (1989) (*The Stories of Eva Luna*, 1991); *El plan infinito* (1991) (*The Infinite Plan*, 1993), a fictionalization of the life of her husband, Gordon, set in California; *Paula* (1994) (*Paula*, 1995), her moving memoir that recounts her daughter's illness and death as well as her own life; *Afrodita: Cuentos, recetas y otros afrodisíacos* (1997) (*Aphrodite: A Memoir of the Senses*, 1998), a delightfully funny as well as useful book on food and aphrodisiacs; *Hija de la fortuna* (1999) (*Daughter of Fortune*, 1999), the story of a young Chilean woman's adventures during the California gold rush; and *Retrato en sepia* (2000) (*Portrait in Sepia*, 2001), a novel that narrates a young woman's search for her past in nineteenth-century Chile and is a bridge between *Daughter of Fortune* and *The House of the Spirits*. Allende has also enjoyed several stints as a visiting professor of literature and creative writing at several institutions in the United States, among them Montclair State University in New Jersey, the University of Virginia, and the University of California, Berkeley.

In 1988, 15 years after the military coup and shortly after her remarriage, Allende returned to Chile for the first time since her exile to cast a vote in the presidential plebiscite that would determine whether Pinochet would serve an eight-year term in a transition to democracy. Months before, she had joined the skillfully organized opposition campaign by sending a videotape to Santiago urging Chileans to vote "no" in the plebiscite. She has movingly related in *Paula* her return to Chile and the enormous difference she experienced between her abrupt and lonely departure from her country in 1975 and her warm return, accompanied by her husband, Gordon, and greeted by fans who had read *The House of the Spirits*. As a result of the negative vote cast for Pinochet, the first national election since Salvador Allende's victory in 1970 was held in Chile in December 1989. Allende returned again to vote in this election that gave a decisive victory to Patricio Aylwin's broad left-center coalition. Her role as commentator and chronicler of her country's history has not only been highlighted in her fiction, but also in her public speaking engagements and a moving article she wrote for the *New York Times* on the arrest of General Pinochet in England in 1998.[21] Despite this involvement, Allende insists that she is not an active participant in Chilean affairs and that she carries in her memory "a personal country, non-existent in reality" (Correas Zapata, 47). Significantly, after more than a decade of writing fiction on topics other than Chile and Chilean history, both appear as major components of *Daughter of Fortune* and *Portrait in Sepia*, creating in the process narratives that may be considered historical novels.

It is impossible, however, to categorize Allende's style of writing with any one label. In consonance with her voracious appetite for life, she feasts eclectically upon such diverse literary models as the family saga, the picaresque novel, testimonial literature, the historical novel, the bildungsroman, and the memoir, creating in the process hybrid texts that resist easy categorization. Regardless of the model, writing for Allende is a very personal affair, as well as one laden with ceremony and spiritual value. In recognition of the success of her first novel, which she began on 8 January, she begins each new book on this date. Surrounded by the photos of her grandmother, Isabel, her mother, Pancha, and her daughter, Paula, she daily lights candles and welcomes the spirits of the book into her room and asks their assistance in helping her write their tale. The rest, she says, is sheer discipline and the solitary but always joyful task of journeying into the dark tunnel of the self to retrieve the pieces of the "huge universal epic from which our collective memory draws its dreams" (Allende, 1992a, 271).

Allende's ultimate goal is "to contribute to the development of a small, spiritual, and happy civilization."[22] If initially this sense of purpose was connected to the complex reality of Latin America, where "words are written with blood,"[23] her entire body of writing encompasses themes that surpass the boundaries of any one continent. Over the years, Allende has offered many reflections on the many reasons why she writes. Most recently, in her foreword to John Rodden's 1999 *Conversations with Isabel Allende,* she framed a complex response that captures different aspects of her personal and literary evolution:

> Writing is a matter of survival: if I don't write I forget, and if I forget it is as if I have not lived. That is one of the main reasons for my writing: to prevent the erosion of time, so that memories will not be blown by the wind. I write to record events and to name each thing. I write for those who want to share the obligation of building a world in which love for our fellow men and love for this beautiful but vulnerable planet will prevail. I write for those who are not pessimists and who believe in their own strength, for those who have the certainty that their struggle for life will defeat all bad omens and preserve hope on earth. But maybe this is too ambitious . . . When I was younger, I thought I wrote only for the sake of those I cared for: the poor, the repressed, the abused, for the growing majority of the afflicted and the distressed of this earth, for those who don't have a voice or those who have been silenced. But now I am more modest. I think of my writing as a humble offering that I put out there with an open heart and a sense of wonder. (Allende, 1999, x)

Allende confesses to having no answers; her goal is to raise questions that make her readers think, that affect their lives, and that alter their perception of reality. To that end, she offers her public a hardy dose of narrative and thematic elements of popular consumption—interesting characters, rich plots, love, and intrigue—and combines them with an underlying belief in the essential goodness of human beings and the need to conquer hate, anger, violence, and despair. Championing the notion that "a book can defy the passage of time" (Allende, 1991b, 258), she has articulated a plea for artistry and creative dreams in the face of political repression and censorship. Significantly, her own literary history is marked not only by the censorship of *The House of the Spirits* in Chile following its publication in Spain, but also by its blacklisting in some Mormon schools in Utah and the serious criticism it received in Virginia, where parents objected to Alba's rape but not to the powerful images of social injustice, political repression, or the military coup.[24]

While each of Allende's novels initially springs from a strong emotion or concern—nostalgia in *The House of the Spirits*, anger in *Of Love and Shadows*, a celebration of writing and female identity in *Eva Luna*, love in *The Infinite Plan*, grief in *Paula*, freedom in *Daughter of Fortune*, memory in *Portrait in Sepia*—the process by which she elaborates these themes is enhanced by detailed and thorough research. Believing that "the novel is a magical trunk where everything fits: poetry, essays, testimonies, fantasies, documentaries" (Allende, 1989, 132), Allende avails herself of multiple sources to construct her tales, including first-hand accounts, interviews, history books, photos, and the lives of family and friends. Her continued success in writing books that have become bestsellers throughout the world has inevitably made her fiction the object of both fervent praise and harsh scrutiny in academic circles as well as the media. She has alternately been acclaimed for her extraordinary skill as a storyteller and rich presentation of the human condition and criticized for her excesses of sentiment and often contrived narrative scenarios. Following the publication of *The House of the Spirits*, it was even suggested that her best-selling first novel and its "seduction of romance merely reproduce[d] the seduction of commodity culture under neoliberalism."[25] This argument was implicitly refuted by others who posited that it was precisely this level of seductiveness and familiarity that enabled Allende's work to be a vehicle for transforming the belief systems of the public.[26] I coincide with the latter point of view and strongly argue that Isabel Allende's fiction challenges her readers rather than mollifies them. The fact that she spins a good tale with abundant doses of love by no means detracts from the underlying political content of her writing.

Allende's fiction is particularly powerful for its critique of all forms of male dominance. Suggesting that a true political literature is one that distributes power between men and women and across class and ethnic boundaries, Allende articulated this challenge in an address to the American Library Association in Texas in January 1996, where she spoke of her dream of seeing "a world where gender, race, nationality, or class will not define or determine people's destinies, a world where tolerance and generosity will prevail."[27] From her earliest writings, Allende has realized different aspects of this goal, engaging in the difficult task of "unsettling the reader's historical, cultural, and psychological assumptions."[28] Her first book, *Civilice a su troglodita* (Civilize your troglodyte), which was

published in Chile in 1974 and is a recompilation of the articles she wrote
for the magazine, *Paula,* is a humorous and satirical attack on male
supremacy specifically designed for a conservative and bourgeois readership and implicitly paying homage to certain aspects of the outdated
feminine mystique. Despite this somewhat contradictory agenda, it is
most successful in anticipating French feminist Annie Leclerc's belief in
the function of laughter as the "best weapon" to "deflate" male
privilege.[29] Allende's pointed and topical assault on the double standard—the absurdity of man the breadwinner by the sweat of his brow in
an age of "magnificent deodorants"[30]—interestingly reappears as a major
component in her 1997 book, *Aphrodite.*

Casting countless barbs at phallic supremacy in her discussions of food
and aphrodisiacs, Allende outrageously proclaims in *Aphrodite* that while
the baguette is "phallic in appearance," it is quite the opposite in tempera-
ment—"modest, trustworthy and never failing" (*A,* 128). Evoking the
much-publicized case of John Wayne Bobbits's cut-off penis that the
police managed to retrieve, she affirms that "they never would have taken
such pains had it been female flesh" (*A,* 97).[31] And gracefully combining
feminism with succulent advice on recipes, she declares, "Sheep vulvas and
cow udders are infallible stimulants . . . but for reasons of feminist solidarity, we omit those recipes" (*A,* 95). While these examples are injected with
light-hearted humor, in a more serious vein, Allende's commitment to
gender issues from her very first novels gives texture to critic Jean Franco's
persuasive argument that feminism in Latin America "is not only a question of individual liberation but of social justice and democratization."[32]
Her female protagonists not only assume the right to speak, but also the
willingness to accept dangerous political risks that further the cause of justice. Underlining the profound relationship between the personal and the
political and the importance of sexuality as "a key to gender hierarchy and
therefore . . . a site of oppression,"[33] Allende further creates a narrative
world that denounces heterosexual male power and provides women with
the space to choose and experience pleasure. Unabashedly aligning herself
in a postfeminist age with feminist causes, Allende considers feminism a
"revolution in progress" (Correas Zapata, 101) for "a more educated
world . . . in which the basic inequality between the sexes will be eliminated" (Allende, 1989, 137–38).

While more radical Latin American women writers such as Tununa
Mercado and Diamela Eltit unsettle their readers' assumptions even fur-
ther by separating "eros" from "romantic love" (Franco, 1996, 231),
Allende is a firm believer that love is, in fact, the best aphrodisiac.

Responding to sharp comments that she is overly sentimental, Allende pointedly observes that if a woman had written *Amor en los tiempos del cólera* (*Love in the Time of Cholera*) instead of Gabriel García Márquez, it would have branded "mushy" and "full of sweet female sentimentality," since "only men can afford the luxury of being sentimental" (Allende, 1992, 274). Further, the difference she suggests between the critical reception of her work and that of García Márquez is one that has been heatedly and extensively discussed by critics of Latin American literature since the publication of *The House of the Spirits* in 1982. Inevitably, initial debates focused on the comparison between the Colombian author's 1967 saga of magical realism, *Cien años de soledad* (*One Hundred Years of Solitude*), and Allende's *House of the Spirits*. Critics, alternately baffled and amazed by the spectacular public reception to Allende's first novel and her seeming lack of literary formation, were both generous and harsh in their evaluation of her book and her sudden place in the "exclusive male club of Latin American novelists."[34] In this regard, it is significant to note that although Allende's first writings are chronologically situated in the post-Boom of Latin American literature—*Boom* referring to the period in the 1960s and early 1970s when Latin American narrative production received worldwide acclaim—her family saga evokes most clearly the best-selling tale of the most famous novelist of the Boom, García Márquez.

Although some critics have labeled *The House of the Spirits* an outright plagiarism of *One Hundred Years*, I argue, as do others, that this judgment reveals a superficial reading of Allende's novel. While this topic will be developed in much greater depth in chapter 2, it is important to stress once again the polemical aspect of Allende's work and the very divided critical responses it has received. Of equal interest is Allende's own response to the continued comparisons between her novel and García Márquez's. While initially she was flattered by such comparisons, in 1991, almost 10 years after the publication of her novel and with four other books under her belt, she pointedly stated that the continued comparisons, which denied her both originality and her own voice as a writer, were beginning to wear thin and make her "mad" (Allende, 1991c, 190). She has further revealed an essential component of the sex bias in literary criticism by expressing disgruntlement at the critics' need to identify a "male mentor" behind every successful woman writer (Correas Zapata, 199).

With regard to the broader issue of Allende's place in contemporary Latin American literature of exile, it is interesting to observe that although

Allende has inevitably acknowledged links between her writing and that of other exiled Latin American authors of her generation—Antonio Skármeta, Manlio Argueta, Cristina Peri Rossi, among others—she has also consistently maintained that she does not feel part of any literary tradition. Her personal comments aside, critics have skillfully highlighted the relationship between her first three novels and the Chilean novel of exile, as well as post-Boom narrative in general with its emphasis on parody, subversion of ideological and cultural norms, and utilization of popular genres.[35] Allende's move to the United States in 1988 has inevitably altered her literary frame of reference. While she has stated that her writing has been influenced by the great contemporary male authors of Latin America— García Márquez, Carlos Fuentes, Jorge Luis Borges, José Donoso, Eduardo Galeano, Mario Vargas Llosa, Julio Cortázar, and her favorite, Pablo Neruda, the "poet of the senses" (Allende, 1994b, 344)—she has also expressed great interest in the fiction of women, many of them minority women, from the United States. Having cited in different interviews the writings of Amy Tan, Louise Erdrich, Barbara Kingsolver, Gloria Naylor, and Toni Morrison, Allende has commented, "I feel that we are sisters in the same search, in the same tone" (Allende, 1994a, 378). Certainly, the importance of storytelling, the blend of rich imagination and social testimony, and the concern for cultural diversity mark the fiction of all these authors, suggesting the potential for further comparative analyses that situate Allende in a broad community of writers.

As a tribute to the importance Allende enjoys in the world of international literature, where she is considered the most widely read Latin American woman writer in the world, she became the first Latin American writer to receive the prestigious Harold Washington Literary Prize in 1996. This award, formerly bestowed upon such writers as Saul Bellow, Susan Sontag, Gwendolyn Brooks, and Studs Terkel, honors the "creative use of the written word to explore themes of contemporary life." Allende has also received over 30 literary awards in her native Chile, Germany, France, Belgium, Mexico, Switzerland, Portugal, England, Italy, and the United States. Most significantly, she became the first woman, the first writer, and the first Latin American to receive in 1998 the Dorothy and Lillian Gish Prize "awarded to a man or woman who has made an outstanding contribution to the beauty of the world and to mankind's enjoyment and understanding of life." Previous recipients of this prize include Frank Gehry, Ingmar Bergman, Robert Wilson, and Bob Dylan.

Allende powerfully reaffirmed her humanitarian beliefs in her acceptance speech of this award, having declared, "I hope for a society where those who have too much will learn to have less. I hope for a culture where creativity, imagination, solidarity, and compassion will prevail. . . . We can all contribute to the beauty of the world."[36] Allende's beliefs translate themselves into concrete acts of philanthropy. She has created the Isabel Allende Foundation to promote the cause of education and the empowerment of women throughout the world. She has established the Paula Scholarship in her daughter's name at the University of California, San Jose, to assist needy students. She specifically earmarked the proceeds from opening night of the movie *Of Love and Shadows* in San Francisco to Survivors International and those from *The House of the Spirits* to the AIDS foundation (Correas Zapata, 93–94).

In the midst of a technological age where the public is continually bombarded by electronic messages, television programs, audiovisual apparatuses, and computers galore, Isabel Allende offers her many readers an experience that transports them back to a time when the written word was valued and the sheer pleasure of the story could soothe a weary soul and fill it with hope. She may not be able to stave off the death of young women, as did her fictional mentor, Scheherazade. But in the space of her imaginative narrative world, she can defy the passage of time as she invites her readers on a journey through the complex human condition where the personal and the political intertwine and the dignity of the individual and the cause of justice are continually affirmed. Earthy, humorous, and often outrageous, Allende is dead set on furthering the utopian project of transforming the world. This ideal not only situates her in the best tradition of Latin American literature, but also evokes the powerful voices of ethnic women writers in the United States. To this degree, Isabel Allende not only straddles two continents in her life, but also powerfully unites them in her work.

Chapter Two

The House of the Spirits

On 8 January 1981, Isabel Allende sat down in her home in Venezuela to write a goodbye letter to her 99-year-old grandfather, who was dying. As she recounts in her memoir, *Paula*, "I wanted to tell him not to worry, that nothing would be lost of the treasury of anecdotes he had told me through the years of our comradeship; I had forgotten nothing. Soon he died, but the story I had begun to tell had enmeshed me, and I couldn't stop. Other voices were speaking through me; I was writing in a trance, with the sensation of unwinding a ball of yarn" (*P*, 9). The narrative threads of this complex tale became Allende's best-selling first novel, *La casa de los espíritus* (1982) (*The House of the Spirits*, 1985), which has traveled far from its birthplace in the South American tropics. Initially rejected by several publishing houses in Venezuela and Argentina because its author was a woman, and, in addition, an unknown, it was finally published in Spain and has been translated into 27 languages, including a pirate edition in Vietnamese and a version in braille. It has also been made into a movie directed by Billie August and starring a cast of renowned actors, among them Jeremy Irons, Meryl Streep, Glenn Close, Vanessa Redgrave, Winona Ryder, and Antonio Banderas.

The odyssey of this novel has been a rather dramatic one marked by the political climate of Allende's native Chile. Subject to censorship by the Pinochet regime until 1983, the novel was smuggled into Chile in diaper bags and even mailed in pieces from abroad to avoid identification.[1] In 1986 it sold for the "equivalent of a month's salary at the minimum wage"[2] and circulated among a vast reading public in the form of photocopies and on loan. Allende has noted that even reactionary Chileans read the novel so as not to be out of touch (Allende, 1985, 450). In Latin America and Europe, it topped best-seller lists; in the United States, it was featured by the Book-of-the-Month Club; and it has even been attributed with awakening "foreign solidarity and sympathy toward Chile and Chilean exiles."[3] As the critic Gerald Martin has perceptively observed, *The House of the Spirits* "is perhaps the only Latin American novel which has ever truly crossed the intellectual divide appearing on bookstands at outlets like Woolworths while being taken seriously by academic readers."[4]

Alternately labeled a family saga and political testimony, it captures—with strong doses of humor, magical realism, and historical accuracy—four generations of the fictitious del Valle and Trueba families from 1920 through to the events preceding and following the Chilean military coup of 1973 and the death of President Salvador Allende. Sweeping the reader along in a whirlwind narrative, Allende eloquently reveals the aspirations and limitations of her complex characters: the founding parents, Severo and Nívea del Valle, whose respective political and feminist activities dramatically affect the lives of their daughters, Rosa and Clara; Esteban Trueba, the domineering patriarch of the conservative ruling class, whose passion for the beautiful Rosa del Valle is transferred, upon her untimely death, to her younger sister, Clara, and whose rape of the peasant girl, Pancha García, determines much of his family's history in later years; the luminous Clara, who resides in a world of spirituality diametrically opposed to her husband's materialism and who records her family's history in her notebooks that bear witness to life; Blanca, Clara and Esteban's daughter, whose love for the peasant, Pedro Tercero García, kindled during their childhood at her country estate survives half a century of personal and political upheavals; Alba, the creative and independent daughter of Blanca and Pedro Tercero García, who awakens to the dramatic changes in her country's politics through her relationship with the guerrilla leader, Miguel, and who reconstructs her family history; Esteban García, Trueba's illegitimate grandchild, whose sole obsession is to seek revenge on those who have dispossessed him, most especially, Alba; Férula, Trueba's sister, whose life acquires meaning in her adoration of her sister-in-law, Clara; and Jaime and Nicolás, Clara and Esteban's sons, who reject their father's values and align themselves respectively with the world of the poor and eccentric bohemians.

Carefully developing the individual and often quirky traits that give depth to their lives, Allende situates her characters in a society marked by rigid conventions of class and gender and by conflicting political ideologies. While not specifically naming the setting of her novel as Chile or the Marxist candidate and later president as her uncle, Salvador Allende, there is no doubt that Isabel Allende chronicles in this work the vast and erratic geography of her native country as well as the political turmoil that led directly to her exile and her desire to "register history and therefore keep alive the memory" (Allende, 1991b, 263). The personal history of her characters and the national history of her home-land not only merge together throughout her novel, but also reflect one another, creating a "kaleidoscope of jumbled mirrors where everything and anything could happen."[5] This sense of endless possibilities defines *The House of the Spirits* and is intricately related to Allende's narrative technique and view of the world.

Magical realism is undoubtedly responsible for part of the unusual happenings in the novel. If according to the Cuban writer, Alejo Carpentier, magical realism, or the "marvelous real," emerges in a heterogeneous Latin America from an "unexpected alteration of reality, a privileged revelation of reality . . . [or] an expansion of the . . . categories of reality,"[6] Allende applies this view to her novel as she continually reveals the fissures in the concept of conventional reality. Clara moves objects by telekinesis, foresees future events, plays "Chopin with the lid of the piano shut" (*HS*, 123), and wanders through the house after her death; a plague of ants suddenly departs from Esteban Trueba's landed estate, Tres Marías, because the elderly peasant, Pedro García, shows them the way out much to the disbelief of the North American agricultural expert; Esteban's sister, Férula, appears in her brother's house to say goodbye after she is already dead; and Trueba shrinks four inches despite the insistence of North American doctors that no such shrinkage has taken place.

While Allende treats all these occurrences with great naturalness, the connotations of magical realism extend far beyond this relationship between the mundane and the unusual. In fact, there are clear underlying political implications to this form of literary expression that is no longer exclusively identified with Latin America and Nobel Laureate, Gabriel García Márquez, but is also associated with the writings of such authors as Toni Morrison, Salman Rushdie, William Kennedy, Tahar ben Jelloun, and Ana Castillo. Premised on the juxtaposition of the real and the magical and the concept of the supernatural as "an everyday occurrence—admitted, accepted, and integrated into the rationality and materiality of literary realism,"[7] magical realism strongly suggests that life, and the representation of life in literature, is not composed of neatly defined categories. Rather, boundaries blur, dichotomies disappear, and new spaces are created for the coming together of such traditionally different spheres as the fictitious and the historical, the spoken and the written, and the male and the female. As Allende herself has stated, "Magic realism is a literary device or a way of seeing in which there is space for the invisible forces that move the world: dreams, legends, myths, emotions, passion, history."[8]

The acknowledgment of these uncontrollable or uncertain domains of human experience and their juxtaposition to more codified forces create the potential for a radical restructuring of reality within the realm of literature. As accepted notions of power and dominance are questioned, subverted, and transformed, readers are implicitly urged to contemplate and "change" their "prejudices" about what constitutes the nature of reality.[9] Allende's own brand of magical realism is one that is intimately connected to the view of women and history she proposes in her novel; it is a kind of "magical feminism," or "magical realism employed in a femino-centric work" (Hart, 29–30). Yet, while unusual happenings are interspersed throughout *The House of the Spirits,* at no time do they obfuscate the compelling portrait of the historical period Allende re-creates. In fact, as historical events leading to the military coup of 1973 become more and more central in the text, the air of magic that permeates the early chapters is gradually diluted, and *"historical* realism" dominates the narrative.[10] The novel's chapter titles suggest this evolution from the mythical or the spiritual to the political, as Allende calls her early chapters "Rosa the Beautiful," "Clara, the Clairvoyant," and "The Time of the Spirits," and the last chapters "The Epoch of Decline," "The Awakening," "The Conspiracy," "The Terror," and "The Hour of Truth." Despite this shift in tone, the blurring between the so-called natural and the unnatural that is at the heart of magical realism can also be viewed as emblematic of the entire novel and related in particular to the realm of sexual politics and the association of men with discourses of power and of women with the private sphere.

From the beginning of her novel Allende challenges this division of male and female into fixed spheres by giving primacy to the female voice in the narrative process. The first sentence of *The House of the Spirits* casts the reader into a complex world in which silence and writing, past and present, and voices defined and unnamed shape the contours of the text: *"Barrabás came to us by sea,* the child Clara wrote in her delicate calligraphy. She was already in the habit of writing down important matters, and afterward, when she was mute, she also recorded trivialities, never suspecting that fifty years later I would use her notebooks to reclaim the past and overcome terrors of my own" (*HS,* 3). While the first-person narrator—Clara and Esteban's granddaughter, Alba—is not revealed to the reader at this time and is quickly subsumed into the third-person narration that informs most of the work, her identity is suggested throughout the text and clarified at the novel's close. In the book's moving epilogue, Alba defines herself as implicit author, narrator, and reader,

piecing together the story of her family and her country. She achieves this
end with the aid of her grandmother's notebooks, the ledgers from her
grandfather's country estate, the letters exchanged between her mother
and her grandmother during Blanca's forced marriage to the Count of
Satigny, family photos, her own experiences, and other sources and documents unidentified to the reader. The fusion of Alba's voice with Clara's
is so strong, in fact, that they effortlessly blend into one another as Alba
writes, "I write, she wrote, that memory is fragile and the space of a
human life is brief, passing so quickly that we never get a chance to see
the relationship between events; we cannot gauge the consequences of
our acts" (*HS,* 367). The novel set before the reader is precisely Alba's
attempt to piece together the relationship between events and to gauge
the consequences of the many acts of violence and love that inform her
family's history and the history of her country.

Alba is joined in this endeavor by her grandfather, Esteban, whose
testimony in first person coexists with her own narration. The presence
of Alba and Esteban as the text's narrators provides a refreshing and
subversive version of what has been called the "double-voiced discourse"
of women's writings—a discourse in which the "dominant" voice is male
and the "muted" voice is female.[11] In *The House of the Spirits,* the dominant voice is Alba's, and the muted voice, reduced to less than 45 pages
of the 367-page novel, is Esteban's. Trueba's voice is not merely a crucial
component for understanding the conservative patriarchal view that
shaped much of Chile's recent history; it is he, in fact, who tells Alba
that they should write their story so that she'll "be able to take [her]
roots" with her if she should "ever have to leave" (*HS,* 366). His suggestion that she write her family history comes at the heel of two more dramatic sources of inspiration. The first is offered by Clara, whose spirit
visits Alba when she is near death in solitary imprisonment during the
military regime; and the second by Ana Díaz, her companion in the concentration camp for women. To this degree, the genesis of Alba's narrative springs from male and female inspiration and highlights Allende's
desire to break down the gender dichotomy that often shapes artistic
endeavors.

Further, Esteban's evolution from a reactionary patriarch imbued
with male privilege and power to a questioning and vulnerable human
being is directly attributable not only to the historical events of his lifetime, but also to the influence that both Clara and Alba have on his
character. Despite one of his initial assertions, "There's nothing I regret"
(*HS,* 48), his written testimony belies this statement. Writing, in fact,

rather than speaking, gives him the opportunity to confront his violent behavior toward the peasants at his estate, Tres Marías; his disillusionment with the military regime he helps triumph; his sense of powerlessness when Alba is taken away by the military in the middle of the night; and his comfort in knowing that Clara's spirit is with him, like a luminous presence in the silence of his house. Although he writes in the style of a first-person monologue that becomes progressively disjointed as he experiences his multiple losses, his narrative is also an implicit conversation with Alba, whose political views he acknowledges though does not support. The fact that Esteban begins his narration on a self-justificatory note and ends it by begging Tránsito Soto to save Alba's life is a telling comment on the disintegration of male dominance in this novel and the profound humanization of Allende's characters, who rarely remain static or immune to change.

At the same time that the author deflates Trueba's discourse of power, she pays homage to what has been considered "classically feminine, *private* genres," among them, the diary and letters.[12] If Allende herself consulted family letters, diaries, and notebooks, as well as interviews and newspaper articles, to create *The House of the Spirits,* she transfers her personal history to the del Valle women and Alba's creative endeavor (Allende, 1986, 50). Foremost in this regard is the presence and influence of Clara's notebooks that bear witness to life; they are not only the most important source for shaping Alba's narrative, but are also symbolic in a broader sense of the power of the written word and its ability to mold and transform life. Clara is so concerned with preserving the clarity of her diaries that she refuses to name either of her two sons Esteban, since "repeating the same name just caused confusion in her notebooks that bore witness to life" (*HS,* 99). That is, life (albeit the fictional one presented in the novel) is molded by the exigencies of the written word, and more specifically, woman's words, which survive history.

This concept is dramatically underscored in the novel through Alba's narration of the mass burning of books that accompanies the early days of the military takeover. The books that are destroyed in the "infamous pyre" (*HS,* 341) are Jaime's medical texts and his edition of the complete works of Karl Marx, Uncle Marcos's collection of fairy tales, Nicolás's esoteric treatise on Nirvana, and Esteban's opera scores—all male-authored texts that noticeably exclude Clara's notebooks. These miraculously escape, not unlike *Don Quixote* itself, shuffled amidst a group of wares in a market in Toledo. While this is a familiar literary ploy to make the reader believe in the reality of the text and its unusual odyssey

from political turmoil to literary history, I would underline that it also
reflects Allende's view of the potency of women's words, words that
cannot be silenced by oppressive regimes. Like Demeter of the classical
world, Clara is powerless to save her granddaughter from rape. She can,
however, give her the power of words to "reclaim the past" (*HS*, 368), a
power that is pitted against the military's attempt to change "world history, erasing every incident, ideology, and historical figure of which the
regime disapproved" (*HS*, 325).

Yet, even as Alba incorporates Clara's journals into her own writing,
Allende suggests the presence of a male-authored text that also contributes to her character's creative endeavors: the fairy tales Alba inherited from Uncle Marcos, the threshold to the world of the fantastic, read
first by Clara, then by Blanca, and finally retold by Alba to the children
in the concentration camp. Much as Alba derives strength and inspiration from her grandmother's notebooks, she is similarly influenced by
the creative rereadings of fairy tales that are part of the bedtime routine
she shared as a young girl with her mother. Blanca's feminist rendition
of such classic stories as *Little Red Riding Hood* and *Sleeping Beauty*, fea-
turing a prince who sleeps for 100 years and a forlorn wolf who is unex-
pectedly disemboweled by a little girl (*HS*, 258), is, in fact, so .com-
pelling that it cannot help but shape Alba's disavowal of patriarchal
norms. But words alone, despite the power they have in Allende's
world, are not substitutes for the sheer force of human will that equally
molds generations of the del Valle–Trueba women and the writing of
their family history.

Allende has indicated that her female protagonists in *The House of the
Spirits* "are feminists in their fashion; that is, they ask to be free and
complete human beings, to be able to fulfill themselves, not to be
dependent on men. Each one battles according to her own characteristics and within the parameters of the epoch in which she happens to be
living" (Allende, 1984, 41). The names Allende gives them, laden with
symbolic meaning, highlight, in particular, her progressive view of history and women's active role in shaping their personal and national his-
tories. Nívea, Clara, Blanca, and Alba capture, most notably in the original Spanish, the idea of a "luminous dimension in ascending gradation"
culminating in a dawn (*alba* in Spanish) that "corresponds to the Marxist
unfolding of history,"[13] or what Allende has called "a state of purity . . .
the purity of facing the world with new eyes, free from contamination,
without prejudice" (Allende, 1991a, 79). The del Valle family matriarch,
Nívea, initiates this concept of progressive ideology by actualizing her

feminist convictions in both the public and private domain. Demonstrating for women's suffrage in public while also influencing the private sphere by ordering that the poplar tree used as a male rite of passage be chopped down, she provides a model for her daughter, Clara, to express her own particular form of revolt. In this context, it is especially significant—as well as magically feminist—that a pregnant and clairvoyant Clara, about to give birth, retrieves from a country road the head of her mother, who had just been decapitated in a car accident. The family legacy of feminism is thus preserved symbolically for generations thereafter, although physically relegated to a hatbox stored in the basement of Esteban and Clara's house.

Clara's role as implicit denouncer of all forms of patriarchal power is made abundantly clear from the beginning of the novel, when as a young girl she speaks back to Father Restrepo in Church and challenges his notion of Hell as a well-made-up story. Years later, as a married woman, she further harnesses this rejection of male power by offering the peasant women of Tres Marías passionate lessons in self-defense and self-esteem. While her endeavor proves as unsuccessful as Nívea's feminist teachings in lower-class urban settings, thus underscoring Allende's belief that issues of class cannot be separated from those of gender, Nívea and Clara's deeds of solidarity anticipate the activism of many Chilean women in the period preceding and following the military coup.

Clara's acts of empowerment also extend to taking upon herself the "Adamic power of literal naming," thus wresting control over her children's names from her husband, the family patriarch.[14] If Clara reserves for herself the right of naming, implicit in this power is the right to name hypocrisy. Unafraid to denounce her husband's classist views, she criticizes his disapproval of Blanca's relationship with the peasant Pedro Tercero García and points out that, he, too, had countless relationships with women from a lower social class, but without the love that Blanca feels for Pedro. By denouncing Esteban's extensive and often violent womanizing with the peasant women of Tres Marías, she brings "Trueba's past from the unspoken to the articulated private" (Foreman, 293) and in the process speaks back to the voice of the master. When Esteban strikes her to regain his power, she turns to silence as a means of voicing her outrage and safeguarding her inner world. Clara's sustained use of silence throughout the novel, initiated in her childhood following her prediction of her sister Rosa's death and ending (for the first time) in the same chapter in which Nívea has the poplar tree cut down, has predictably generated passionate critical responses.[15] While Allende herself has curiously stated that Clara "hides in silence" and that "she is always escaping,"[16] other readers have noted that Allende does not "simply reproduce culturally ordained silence" but rather seeks to "reinscribe female silence as subversive alternatives."[17] I would argue, in fact, that at no point is Clara's power over her husband greater than when she denies him words and resorts to addressing him through others or through written messages. Clara's presence in the novel is ultimately a testimony to the varied forms of communication—verbal, nonverbal, written—that women have historically used to sustain their own private rebellion against patriarchal domination.

While Clara's daughter, Blanca, is unable to subvert the master's authority in such direct terms and is given to solitude and isolation, her love affair with Pedro Tercero and her ability to cross the severely sanctioned boundaries of class save her from the conventions ordained for upper-class women and enable her to fashion her own style of private rebellion. Thus, despite Nívea, Blanca, and Alba's "social and economic independence" on their paternal home,[18] their attempts to speak back and the strong mother-daughter bonds they share create private forms of transgression and empowerment that "the patriarch cannot control"[19] and that become increasingly more politicized as the novel progresses.

Also significant in this novel in which female characters "challenge . . . social and sexual prejudices, dictatorship, and political repression"[20] are several marginal characters whose presence in the novel allows for additional reflections on the nature of power. Most notable among them is the prostitute Tránsito Soto, whose ambition provides a mirror reflection of Esteban Trueba's, and who is pivotal to Alba's salvation at the end of the work. Borrowing money from Trueba as a young girl so she can leave her small town brothel and make it big in the capital, her goal is to create a cooperative run by prostitutes, without the tyranny of pimps who use and abuse them. Although this model authorizes female autonomy and defies the master of the brothel, Tránsito's stance is, in fact, dubious. Successful and thriving not only because of her brains and business sense, but also because she collaborates with those in power and maintains equally good relations with Marxists and fascists alike, she uses her contacts with the army generals to get Alba released from jail and thus repays her *patrón's* favor to her decades before. Seemingly peripheral yet occupying "a central position of power" (Panjabi, 15), her transformation from small-town prostitute to influential madam reveals the fluctuating terrain between structures of "dependency and dominance"[21] that Allende forcefully dismantles throughout her text.

The continual involvement of Allende's characters in the political realm and the compelling relationship between fiction and historical representation that informs much of *The House of the Spirits* distinguishes it in great measure from its 1967 predecessor, *Cien años de soledad* (*One Hundred Years of Solitude*). Critical opinion has been sharply divided in evaluating the relationship between these two Latin American novels that have enjoyed meteoric success throughout the world. Some insist that Allende's novel is nothing more than a pale imitation or "Chilean version"[22] of the Nobel Laureate's text, while others stress that it "reads, initially like a parody of García Márquez's novel, though not a *conscious* sort of parody" (Antoni, 16). While *One Hundred Years of Solitude* may well represent for Allende what Uncle Marcos's fairy tales represent for Alba—a male-authored text that coexists with female literary models in helping to parent her novel[23]—I would argue that the two works are, in fact, more different than they are similar. Despite a likeness in certain basic aspects—the chronicle of a family saga; the similarity between certain characters; the coexistence of the real and the magical; the narrative techniques of foreshadowing and *mise en abîme*, or mirror reflections of the main structure of the work; and the presence of a metafictional mode or writing about writing—the vision of the world that both authors present is sufficiently different to verify Allende's "healthy respect for the master's voice" combined with an "unwillingness to be seduced by the *maestro*."[24]

Foremost in this regard is the fact that the Colombian author's novel is a mirror reflection of a male-authored world penned by one man (García Márquez), restated by another (Melquíades), and finally interpreted by a third (Aureliano) in a "room of his own" from which women are zealously excluded. Allende's text, on the other hand, is a mirror reflection of a female-authored world. Allende now occupies the seat of García Márquez, whereas Clara, the spiritual grandmother whose rich imagination and prophetic gifts mirror those of Melquíades, gently pushes the gypsy aside to transcribe her own tale. Finally, Alba's mission, like that of Aureliano, is to read the tale and to enhance it. But whereas Aureliano's manuscript disappears in the cataclysm that annihilates Macondo, Alba's survives and is generated by her pen and her womb—writing and gestation—an androgynous fusion of male and female symbols. Further, the devoured fetus in *One Hundred Years of Solitude* that marks the definitive end of a family and civilization may be contrasted in no uncertain terms with Alba's awaited child, a daughter, she intuits, "marked by the rape of society," but also "the hope . . . of a better society."[25]

Of equal significance in evaluating the relationship between these two novels is the role that history plays in the development of narrative tension. According to one critical account, "Allende's ultimate allegiance to the political and historical marks her text's difference from García Márquez's" (Foreman, 294). In fact, the political content of the last four chapters and the novel's epilogue read much like a fictionalized version of the accounts of Chilean history recorded by historians and novelists alike. Allende is highly successful in communicating the complex events leading up to the military coup of 1973 precisely because she skillfully uses many characters and foreshadowing techniques to give voice to the different political views that clashed headfirst during the Salvador Allende presidency and in the period following his death.

From the beginning of her novel, Allende suggests the political events that transformed Chilean society in the 1970s. Implicitly linking the innovations of Uncle Marcos's airplane with the program of social reform proposed by Salvador Allende, the author describes the crowds who come from all over to see Marcos's plane take off and adds: "No political gathering managed to attract so many people until half a century later, when the first Marxist candidate attempted, through strictly democratic channels, to become President" (HS, 13). Similarly, amidst the varied guests of importance who visit the Trueba–del Valle house and participate in social gatherings, animated discussions, and spiritualist meetings, Allende implicitly underlines the presence of the Poet, Pablo Neruda, and links his life to Alba's: "In those days a large number of guests ate and drank in the big house on the corner. . . . Among them was the Poet—years later considered the greatest of the century and translated into all the known languages on earth—on whose knees Alba often sat, little suspecting that one day she would walk behind his casket, with a bunch of bloody carnations in her hand, between two rows of machine guns" (HS, 239).

Through dramatically charged sentences as these fraught with suspense and auguries of violence, as well as other foreshadowings that result equally ominous, such as when Alba has a nightmare at age 14 that Esteban "García was . . . the beast waiting for her in the shadows, ready to jump on top of her at any turn of life" without "knowing it was a premonition" (HS, 279), Allende projects her characters into the historical realm that is present in the novel significantly before the mention of Salvador Allende's candidacy but that assumes immediacy during his presidency. Historians have assiduously documented the initiatives of agrarian reform undertaken by the Allende government that often did not come to fruition fast enough to meet the peasant demands. *The House of the Spirits* gives a human face to this issue by dramatizing the reaction of a furious Esteban Trueba held hostage by the peasants of Tres Marías and rescued from total humiliation by Blanca and Pedro Tercero García. Although Allende does not explore the complexities of the peasant point of view with the same depth that she gives to issues of gender, she highlights in no uncertain terms the class conflict that is so prevalent in Chilean society. While presenting a society stratified by class differences, she utilizes narrative intrigue and unabashed sentimentalism to underscore the means for breaking down such barriers. The sustained love affair between Blanca, the *patrón's* daughter, and Pedro Tercero García—the son of Trueba's foreman—modeled after the revolutionary singer, Víctor Jara—suggests a concerted attempt to unite two radically opposed social classes. The fact that Alba, the result of their illicit union, is the pride and joy of her grandfather further signals a tentative fissure in the unyielding posture of the ruling class.

Trueba's political beliefs ultimately serve Allende's purpose of denouncing the various means used by reactionary forces to achieve a monolithic political agenda. The complex strategies employed in reality against the Allende government—teamsters' strikes, sabotage of consumer goods, slurs and false rumors against the president, utilization of upper-class women to protest shortages in the stores, graphic images of Communist soldiers seizing little children and sending them to Moscow, alliances with the United States—are faithfully recorded as the author describes an increasingly obsessed Esteban Trueba, isolated from his family and intent on restoring "the values of family, tradition, private property, law and order" (*HS*, 261). He plots with fellow congressmen and gringos from the United States to help overthrow the government. He stockpiles weapons in his home, a material manifestation of the stockpiling of "hatred" (*HS*, 291) generated by the upper class. And he molds words to his political ideology, labeling the left "the enemy of democracy" (*HS*, 262).

In marked contrast to his monolithic discourse of social and political vigilance are the words and actions of other characters of the novel who represent a broad spectrum of political opinions. Jaime's support of socialism but horror of extremism and violence is contrasted to the guerrilla leader Miguel's belief that "the violence of the system needed to be answered with the violence of revolution" (*HS*, 271). Despite Jaime's abhorrence of armed measures, he, nonetheless, assists Alba in hiding the weapons she has sequestered from her grandfather's stockpile and comes to respect Miguel once he meets him in person. Alba, for her part, implicitly influenced by the tales of social inequalities Pedro Tercero tells her on their Sunday outings with Blanca and moved by a strong humanitarian spirit that is part of the del Valle family legacy, openly confronts her grandfather, but, at the same time, never stops loving him despite his reactionary views.

Allende's skills as narrator together with her rich background as a journalist are particularly brought to bear in her moving description of the military coup of 11 September 1973, a violent usurpation of power that "happened in a country that prided itself on its deeply grounded democratic traditions" (Skidmore and Smith, 141). It brought in its wake murder, torture, terror, disappearances, censorship, the dissolution of Congress, the reconfiguration of culture, and "the rigid control of ideological processes,"[26] virtually eliminating overnight the vast agenda of social reform initiated by the Allende government. Juxtaposing Trueba's celebration of the military coup with the description of his son Jaime's torture at the hands of the same military, Allende moves effortlessly between individual history and national history, continually seeking to present telling details from the viewpoint of both the victors and the victims while clearly sympathizing with the latter. Paying homage to both her uncle, Salvador Allende, whose farewell speech to the Chilean people is included word for word in the text, and to the Nobel Laureate Pablo Neruda, whose funeral procession through the streets of Santiago shortly after the coup is representative of "the symbolic burial of freedom" (HS, 329), Allende weaves a narrative of unparalleled tension that reaches its culmination in the last two chapters when Alba is seized by the military and subject to countless acts of torture.

Allende has stated that writing The House of the Spirits was "a kind of therapy" for her, "a way of drawing out all the sadness that had built up inside, of trying to share the painful experience" that she didn't go through but that so many Chileans had lived (Allende, 1991a, 78). Unlike such Latin American authors as the Argentinean Omar Rivabella, who documents with horrendous imagery the torture experienced by his protagonist in Requiem for a Woman's Soul, Allende chooses to suggest, rather than to describe, Alba's rape and mutilation and the rape of countless other women whom she meets in the concentration camp. While Allende has said that her goal is to "force the reader into the mood of terror and let him imagine the details,"[27] I would add that she also wants her reader to be empowered by a spirit of resistance rather than defeated by overwhelming details of atrocities. This sense of empowerment that extends from author to character and reader is most eloquently expressed through Alba's ability to convert her personal tale of horror into a narrative that forgives but does not forget. To this degree, her words are a testimony to Eduardo Galeano's belief that "Latin America's contemporary reality does not derive from some indecipherable course" but can provide a new space where "the victims and the defeated of the past might become the protagonists of the present" (Martin, 359).[28]

Within this context, it is easy to understand the heated controversy that has been generated by the conclusion of the novel and the events leading up to it. These include the rise in power of Esteban Trueba's bastard grandson, Colonel Esteban García, and his use of state-sanctioned oppression as a vehicle to seek revenge on Alba, who has been involved in clandestine activities against the military regime. Clearly demonstrating a basic tenet of patriarchal society that posits the female body as a "primary location of power, around which domination is exercised,"[29] García subjects Alba to multiple forms of torture including rape, electroshocks, and extended solitary confinement in a doghouse. He also amputates three of her fingers, an act that parallels Trueba's mutilation of Pedro Tercero García's fingers in the past. The extent to which his private obsession and the official approval for such actions are joined together in the novel provides a telling testimony on how these two realms cannot, in fact, be separated. The private spills over to the political, and vice versa, Allende suggests, much as she illustrates the same concept in the beginning of her novel when the death of Clara's sister, Rosa, is inadvertently caused by a political opponent of her father. Hence, Alba's response to and recognition of the motives of her torturer must necessarily involve both spheres.

As Michel Foucault and others have theorized, where there is power, there is resistance. Alba amply demonstrates this through her strength in surviving solitary confinement and her ability to follow, while in the doghouse, Clara's idea that she "write a testimony that might one day call attention to the terrible secret she was living through, so that the world would know about this horror that was taking place parallel to the peaceful existence of those who did not want to know" (*HS*, 351–52). Composing words in her head while dying of starvation, she symbolically writes her passage from dehumanized enclosure to the "liberating space of female truth" (Meyer, 362). Further, by acknowledging the acts of resistance of the other women who helped her survive—the indomitable Ana Díaz, the women in the concentration camp, the unnamed woman who gives her refuge when she is left by a garbage dump following her release from jail—Alba's personal tale becomes one piece of a broader political context that underscores Allende's belief in the solidarity among women and their role in opposing the military regime. If, as Allende has noted, "terror works . . . by first separating people, isolating them" (Allende, 1994c, 389), she implicitly reveals the fissures in this strategy through the courageous efforts of her female characters who duplicate in fiction the tremendous risks Chilean women have taken in reality in dangerous political situations.[30] Although it may be argued that Alba is not representative of all women because she, in fact, belongs to the upper class, her attempt to pay homage to women of different social classes is indicative of how "privilege" can be used "to destroy privilege" generated by ideology, class, and gender.[31] Finally, by breaking the cycle of hatred and vengeance that has been part of her family legacy as well as of the classist and sexist Chilean society, Alba and Allende suggest the possibility of dislodging "the prison houses of . . . cultural order."[32]

Precisely because the end of the novel is so charged with political meaning, it has become a target for various readers and critics to map out their ideological terrain. Many have failed to see the intimate relationship between the personal and the political and have attributed Colonel García's violence exclusively to "personal, rather than political, motives."[33] Others have focused on what they consider Alba's passive role at the novel's close and her desire to wait for Miguel and nurture the growing life within her. Such critics have concluded that Alba's posture "undoes and weakens certain premises" of the novel that appeared to be "progressive."[34] Allende herself, acutely aware of the criticism generated by her message of reconciliation from Chileans on the left, who were unable to embrace the notion of foregiveness at that time, and by Chileans on the right, who wanted to deny the reality she presented,[35] has actively and vociferously defended her novel on various levels. In the most general sense, she argues as does Simon Wiesenthal that "only victims can forgive."[36] In a 1988 interview, she forcefully states the following:

> We can't torture the person who has tortured us because then it's a never-ending chain of fear and hate and anger and violence. We have to stop it because we are better. . . . This is not something I have invented or I felt myself. I learned it from the people who have suffered much more than I, who have *really* suffered and those people don't have any wish for revenge. They want justice . . . They don't want to forget, but they want to for-

give. They are not willing to kidnap the children of the kidnappers or torture the torturer or kill the criminal. (Allende, 1991b, 263)

On still another level, perhaps a more literary one, I would add that
Alba's response to her rape and victimization by Colonel García is tem-
pered not only by her actual experience, but also by Clara's notebooks
and other documents that she has on hand upon her release from jail. In
these writings, she finds transcribed the story of Pancha García's rape by
her grandfather, Esteban, and the twisted development of Pancha's
grandson, Colonel Esteban García, who tries to avenge his grandmother
and himself by raping her. By juxtaposing one grandmother's tale of dispossession and humiliation (Pancha's) with the other grandmother's tale
of self-possession and authority (Clara's), Allende artfully creates a compelling thesis for the pernicious or inspirational effect family history has
on those who receive its legacy. Alba's decision to reverse the cycle of
hatred and vengeance generated by Pancha's rape may thus be viewed,
in part, as a direct result of her metamorphosis through the written
word. As she explains at the end of the novel:

> When I was in the doghouse, I wrote in my mind that one day Colonel
> García would stand before me in defeat and that I would avenge myself
> on all those who need to be avenged. But now I have begun to question
> my own hatred. Within a few short weeks, ever since I returned to the
> house, it seems to have become diluted, to have lost its sharp edge. . . . I
> feel its flame going out as I come to understand the existence of Colonel
> García and the others like him, as I understand my grandfather and piece
> things together from Clara's notebooks, my mother's letters, the ledgers
> of Tres Marías, and the many other documents spread before me on the
> table. It would be very difficult for me to avenge all those who should be
> avenged, because my revenge would be just another part of the same
> inexorable rite. (*HS*, 367–68)

While Esteban Trueba is initially unable to comprehend the relationship between his own violent past and the frightening events that befall
his granddaughter and thus to realize that "Alba is the human instrument through which [he] is made to pay psychologically for a lifetime of
large- and small-scale transgressions" (Earle, 548), Allende clearly
demonstrates that Trueba's abuse of power proliferates beyond his control and encompasses both his personal past and future events in his
country. Alba's role of pardoner rather than avenger thus springs from

her acknowledgment of Colonel García's particular pathos and from her desire to revise her family history and participate in a creative reconfiguration of reality, similar to Blanca's molding of clay figures that were half beast and half human and her Aunt Rosa's embroidery of original mythological creatures. Armed with her pen and carrying a child in her womb—"the daughter of so many rapes or perhaps of Miguel, but above all, my own daughter" (*HS*, 368)—Alba, like many women artists before her, journeys "through the cratered night of female memory to revitalize the darkness, to retrieve what has been lost, to regenerate, reconceive, and give birth."[37]

To this degree, despite the fact that *The House of the Spirits* ends with the same words with which it was started, "*Barrabás came to us by sea . . .*" (*HS*, 368), it is by no means circular in meaning but progressive in its underlying message. As Allende herself has observed, "History never repeats itself exactly the same. I don't think we walk in circles, but in a slow spiral in which each turn takes us a little higher."[38] It is this articulation of a higher ground that makes Allende's novel a reflection of how literature can be used to advance the cause of justice. As in a Chinese-box construction, the suggestive image of reconciliation that closes the novel similarly provides a mirror reflection of countless other unions of disparate characters and events. Much like the big house on the corner whose configurations respond both to Trueba's initial design and to the additional rooms Clara added at random to accommodate her friends, Allende continually seeks that hybrid zone where traditional categories are dismantled and differences coexist or fuse into one.

While this aspect has already been discussed with regard to the complex issue of male and female power, it extends to other aspects of the novel as well. From the first pages of the novel where Rosa inhabits the "tenuous line between a human being and a creature of myth" (*HS*, 6) and the tablecloth she embroiders is filled with "creatures that were half bird and half mammal" (*HS*, 6), Allende suggests that creativity and innovation require a transgression of fixed boundaries. Recognizing that feats of human endeavor cannot be accomplished with just imagination or the laws of logic but rather require a healthy combination of the two, Allende describes how Uncle Marcos was able to assemble an airplane whose instructions were written in English "thanks to his invincible imagination and a small dictionary" (*HS*, 12). Similarly, she notes that as a young girl, Clara read everything, from the magic books of her Uncle Marcos to liberal-party documents. And in her most detailed description of the fusion of opposites, she highlights how Alba was brought up by an assortment of eccentric relatives who introduced her to vegetarian diets, spiritism, Japanese martial arts, unorthodox fairy tales, Tibetan dance, uncensored vocabulary, anatomy lessons, and yogic breathing, leading her into adolescence "completely ignorant of the boundary between the human and the divine, the possible and the impossible" (*HS*, 255).

While these examples suggest the coexistence of different realms of human experience within one subject, Allende also provides compelling portraits of the blending of characters previously located in different ideological spheres. Foremost among them is the reconciliation between Esteban and Clara long after Clara has died. Unable to possess her in life, and acutely aware of inhabiting, physically and spiritually, a different space from his wife, Trueba slowly becomes "clarified" during the course of the novel. Like Clara before him, he feels the presence and laughter of the spirits who inhabit his house, most notably that of his wife, and recognizes that "the irremediable fact of her death did nothing to alter our reunion. We were finally reconciled" (*HS*, 249). Blocked from verbalizing the pain he feels after she dies, he says, "I'll try to write it" (*HS*, 248), thus paying implicit tribute to Clara's retreat into silence and her use of the written word as a vehicle for self-expression. Even his shrinkage, the material representation of his increasingly narrow political ideology as well as the fulfillment of his sister Férula's curse that his body and soul shrink to nothing, has a potentially positive connotation; it can be viewed as the ultimate leveling-off process between Clara and Esteban. If during her life, he "had always felt like a giant next to her" (*HS*, 249), at her death, they are almost the same size.

In addition to this blending of lives, Allende offers mirror reflections of different events separated by time whose intention is to provide texture to her assertion that "the past and the future formed part of a single unit" (*HS*, 72). Thus, Pedro Tercero and Blanca make love in the same place where Esteban Trueba raped Pedro's great-aunt, Pancha García, but the site itself becomes recontextualized as class and gender domination are replaced by an equalization of social and sexual differences. In much the same vein, exact words are repeated in different situations, as when Pedro Tercero rescues Esteban from his hostage situation at the Tres Marías because Blanca asked him to, and when Trueba similarly rescues Pedro Tercero from political risk during the military regime because Blanca requested the same. The repetition of similar events lived differently by Allende's characters provides telling glances into their inner worlds and reveals the degree to which they are able to overcome their hatred and open themselves to humanitarian forces that reconcile rather than divide. This is perhaps, the most salient aspect of *The House of the Spirits,* which accounts for much of its appeal. Without sacrificing psychological truth or historical accuracy, Allende creates the profound drama of human beings who continually push themselves beyond their limits to break ingrained patterns and to fashion a better world.

In this context, if the process of writing *The House of the Spirits* enabled Allende to recover "those memories that were being blown by the wind, the wind of exile,"[39] her novel pays homage to those who stayed in Chile to fight against oppression—Miguel, Alba, Ana Díaz—to those who died as a result of the military coup—Jaime, Amanda—and to those who sought political asylum in exile—Blanca, Pedro Tercero García. Each of their stories, different faces of the Chilean resistance and diaspora, is an implicit challenge to the sinister voice of power most clearly represented by Colonel Esteban García. To read or reread this novel decades after the Chilean coup and with General Pinochet stripped of immunity from prosecution in Chile is to contemplate the enormous changes in Chilean politics and to reflect on a different kind of power, the power that narrative still has at the beginning of a new millennium.

Despite the almost four centuries that separate Miguel de Cervantes, the consummate narrator, and Isabel Allende, it is obvious that narrative still moves the reader today as it did in Cervantes's time, enabling human beings to transcend their national borders and to participate in a "shared reality."[40] The shared reality that Allende communicates is one that enables her public to believe that human beings can change and evolve, that there is a sense of justice in life, and that the forces of oppression cannot annihilate individual will. This spirit of reconciliation permeates her narrative vision and even extends to her view of the somber force behind *The House of the Spirits,* Pinochet himself. In a 1999 article published in the *New York Times Magazine* following Pinochet's arrest in England for crimes against humanity, Allende wrote: "I merely wish that in the winter of his life the general would ask forgiveness of all those whose lives he destroyed, the families of the dead and disappeared, the exiled and tortured; that he would reveal where the bodies of his victims can be found. Only then, with the recognition of past errors, will a true reconciliation among Chileans begin."[41]

Precisely because Allende never moralizes or imposes a didactic tone on her work but instead creates a sense of intimacy and familiarity, *The House of the Spirits* invites its readers to think about issues of freedom and oppression and to reread their own personal and national history. In this sense, it is particularly effective in "touching an emotional nerve and jolting the reader into a new awareness."[42] The fact that it is read and studied and discussed in countries as different as Vietnam and the United States is ultimately a tribute to Allende's creative and magical imagination and extraordinary talent as chronicler of her country's history.

Chapter Three
Of Love and Shadows

When Isabel Allende completed *The House of the Spirits* in 1982, she had a concern that many first novelists face: Would she be able to write another novel? This preoccupation did not last long; slowly another story started taking shape in her mind, one that in fact concerned her since her days of political activism in Chile following the 1973 military coup. It was a story that expanded the range of horrors of the Pinochet regime from the vivid suggestions of rape and torture in her first novel to a dramatic portrayal of the plight of the disappeared and their families. *De amor y de sombra* (1984) (*Of Love and Shadows*, 1987) is Allende's tribute to those who were "disappeared" by a sinister web of repression that found fertile terrain in the 1970s in many countries in Latin America, such as Chile, Argentina, Guatemala, and Uruguay.

Of Love and Shadows is a novel that not only draws from Allende's interviews with victims and families of the persecuted, but also from an event that threatened to disturb the complacency of Chile's military dictatorship in November of 1978: the discovery of the bodies of 15 murdered peasants in abandoned mine kilns in the region of Lonquén, 50 miles from the capital city, Santiago. According to Allende's own account, she was living in Venezuela when the news of the bodies of the 15 *desaparecidos* (disappeared) was published throughout the world. The Catholic Church in Chile, one of the few institutions that was active in helping victims of persecution and poverty following the coup, had received notice of the discovery of dead bodies in the mine kilns and sent a delegation of church officials, lawyers, and journalists to verify the report. Upon finding body parts and tattered vestiges of clothing in the mine, the commission requested that the president of the Chilean Supreme Court undertake an investigation to identify both the victims and the perpetrators of the crime. Obliged to comply with the externals of the judicial process, the regime brought to trial eight members of Chile's militarized police (*carabineros*) held responsible. Although convicted of murder, they never went to jail. Instead, they benefitted from the Amnesty Law decreed by the Pinochet regime in April 1978, which absolved all those guilty of crimes committed up to and including that year. Having sought further to erase from public memory the Lonquén chapter and its political symbolism, the military government authorized, in 1980, the dynamiting of the kilns and the construction of a fence to block the area off from the frequent pilgrimages of inhabitants of the region.[1]

Two years after the discovery of the bodies in the mine, Máximo Pacheco, vice-president of the Chilean Commission on Human Rights and one of the lawyers who initially went to Lonquén to investigate the report, published an exhaustive study of the trial that ensued, complete with the testimony of the families of the disappeared, the accused, and medical examiners, as well as declarations by the Supreme Court and the Archbishop of Santiago. His 1980 book, *Lonquén,* reached Isabel Allende's hands and provided additional information to the countless press clippings on the event she carefully guarded in her Caracas home. As Allende herself describes in her memoir, *Paula:*

> What happened in Lonquén was like a knife in my belly, I felt the pain for years. Five men from the same family, the Maureiras, had died, murdered by *carabineros.* Sometimes I would be driving down the highway and suddenly be assaulted by the disturbing vision of the Maureira women searching for their men, years of asking their futile questions in prisons and concentration camps and hospitals and barracks, like the thousands and thousands of other persons in other places trying to find their loved ones. . . . Every time I thought of them, I was transported with implacable clarity to the times I lived in Chile under the heavy mantle of terror: censorship and self-censorship, denunciations, curfew, soldiers with faces camouflaged so they couldn't be recognized. . . .
> (*P,* 281–82)

Compelled to record their story and to bear witness to their tragedy, Allende began *Of Love and Shadows* on 8 January 1983, exactly two years after she had started to write her first novel. She blends fiction with fact to create a powerful work that straddles several literary genres and situates itself in the middle of testimonial literature, a police novel fraught with suspense, and a tender story of love. Much more limited in chronological range than *The House of the Spirits,* Allende's second novel takes place during several months of "Another Spring," the title of the first part of the book. Though careful not to refer to either precise chronology or the country's name, the allusions to the military coup five years before, the bombing of the presidential palace, the dissolution of Congress, and the portrayal of the General with his black lens glasses clearly suggest 1978 and Chile as the focal point of the unfolding action.

The plot is rather complex and warrants a summary: Irene Beltrán, a flamboyant and unconventional young journalist from an upper-class family, is sent by her magazine to Los Riscos to cover the story of a so-called saint. The saint is 15-year-old Evangelina Ranquileo, who is said to perform miracles while in a convulsive trance characterized by erotic body movements and tremors in her house. Irene is accompanied by the photographer, Francisco Leal, the son of exiles of republican Spain and a committed militant engaged in clandestine activities against the regime. Evangelina's noontime fit is interrupted by the arrival of a group of soldiers led by Lieutenant Juan de Dios Ramírez. Ramírez panics at the bulletlike sound of stones rolling down the roof—part of the disorder of the natural world produced by Evangelina's condition—and orders his soldiers to take fire. Disconcerted by his inability to subdue the writhing girl, he approaches Evangelina with the intent of taking her prisoner and is promptly punched in the face and carried out of the house by this 15-year-old girl who acquires the strength of a man during her mysterious trance. Although the soldiers depart in a state of complete humiliation, Ramírez subsequently reappears and takes off with Evangelina, who is never seen again.

Thus begins the suspenseful political intrigue of the novel, as Irene, gradually awakened to the brutality in her country, attempts, with Francisco's help, to ascertain Evangelina's whereabouts. Her persistent efforts lead her to the discovery of an abandoned mine in Los Riscos where she and Francisco find not only the dead body of Evangelina, but also the corpses of the campesinos from the region who had disappeared in the early days of the military uprising. Five of the victims are from the Flores family and include Evangelina's biological father and brothers. As Allende recounts in the novel, Evangelina was switched at birth and confused with the newborn baby of the Flores family. When the incompetent and intransigent hospital staff refused to acknowledge its error, the two families brought home little girls who weren't their own, but whom they raised as if they were. Evangelina is brought up by her adopted parents, Digna and Hipólito Ranquileo, and their other children. Among them is their oldest son, Pradelio, who falls madly in love with the young woman he has come to know as his sister, and who is so disturbed by her convulsive fits that he confides his worries to his superior, Lieutenant Ramírez.

The girl who belongs by birth to the Ranquileo family is also named Evangelina and is brought up, in turn, by the Flores family, who was active in the Farmer's Union during the period of reform, a clear allusion to the Salvador Allende presidency. It is Evangelina Flores who eventually assumes the difficult role of identifying the remains and torn vestiges of the men she considers her father and brothers. She also provides Irene and Francisco with countless details about the events that occurred the day her family members were arrested and the fruitless journey she and her mother underwent through the legal system. Finally her involvement in solving the crime leads to her exile and her mission of testifying in future years about the plight of the *desaparecidos* before the United Nations and other international organizations "to insure that the men, women, and children swallowed up by that violence would never be forgotten."[2] Her story, as well as that of others who were involved in the two crimes, becomes an obsession for Irene. With the active support of the Catholic Church and the prestige of the Cardinal of Santiago, she exposes to the press the web of duplicity and violence behind the crimes and is gunned down as a result. She subsequently heals and is surreptitiously aided in leaving the country together with Francisco, thus beginning the long process of exile that has marked the life of Allende herself and the lives of many other Chileans and Latin Americans in the 1970s.

A plot of this nature heavily weighted with a deep-seated commitment to a pressing political reality and imbued with traditional narrative elements of popular appeal—fast-paced action, unusual events that somehow fit together, violence, unbridled passion, and love—makes *Of Love and Shadows* a hybrid text that bears resemblance to the diverse examples of testimonial fiction cultivated in recent decades in Latin America. Written with the intent of using the printed word and a body of fiction to give meaning to the bodies of those who have disappeared or who lack the resources to have their stories told, testimony becomes "a form of combat," a means by which "images of pain and terror are transmuted . . . into witnesses of survival."[3] Although the form of the narrative may vary and range from fragments of real stories included in fictional texts to complete renditions of life stories often "related by a member of the subaltern classes to a transcriber who is a member of the intelligentsia,"[4] the role of the author as witness and recipient of another's plight is a central component of the testimonial agenda. Alicia Partnoy summons from memory the voices of her friends in Argentina's detention camps in her testimonial work, *The Little School: Tales of Disappearance and Survival in Argentina* (1986). Elena Poniatowska portrays in her 1969 *Hasta no verte, Jesús mío* (*Here's to You, Jesusa!*) the account of Jesusa Palancares, a working-class Mexican woman whose long life includes participation in the Mexican Revolution. Isabel Allende, in turn, blends the historical reality of the Lonquén discovery and the tragedy of the Maureira family with the fictional story of Los Riscos, the two Evangelinas, the Flores family, Irene Beltrán, and the other characters who assume a pivotal role in *Of Love and Shadows*. Much as the Maureira women's courage and, in particular, the daughter who spoke before the Commission on Human Rights in Geneva inspire Isabel Allende, and much as countless women have been moved to action by the deeds of the Guatemalan activist, Rigoberta Menchú, Evangelina Flores's determination inspires Irene Beltrán to publicize her story (Allende, 1986, 53).

The fusion of the historical and the imaginative and the different demands each one imposes on a narrative structure invite speculations on the thoughtful question the critic and historian, Hayden White, has raised: "What kind of insight does narrative give into the nature of real events?"[5] Allende's deceptively straightforward text, composed, in fact, of suggestive imagery and countless levels of symbolism, provides stark insights into the complex web of Chilean social and political life during the military regime. I would even suggest that Evangelina Ranquileo's mysterious state, the catalyst for Allende's plot and pointed analysis, transcends its particular circumstance and becomes a representation of disruptive forces in Chile. If, as the writer Raúl Zurita has observed, following the 1973 military coup, truth "sought refuge in . . . zones of experience" beyond language,[6] Evangelina's trance provides a graphic representation of this phenomenon. Her particular truth—manifested in bodily functions beyond the realm of language—is intimately connected to her family dynamics. Evangelina has not only been deprived since birth of her right to live with her biological parents; she has also been deprived of the possibility of actualizing the erotic desire she feels for Pradelio Ranquileo.[7] Her adopted father, Hipólito, fearing an incestuous bond between Evangelina and Pradelio—one that in fact has no basis in reality since the two are not related by blood—chastises his son for his physical attachment toward his so-called sister, thereby creating a mechanism of repression that produces severe consequences for both Evangelina and Pradelio.

Within a broader context, the Chilean sociologist, Julieta Kirkwood, has persuasively argued that the authoritarianism emblematic of Chilean society during the Pinochet regime was manifested not only in the military rule that permeated all aspects of public life, but also in the private sphere. The family, in particular, may be viewed as one of the most powerful enforcers of authoritarian culture in all social classes, from the intelligentsia to workers and peasants, even exercising its regulatory rules on "the proletarian family . . . the basic revolutionary unit."[8] Allende appears to substantiate this theory in *Of Love and Shadows*. Although she cedes to Hipólito's wife, Digna, a level of autonomy in family affairs when her husband is away working as a clown in a traveling circus, she underlines that Digna takes backseat to him upon his return. Digna is notably silent about his harsh rebukes of Pradelio and her son's subsequent decision to join the armed forces as a means of escaping from the family domain. Given Evangelina's strong desire for Pradelio, a desire that cannot be verbalized; the unusual circumstance of her birth; and the extreme economic deprivation of her daily life, it is not difficult to conclude, as Francisco's father, Professor Leal suggests, that Evangelina is "the abnormal product of a society gone mad: poverty, the concept of sin, repressed sexual desire, and isolation had provoked her sickness" (*OLS*, 100).

The unleashing of "the vortex of forces too long held in check"[9] ultimately leads to Evangelina's death. The defiance of authority underscored in her aggressive behavior toward Lieutenant Ramírez and her implicit transgression of gender norms must be disappeared to maintain a society predicated on the suppression of truth. Yet, even before her disappearance and despite the obvious psychological overtones behind Evangelina's behavior, Allende reveals that no one in the community is able to grasp the nature of her problem. Education and social class are not the only factors that intervene in the community's inability to understand the young woman. Rather, Allende suggests that Evangelina—much like a literary text—is read according to the vested interests of those who have interpretive powers in society. Since no reading is ever neutral but infused with ideology, each social or religious institution interprets the Evangelina phenomenon according to its own strategic role in society. The doctor at the local hospital declares that her problem is hysteria and that she needs tranquilizers and electric shocks; the Protestant reverend attributes the problem to Hipólito's drinking and affirms that Evangelina is the vehicle through which God is calling out to her father to repent; the Catholic priest is convinced that Digna's Protestantism is the root of Evangelina's illness and that God is showing displeasure with her mother's abandonment of the Holy Church; and the earthy midwife of Los Riscos, for whom affairs of the body are a central concern, issues the simple pronouncement, "The girl needs a man" (*OLS*, 58).

The chorus of voices that intervene in offering their judgments further reveals how the hidden forces and desires that are expressed in Evangelina's trance become part of the public domain, disrupting the so-called normal order of events. Her sickness curiously emerges the day an invasion of frogs covers 270 meters of the main road in Los Riscos, creating the illusion of a "glistening carpet of moss" (*OLS*, 36).[10] While Allende is not interested in developing in her second novel the same tone of magical realism that permeates the initial chapters of *The House of the Spirits*, she does suggest a parallel between this bizarre disruption of everyday occurrences and Evangelina's trance. As witnessed by Irene and Francisco, the following occurs in the first part of the novel:

> At twelve o'clock noon Evangelina fell back on the bed. Her body trembled and a deep long moan, like a love call, ran through her. She began to shake convulsively; her body arched backward with superhuman force. The girlish expression of a few minutes earlier was erased from her disfigured face and she was suddenly years older. A grimace of ecstasy, pain, or lust marked her features. . . . Outside the dogs howled an interminable lamentation of catastrophe in accompaniment to the sounds of song and prayer. Tin utensils danced in the cupboards, and a strange clatter lashed the roof tiles like a hailstorm of pebbles. A continuous tremor shook a platform in the rafters where the family stored their provisions, seeds, and work tools. . . . On the bed, Evangelina Ranquileo writhed and twisted, the victim of impenetrable hallucinations and mysterious urgencies. (*OLS*, 70–71)

The contrast between the dutiful girlish Evangelina and the tormented lustful woman—a radical split in personality—clearly suggests a relationship between schizophrenia and repressed desire.[11] Yet, on a political level, this division in self may be interpreted as symbolic of the divided body politic in Chile during the military regime. In a 1986 interview, Allende described Chilean reality in terms that apply both to Evangelina and to society in general: "There is an invisible frontier that separates the apparently ordered world where we live and whose laws we believe we understand, from another world which exists simultaneously, that surrounds us and covers a most terrible orbit" (Allende, 1986, 54). This "terrible" space that tries to hide its presence behind the appearance of normalcy is the sphere of unrestrained violence with its concomitant series of prohibitions. Just as Evangelina's desire for Pradelio cannot be articulated within a family and social structure that represses disorderly forces, Chilean political life in the 1970s is premised on the eradication of disruptive concepts. As Allende narrates in her novel, "'Justice' was an almost forgotten term, no longer mentioned because, like the word 'liberty,' it had subversive overtones" (*OLS*, 214).

Class divisions and the pointed dichotomy between the rich and the poor are similarly reflected in Allende's description of the city itself, presumably Santiago, where most of the action occurs. Seen through the eyes of Irene's mother, Beatriz, who shares the regime's enthusiasm for an economic prosperity that only benefits the wealthy, the city glitters with "exotic merchandise that once had been unknown in this country . . . spiral buildings housing luxury boutiques to satisfy the whims of the newly rich; and high walls hiding the slums of the city, where life did not follow the order of time and the laws of God" (*OLS,* 177). *Of Love and Shadows* powerfully demonstrates that the high walls hiding the other side of the city are not sufficient to conceal the truth; in fact, they are gradually eroded throughout the text as Allende suggests that the two worlds of Santiago are emblematic of the entire country in the late 1970s. In the words of the critic Bernardo Subercaseaux, Chile is "a schizophrenic country or rather two countries. . . . Standing in opposition to this country of gilded store windows suffering from cultural amnesia, another country persists, however, one that is invisible, that doesn't show itself but that, nevertheless, exists. . . . "[12] This pressing awareness of a divided nation is highlighted most clearly in the novel by the description of "two countries [that] were functioning within the same national boundaries: one for a golden and powerful élite, the other for the excluded and silent masses" (*OLS,* 177). Irene herself, personalizing this division, intuits that "Evangelina, the saint of the dubious miracles, was the borderline between her orderly world and a dark unknown region" (*OLS,* 127). The bodies of the disappeared buried within the darkness of the mine thus become a compelling metonym for the burial of the dissenting body politic that is exhumed in the second part of the novel—appropriately entitled "Shadows"—and that threatens to alter the foundation of the orderly public sphere.

Allende's narrative skill in symbolically reflecting the divisions in Chilean society is also apparent in her fictionalization of the complex relationship between repressive social practices and the individual. The disturbing images of mutilated body parts that are found in the mine graphically represent the psychological alteration, and in some cases, the disintegration, experienced by those forced to live under the dictatorial regime. Further, the suggestive image of the hidden self crystallized in Evangelina Ranquileo's trance reappears in less dramatic form in several other characters, providing subversive models of resistance to the seemingly monolithic body politic. Francisco Leal, trained as a psychologist with a doctorate from abroad, is an example. Suspended from his position at the university after the military coup because "the School of Psychology was closed for being a hotbed of pernicious ideas" (*OLS,* 47) and unable to find work as a practicing psychologist in a society where those who need him the most—the disenfranchised and alienated—do not have recourse to his services, he takes a job as a photographer at a slick magazine to make ends meet.

While pointedly critiquing through Francisco's story the dictatorship's overt repression of the hidden demons of the psyche, Allende does not condemn her character to social irrelevancy. Rather, his other life, as hidden as the bodies in the mine, evokes details of Allende's own clandestine activities in Chile before her exile to Venezuela. Francisco assists opposition members who enter the country and fugitives who leave it; he aids survivors who hide from the police; and he gathers information on the torturers and compiles reports that are smuggled outside the country "in the soles of priests' shoes and in dolls' wigs" (*OLS,* 208). In his dual role as militant and photographer, he daily traverses the contours of a divided city and inhabits both a world of pure surface where the illusion of prosperity is projected into the public sphere through the glitzy pages of his magazine and a world of harsh realities where the surface must always be disguised. As Allende narrates: "The same day that he photographed exquisite dresses of muslin and lace, in his brother José's barrio he treated the little girl who had been raped by her father, then carried the latest list of victims to the airport where, after reciting the password, he delivered it to a messenger he had never seen before. He had one foot in compulsory illusion and the other in secret reality" (*OLS,* 83).

Francisco's fragmented existence is similarly reflected in the travails of his brother José, whose spiritual work as a priest is accompanied by his political work in the Vicariate of Solidarity, locating the remains of the *desaparecidos,* and in the activism of the hairstylist, Mario, whose professional devotion to the cult of surface beauty belies his commitment to exposing the regime's ugly practices. Although these examples, similar to the models of female and male activism in *The House of the Spirits,* implicitly celebrate the indomitable will of human beings to resist oppression, Allende's novel also suggests the spiritual mutilation of those who lack such inner resources. Francisco's brother Javier, a biologist by profession, is unable to withstand the loss of identity he experiences when he is fired from his job because of his union activities. Isolated, depressed, and seemingly useless, he commits suicide, thereby completing the process of disappearance the regime initiated. While

Allende clearly stresses that personal nullification is much more serious when the forces of unbridled violence intervene, she believes it is also severely damaging on the psychological level when practiced by state apparatuses intent on maintaining power. Deeply concerned about the profound effect of such practices on the individual, she reserves for her protagonist, Irene Beltrán, the most complex transformation of character, a direct consequence of her submergence in the world of shadows.

Initially portrayed as politically naive and accepting of many upperclass values—among them, the justification for the military coup adamantly proclaimed by her fiancé, Captain Gustavo Morante—Irene's odyssey throughout the novel is marked by an increasing sense of separation from her social class, her fiancé, and finally, her country itself. The transformation in her physical appearance from wavy manes and peasant skirts to tied-back hair and long pants and the shifting of her emotional attachment from Gustavo to Francisco are the most obvious signs of the shedding of the external trappings of her former self. Uninhibited and daring, but also "educated to deny any unpleasantness, discounting it as a distortion of the facts," her "angelic ignorance" (*OLS*, 117) is sullied the day she enters the morgue in search of Evangelina Ranquileo's body. Unable to discount the "extensive marks of beatings" on the body of a young woman, "the burned face, the amputated hands" (*OLS*, 118) as a distortion of the facts, she confronts for the first time the images and smells she had tried to block out and that reappear in her mind as part of a political reality she can no longer deny—"the smoke of bonfires burning blacklisted books . . . the outlines of a human body floating in the dark waters of the canal" (*OLS*, 117–118).

Similar to Allende, whose awakening to the abuses of the military regime was also marked by a desire to use her journalistic skills to tape interviews and to help victims of oppression, Irene's activism has a catalytic effect on other characters in the work and ultimately serves to reveal the potholes in the regime's monolithic discourse. In fact, much as individuals in the novel are mutilated by the incestuous union of the State and the armed forces—two bodies that warrant far more separation than that imposed upon Evangelina and Pradelio—Irene's investigative reporting uncovers signs of disintegration in the military body as well. The sense of unity that is apparent in the military at the beginning of the text when the soldiers appear at the Ranquileo household and invade "in a body . . . with weapons in hand" (*OLS*, 71) is carefully eroded in subsequent sections of the novel, much as the corpses buried in the mine. The narrative strategies that Allende employs in the novel and in particular the introduction of first-person accounts contribute to this endeavor by creating the effect of taped testimonies that capture the voices of those who witness the disappearance of both Evangelina Ranquileo and the peasants following the military coup. Their diverse and colliding versions, a heterogeneous body of discourse that plays havoc with absolute notions of truth, implicitly disavow the "official, public and authoritarian discourse" of the regime engaged in a perpetual "monologue" with itself "that leaves no room for reply."[13]

Further, the inclusion in the novel of two different crimes committed by the military, strictly necessary from a narrative point of view because the investigation of Evangelina's disappearance leads to the subsequent discovery of the bodies in the mine, invites countless questions about the nature of power and its exercise in both the private and public terrain. Do the arrest, rape, and murder of one person, Evangelina Ranquileo, purely fictional crimes invented by Allende, seem unimportant when compared to the brutal assassinations of 15 campesinos, a historical event documented by Máximo Pacheco and cited almost textually in *Of Love and Shadows*? Is the reader meant to interpret Evangelina's disappearance as the result of the violent excesses of one man alone, Lieutenant Ramírez, intent on "recovering the macho pride she snatched from him that day in the patio of her house" (*OLS*, 242)? Or does the impunity enjoyed by the military "in all its activities" (*OLS*, 214), the total lack of accountability for abuse of power, provide carte blanche for its officers to redefine, as convenient, the "internal enemies" (*OLS*, 132) they have been told to eliminate? Allende's second novel, as well as *The House of the Spirits*, reflects her belief that "there is a direct line from machismo to militarism [and that] the military mentality . . . is the synthesis, the exaltation, the ultimate exaggeration of machismo."[14] Within this context, both crimes may be read as a grotesque example of the way in which the rhetoric of the State merges with the unleashed force of the military to "disappear" all those who are deemed disruptive or dissident.

Despite Allende's obvious critique of the armed forces, her novel resists, in some measure, the presentation of the military in stereotypical terms. Even her most unsympathetic portrayal, that of Lieutenant Ramírez, is complemented by Captain Rivera's testimony to Irene about Ramírez's transformation from an officer haunted by his first execution to a man consumed with his own sense of power. Further, she convincingly tears apart Ramírez's blind belief that "the armed forces must be monolithic" (*OLS*, 128) through Rivera's denunciation of Ramírez's crime to Irene and more significantly by Gustavo Morante's aborted attempt at a military coup designed to restore "the honor of the institution" (*OLS*, 255). While these examples add texture to her novel, I wonder if Allende is not presenting, in fact, a more favorable portrait of the military than is corroborated by reality. Allende herself has been characteristically forthcoming in defending her view of the seeds of discord and remorse within the armed forces. Revealing in interviews and in her memoir, *Paula*, the genesis of several of her characters (Allende, 1986, 52), she describes at length different sources behind the inspiration for Captain Gustavo Morante. Among them she cites the story of a Chilean officer in exile in Venezuela who refused the order to kill and was expelled from the country (Correas Zapata, 91) and the case of a young officer who shared his story with her in Santiago in 1974. His story—one that is reproduced in *Of Love and Shadows* but attributed to Lieutenant Ramírez and not to Gustavo Morante—describes the officer's first execution of a political prisoner whom he had to shoot in the temple because the prisoner, tranquil and "beyond fear," (*P*, 283), was still alive after his soldiers' round of fire. Unable to exorcize the haunting image from his mind, he reveals it to Allende so that she "may be able to make use of it," and understand that "not all the military are murderers, as is being said; many of us have a conscience" (*P*, 283).

While Allende's novel clearly depicts the evil that exists in human beings, an evil that the system itself foments, it also bears tribute to her belief that "for one torturer you have a thousand people who have risked their lives for freedom, for justice, to help each other" (Allende, 1991b, 262). This belief is significantly given the most credibility in her novel through her detailed account of the role of the Catholic Church in providing the solidarity, means of diffusion, and courage needed to publicize the Los Riscos crimes. As Raúl Zurita observes, after 1973, the sense of "community space" in Chile was severely restricted (Zurita, 313); while organizations such as the Chilean Association of the Relatives of the Detained and Disappeared were formed in 1974, building a solid network of support among its members, the Catholic Church remained, according to the opinion of many, "the only viable institution independent of the police state" (Moody, 40). *Of Love and Shadows* pays particular homage to the Cardinal of the Catholic Church and his staunch commitment to the cause of justice:

> This leader of the Church took upon his own shoulders the burden of defending the victims of the new order, placing his formidable organization at the service of the persecuted. If the situation became dangerous,

he changed his strategy, backed by two thousand years of prudence and acquaintance with power. He avoided open confrontation between the representatives of the Church and those of the General. On occasion he gave the impression of retreat, but soon it was apparent that this was merely an emergency tactical maneuver. He did not deviate one iota from his task of sheltering widows and orphans, ministering to prisoners, keeping count of the dead, and substituting charity for justice if that became necessary. (*OLS*, 220)

Drawing heavily on Pacheco's *Lonquén* as a crucial source in her portrayal of Church solidarity yet relying also on her own imagination to fill in certain gaps, Allende reveals that her novel and the exigencies of fiction curiously coincide in a strange way with reality itself and political expediency. As an illustration, she cites the part in *Of Love and Shadows* when Irene and Francisco ride by motorcycle to the sealed-off mine in Los Riscos to photograph the corpses and then deliver the photos to Francisco's brother José, who in turn gives them to the Cardinal. Although Allende's mother—her favorite critic and editor—protested the improbability of such a daring venture during the perilous curfew imposed by the regime, Allende decided to leave it in, citing "literary license" (*P*, 284). Reality, however, subsequently made the implausible plausible. During Allende's return to Chile in 1988 to vote in the national plebiscite, she was visited by a priest who informed her that he had been told in confession about the bodies in the Lonquén mine and had gone there on motorcycle, during curfew, to photograph the remains and deliver the packet to the Cardinal (*P*, 283–84). Allende's text had unwittingly duplicated his experience, thus underscoring another way in which narrative not only provides insights into the nature of real events, but also mirrors them in an uncanny fashion.

The imaginative force of the novelist, nonetheless, pales when compared to the fabrications propagated by those in power to justify their actions. A case in point: Lieutenant Ramírez testifies to the court that the Flores men were arrested because they constituted "a threat to national security because of their affiliation with a leftist group," because they had plans to attack the military barracks in Los Riscos, and because they were being trained by "foreign agents who had infiltrated the country by sea" (*OLS*, 262). He further describes how they were brought to military headquarters for questioning and were subsequently destined for the detention camp at the National Stadium. On route to the stadium, they asked to be taken to the mine in Los Riscos where they said arms were hidden. Arriving there, the soldiers and their prisoners were met by a fusillade from unknown attackers that resulted in the deaths of all the prisoners and the survival of all the soldiers. Fearing retaliation against himself and his soldiers, Ramírez ordered the bodies to be sealed within the mine and reported that the men had indeed been sent to the stadium as planned. While this version might well be considered an example of magical realism worthy of García Márquez, if not Allende, it corresponds in fact, word for word, to the actual testimony of Captain Lautaro Eugenio Castro Mendoza concerning the arrests on the Island of Maipo on 7 October 1973 and the deaths at Lonquén a few days later.[15]

The juxtaposition of the convoluted reasoning of the perpetrators of the crime and the government's official organ, *El Mercurio,* with the straightforward voices of denunciation of the victims' families and their advocates in Pacheco's book, and to a lesser degree in Allende's novel, provides further testimony of the marked division between the official and unofficial story. Most significant in this regard are the excerpts from *El Mercurio* (Pacheco, 211), which Allende reproduces in *Of Love and Shadows.* Implicitly distinguishing between the events that occurred right after the military coup and the state of the nation five years later, the newspaper urges Chileans "to continue our march on the road of progress, striving to heal our wounds and overcome animosities; dwelling upon cadavers merely hinders that endeavor" (*OLS*, 233). Within the context of Allende's novel and the relationship between the two crimes, the cadavers do not, in fact, belong to the past but are a crucial part of a sordid present.

Given the marked presence of political themes in *Of Love and Shadows,* it is not surprising that the novel was originally "meant to be a book about death and torture, repression, crime, horror" (Allende, 1991b, 262). However, Allende's unbridled romanticism, belief in solidarity, and conversations with victims ultimately transformed it into another story, one of love and hope. Allende emphasizes this aspect from the very epigraph of the novel, which also clarifies her own role as narrator of the novel: "This is the story of a woman and a man who loved one another so deeply that they saved themselves from a banal existence. I have carried it in my memory . . . and it is only now . . . that I can finally tell it." Blending together political drama with unabashed sentimentality, Allende traces Irene and Francisco's journey from their discovery of the Los Riscos crimes to their discovery of love. If her political descriptions are notably crisp and reflective of her concise journalistic skills, her descriptions of love—not only that shared by Francisco and Irene, but also by Francisco's parents, Luis and Hilda Leal, and by Digna and Hipólito Ranquileo—are more uneven, achieving at times moments of lyricism and at others shades of clichéd prose as when Francisco finds Irene "without blemish, like the heart of a fruit waiting to ripen" (*OLS*, 107) and knows that she "would be his because it had been written from the beginning of time" (*OLS*, 194).

Ultimately, however, the refreshing view of romance and sexual politics that Allende presents in her novel overshadows minor defects in style. Unlike the more traditional marriages of the Leals and the Ranquileos, where, despite the strength of both Hilda and Digna, their husbands exercise considerable power in the family sphere, the relationship between Irene and Francisco offers a reconfiguration of conventional roles. Irene's self-confidence and determination coupled with Francisco's gentle and open nature produce an egalitarian union with shifting roles depending on the circumstance. Thus, when the two contemplate the wisdom of entering the abandoned mine at Los Riscos, and Francisco, in particular, debates "the prudence of taking Irene along on an adventure whose outcome he could not foresee," Allende narrates Irene's response and Francisco's reaction to it: "'You're not taking me anywhere. I'm the one who's taking you,' she had joked, and perhaps she was right" (*OLS*, 188). The mutuality in their relationship is also expressed in their first act of lovemaking, which Allende narrates with considerable detail and special attention to the pleasure each one feels:

> Irene had not loved like this; she had not known surrender without barriers, fear, or reserve; she did not remember having felt such pleasure, such profound communication, such mutual exchange. . . . Never had she experienced such joy in the fiesta of the senses: take me, possess me, receive me, because in this way I take you, possess you, receive you. . . . Francisco smiled in total happiness: he had found the woman he had been pursuing since his adolescent fantasies, had sought in every body through the years: his friend, his sister, his lover, his companion. Slowly, without haste, in the peace of the night, he dwelled in her, pausing at the threshold of each sensation, greeting pleasure, possessing at the same time he surrendered himself. (*OLS*, 196)

Their love becomes so strong that it keeps at bay the encroaching shadows that often envelop them and that are alternately described in the novel as the shifting shadows of the unknown, death, presentiment, darkness, political clandestineness, and fear. Violeta Parra's moving verse that opens the first section of the novel, "Only love with its science makes us so innocent," captures the total lack of pretense that characterizes the two lovers as they plan their escape from the shadows. The pain of exile and the loss of the homeland, one that Allende knows well, is mitigated in the novel by a verse from the Chilean poet Pablo Neruda that serves as the epigraph for the third section of the book, entitled "Sweet Land": "I carry our nation wherever I go, and the oh-so-far-away essences of my elongated homeland live within me." Transforming Neruda's poetic image into concrete reality and imitating the act of Allende herself when she left Chile, Irene takes with her soil from her garden, a gift from her Nana Rosa, "so that she could plant forget-me-nots on to the other side of the sea" (*OLS*, 288). Irene's and Francisco's final words, "We will return" (*OLS*, 290), not only echo Allende's upon leaving Chile (*P*, 229), but also provide a fitting end for a novel that begins with Irene's separation from her social class and closes with her separation from country. In the middle of these two processes, she forges bonds with others, and more importantly, with the most courageous part of her own being.

Of Love and Shadows, a best-seller in Allende's native Chile, as well as in Germany, has garnered diverse critical reaction since its publication in 1984; like *The House of the Spirits*, it was made into a movie that enjoyed particular success in Latin America and starred Antonio Banderas and Jennifer Connelly.[16] It has alternately been described as too sentimental, too political, or not political enough, and even as "too direct" by the author herself (Allende, 1991c, 195). Some have taken exception to Irene and Francisco's act of lovemaking right after their discovery of Evangelina's body in the mine. Allende, well aware of this criticism, has defended the inclusion of such an erotic scene in her novel, stating that "making love brings them back from hell to life, to the paradise of love, in which they are safe."[17] While one critic, anticipating Allende's view, has perceptively characterized their lovemaking as the affirmation of Eros over Thanatos,[18] I would add that Irene's expression of sheer sexual pleasure reinstates the female body as a whole in the face of its mutilation in the mine.

Of Love and Shadows acquires special meaning in the context of the report of the Rettig Commission—also called the National Commission of Truth and Reconciliation—founded by President Patricio Aylwin of Chile and released in 1991. While limited in its focus to disappearances, executions, torture, and assaults that resulted in death during the period from September 1973 to March 1990, the Rettig Commission provided the opportunity for groups committed to human rights to stress their view that "genuine reconciliation was possible only on the basis of truth coupled with justice."[19] Allende's novel, while unable to provide the means for reconciliation, offers a compelling testimony of historical truth. Committed to disproving the General's claim that the "public has a short memory" (*OLS*, 229), Allende retrieves from her own memory and the lives of others a chapter in Chile's political life and presents it to her vast reading public.[20] Her ultimate intent, as she lyrically states in the novel's epigraph, is to bear tribute to those who have confided their lives to her and have said, "Here, write it, or it will be erased by the wind."

Chapter Four

Eva Luna

"My name is Eva, which means 'life,' according to a book of names my mother consulted."[1] With these words, Allende begins her third novel and gives birth to a protagonist who has the singular distinction of being her favorite female character (Correas Zapata, 103) and the one who expresses most clearly her views about life, revolution, men, and literature.[2] Independent, creative, resourceful, generous, and sensual, Eva is, above all, the consummate storyteller. Her gift for spinning a tale and for befriending men and women alike with her rich imagination reflects Allende's love of storytelling and her sense of having arrived as an author following the publication of her two previous novels. No longer juggling her double life as a school administrator by day and a writer by night, Allende created the characters who populate this work "in the full light of day" (*P*, 288) and in a room of her own in her new house in Caracas. As she recounts in her memoir, *Paula*, "With *Eva Luna*, I was finally aware that my path was literary, and for the first time dared say, 'I am a writer.' When I sat down to begin that book, I did not do so as I had with the two earlier ones, filled with excuses and doubts, but in full control of my will and even with a certain measure of arrogance" (*P*, 289).

This sense of authorial self-confidence and mastery infuses Allende's novel and is transferred, in turn, to her protagonist. *Eva Luna* (1987) (*Eva Luna*, 1988) is, above all, a celebratory novel that bears tribute to the power of words and the imagination, the joys of sensuality and friendship, the ability of human beings to overcome social barriers, and the re-creation of reality through the lens of fiction. While these elements have also been present in Allende's previous two novels, *Eva Luna* is markedly different from *The House of the Spirits* and *Of Love and Shadows*, which both have a strong inflection of Chilean politics. Allende's third novel is clearly the offspring of the tropics and of the blend of cultures and races that characterize Venezuelan life. While the author herself has noted that she wrote this novel with a clear consciousness of "the two cultures she lived in, that of the south and that of the Caribbean" (Correas Zapata, 102), her suggestive image of cultural blending, or *mestizaje,* actually encompasses much more than ethnic or geographical

relationships. It provides, in fact, a compelling metaphor for understanding the complexities of this text in which different races, religions,
cultural forms, fictional modes, characters, and concepts of gender fuse
together to create a novel whose hybrid nature not only reflects aspects
of Latin American reality, but also Allende's contribution to erasing the
barriers that divide people and ideas.[3]

Since ideology and narrative form continually work together in
Allende's fiction to create a cohesive whole, it is fitting that a text so
devoted to blending differences should have a narrative structure centered around two characters, Eva Luna and Rolf Carlé, from two different worlds, South America and Europe, respectively, who come together
in chapter 10 and become lovers at the end of the work. Narrated in
first person by Eva Luna and consisting of 11 chapters and A Final
Word, the novel devotes chapters 1, 3, 5, 6, and 8 to Eva's life from her
birth in 1943 to her arrival as a 17-year-old girl in the capital city.
Chapters 2, 4, and 7 are centered, in turn, on Rolf Carlé from the time
of his upbringing in northern Austria to his emigration to a small village
in a tropical country in South America and his arrival in the capital city.
Chapter 9, initially devoted to Rolf's career as a filmmaker, instead
develops Eva's reunion with her childhood friend, Huberto Naranjo.
Chapters 10 and 11, in turn, describe the meeting of Eva and Rolf, their
joint participation in a daring political feat, and the moment when Eva
sits down and inscribes on "a clean white piece of paper—like a sheet
freshly ironed for making love" (*EL,* 251) the story of her life contained
in her television script, *Bolero.* The novel's conclusion, or final word—an
ending that simultaneously forms part of Eva's *Bolero*—provides two
different versions of Eva and Rolf's relationship, which alternately rein-
force and undermine heterosexual romance, thus highlighting another
concept key to this novel: certainty and fixed notions of truth are
replaced by ambiguity and open-endedness.

Allende's concerted attempt to rewrite and fuse together in *Eva Luna*
varied canonized forms, be they mythical, political, or sexual, also
extends to the hybrid nature of her novel's narrative components. Resem-
bling at once a picaresque novel, a contemporary refashioning of the
Thousand and One Nights, a postmodern work, a female bildungsroman,
and a tale of romance, *Eva Luna* is, above all, the space where these different fictional modalities coincide and coalesce to shape an original narrative decidedly more complex than its individual parts.[4] If as the critic
Hayden White has theorized, ". . . every narrative discourse consists,
not of one single code monolithically utilized, but of a complex set of

codes the interweaving of which by the author . . . attests to his talents as an artist, as master rather than servant of the codes available for his use",[5] Allende amply demonstrates her mastery and creative blending of multiple narrative codes in *Eva Luna*.

The picaresque mode is most easily discernible in such aspects of the novel as Eva's first-person account with its episodic structure; her marginalized status as orphan and domestic servant at the tender age of seven; her ability to survive in an environment often populated with unkind masters; her streetwise sense cultivated at an early age with assistance from her friend Huberto Naranjo; her diverse experiences in different social classes; and her ultimate reliance on her wits as a means to prosper. Yet, even given the elasticity of the picaresque modality that has accommodated such feminist variations as Erica Jong's 1980 *Fanny, Being the True History of the Adventures of Fanny Hackabout-Jones*, Allende's philosophy of life cannot possibly be contained in such a narrative convention. Acts of cruelty in *Eva Luna* are continually juxtaposed with acts of kindness; tyrannical masters are replaced by benevolent father and mother figures; representatives of the political establishment are humanized; Eva's physical attributes and sexuality are exempt from a process of objectification; and most importantly, reality is continually transformed by the imagination to such an extent that the compelling presence of social forces typical of the picaresque is ultimately reduced to one more aspect of the artifice of the text.

This last point warrants far greater explanation to be understood and is ultimately related to the view of storytelling and writing that informs Allende's novel and her particular debt to one of her literary precursors, the *Thousand and One Nights*. The epigraph of *Eva Luna* introduces the reader to the importance of this book and cites from a passage where Scheherazade is asked "for the sake of Allah, [to] tell us a story that will help pass the night." Scheherazade's mission, in fact, was not only to tell tales to help pass the night, but also to tell stories so compelling, so filled with the complete gallery of human types and experiences, and so intricate that one would lead to another and another and another for 1,001 nights. All to dissuade her husband, King Shahriyar, from beheading her as he had done with his first unfaithful wife and many deflowered virgins thereafter. The fact that Scheherazade, a learned and erudite young woman with a finely tuned knowledge of philosophy, literature, and medicine, was skilled enough to captivate the king and soothe his angry heart is a tribute to what may be viewed as the "emancipatory potential of the aesthetic and cultural realm,"[6] and specifically, storytelling.

Isabel Allende and Eva Luna clearly share Scheherazade's belief in the transformational power of stories and their potential for freeing the human spirit; both record in passionate terms their first encounter with the *Thousand and One Nights* and the sense of fantasy, magic, imagination, eroticism, and sensuality that flowed from its pages onto their impressionable souls. Isabel Allende writes that "the world has never been the same" since she first savored the rich "descriptions of food, landscapes, palaces, markets, smells, tastes, and textures" found in this work (*P,* 71); Eva Luna notes that the reading of this text turned "the known order of things upside down" and made her lose "sight of reality" (*EL,* 153). Significantly, the many motifs that shape *The Arabian Nights,* including the wide spectrum of social types; the dazzling display of story upon story and the presence of storytellers, amateur and professional alike; the accounts of police brutality and corruption; the blending of such different realms as politics and religion; and the varied sexual scenarios similarly emerge in Allende's narrative, a tribute to her literary model.[7]

The experience of entering unknown and unchartered territories, which both Allende and Eva feel, as readers of the *Thousand and One Nights,* is transferred, in turn, to the narratives they produce. The result is the creation of fictional worlds where the boundary between the real and the imaginary becomes increasingly blurred, and the only thing that is ultimately real is the story itself. Reflecting in a self-conscious mode on the experience of writing, Eva, jointly practitioner and theorist of the craft of fiction, alerts her reader that when she writes, she describes life as she "would like it to be" (*EL,* 301), and that at times she feels that "the universe fabricated from the power of the imagination had stronger and more lasting contours than the blurred realm of the flesh-and-blood creatures around [her]" (*EL,* 188).[8] Nowhere is this communicated more powerfully than in the last story Eva tells Rolf Carlé. It is a story about a warrior who asks a storyteller to sell him a past because his "is filled with blood and lamentation" (*EL,* 281). The storyteller, a sensitive and imaginative woman who recognizes the importance of good memories for personal survival, gives him a past and a memory, none other than her own. Thus, her life becomes interwoven with his to such an extent that she no longer knows where the boundary lies between his past and hers. Fiction replaces experience for both the storyteller in Eva's story and Eva herself, emphasizing the importance of artifice in the novel.

Reality is, in fact, replaced by multiple levels of artistic representation throughout the entire novel, providing countless mirror reflections of the writer's magical feats with words. Eva's first master, the scientist

Professor Jones, embalms dead bodies with such success that they are considered as real as their live models. His success is so great, in fact, that following the death of the country's dictator, the latter's advisors contemplate concealing his death, having his body embalmed, and parading it before the country as if nothing had happened. Another of Eva's *patronas* fashions objects out of a doughlike mass called "Universal Matter," and the results are so felicitous that Eva herself creates hand grenades out of the same material years later to help Huberto Naranjo rescue fellow guerrilla fighters from prison.[9] But there is a notable difference between these objects immobilized in space and fixed in hardened materials and the tales Eva tells to her friends and *patrones* alike. Just as the Argentinean short story master, Jorge Luis Borges, remarked about the *Thousand and One Nights*, "One knows that entering that book one can forget one's poor human fate,"[10] so too, fictitious as Eva Luna's tales may be, they enliven and soothe the weary soul and uplift the human spirit with their humor, unexpected turns, and delightful sense of irreverence. The rest is sheer trickery or parody. Eva herself makes notably clear the distinction between her desire to mold reality and create a world of her own "populated with living people" and the "parody of reality" that characterized the sphinxes and musketeers of her Yugoslavian *patrona* (*EL*, 188).

Yet, despite this crucial difference in different kinds of artifice, *Eva Luna* makes us wonder if Allende is not suggesting, in a broader ideological context, that many social and political practices are also constructs, despite claims to the contrary of those who exercise power. Huberto Naranjo forcefully argues to Eva that "injustice" is "not part of the natural order of things, as he had supposed, but an aberration" created by governments to maintain inequality (*EL*, 181). Similarly, sexuality—a polemical territory of thought where the word *natural* is fraught with political implications—is, in a particular instance of the novel, conceptualized as one more construct, one more artifice. The story of Eva's friend, Melesio/Mimí, is a case in point: born with a man's body but a woman's soul, Melesio experiences his female identity through his performance as Mimí in a cabaret for transvestites. Throughout the novel, he undertakes the painful process of feminizing himself until Melesio is finally transformed into Mimí complete with external beauty and atrophied male sexual organs. Mimí's story functions in the text on many levels and is at once a cautionary tale about resistance and conformity. Mimí, rejecting the notion of inborn sexuality as a natural state, cedes to gender as a social construct and artificially creates a female identity to

match the desires of a male-dominated society, much as Eva creates stories to fulfill the desires of her listeners (Karrer, 161). In still another
sense, the coexistence or fusion of female and male in Mimí's being provides one more mirror reflection of the creation of hybrid spheres that
shapes Allende's novel, urging her readers to consider the dissolution of
concepts of certainty as defining aspects of contemporary reality. In this
regard, Allende, previously the re-creator of the picaresque mode, as
well as a Latin American Scheherazade, imbues her novel with the postmodern endeavor of offering "multiple . . . alternatives to traditional,
fixed unitary concepts"[11] and dismantles, in the process, a wide range of
culturally engendered constructs.

   This intent to undermine conventional beliefs is crystallized most
clearly in the view of *Eva Luna* as a female bildungsroman, a novel of a
young woman's psychological, intellectual, and moral development. As is
easily surmised from the protagonist's name, Eva Luna's conception is
heavily immersed in mythical and archetypal symbolism of a hybrid
nature. Her parents, in fact, initially inhabit regions seemingly unmarked
by conventional time and space. Consuelo, Eva's mother, of European
stock and "long red hair like a whip of fire" (*EL,* 3), spends her childhood
"in an enchanted region" (*EL,* 1) of an "eternal green" (*EL,* 3) that bears
resemblance to the "green world" archetype of freedom.[12] Her father, "an
Indian with yellow eyes," comes "from the place where the hundred rivers
meet" (*EL,* 1). These resonances of tropical Caribbean geography are later
combined with biblical overtones as the two are joined together in a garden where the Indian is bitten by a snake. Consuelo, fearing the eager
plans of her *patrón,* the scientist Professor Jones, to convert the dying
Indian gardener into "an indigenous mummy posed as if pruning" (*EL,*
17), rebels against her master, sucks the venom out of his wound, and
offers him her virgin's body as a last consolation to his suffering. His gan-
grene miraculously subsides under Consuelo's erotic cure, and he soon
departs. Consuelo, relishing the memory of their passionate lovemaking,
subsequently gives birth to a daughter, whom she names Eva, "so she will
love life" (*EL,* 21), and Luna, because her father was a member of the
Luna tribe, "the Children of the Moon" (*EL,* 21).

   Although Allende does not associate Eva's father with the Guajiro
tribe that resides in select areas of Venezuela, the Moon, or Kashi, is
considered the father of the Guajiro.[13] Similarly, according to Guajiro
folklore, the snake, a representation of sickness, death, and danger, may
be relieved of its potential for destruction when it is killed and water, the
"principle of life," is extracted from it (Perrin, 128). Given the phallic

symbolism of the snake in the worship of the Moon goddess[14] and the fact that in Apollo's shrine, there was a sacred snake fed by a naked virgin (Harding 53), it is fascinating to see how Allende interweaves these different symbolic meanings into her newly transformed myth of her protagonist's creation.[15] The Biblical serpent in the Garden of Eden who tempts Eve is now jointly converted into a phallic symbol and a representation of the Guajiro snake, emptied of its water or semen during the sexual act, to relieve it of its death-producing force and to reunite it with its life-affirming opposite. Eva, the offspring of this hybrid combination of mythological symbols, while owing her existence to her mother's rebellion, is born with a legacy of life-bearing forces, femininity, and renewal, suggested by *luna*, or moon. Eva herself seems acutely aware of her symbolic heritage and remarks toward the close of the novel, "as always, I was calmed by the moon" (*EL*, 277); "It seemed as if I had lived many lives, that I had turned to smoke each night, and been reborn each morning" (*EL*, 287).

Yet, lest the reader assume too much of an unequivocal identification between Eva and the moon, Allende provides an interesting twist consistent with the ambiguities that characterize this text. Unlike the moon's association with fertility, renewal, and menstrual cycles, Eva ceases to menstruate at age 17 following her traumatic reaction over her *patrona* Zulema's suicide and doesn't resume menstruation until nearly 10 years later, when she is able to shed the ghosts of the past. I would venture to say that the inclusion of such a detail in the text extends far beyond the paradoxical meaning it lends to Eva's last name, the interesting association it offers between psychological stress and physiological functions, and the suggestion of freedom it implies from biological determinism and fear of pregnancy. Rather, I would argue that the suppression of natural bodily functions is a corporeal version of a complex process of suppression that envelops the entire text and is again related to the underlying principle of the artistic or artificial construction of reality that dominates the narrative. Eva herself declares, "I . . . suppressed bad memories so I could remember my past as happy" (*EL*, 157).

While a certain element of narrative distance is understandable, given the fact that the adult Eva relates the story of her life from the time of her birth to her present, the detached tone that often informs her story suggests more than chronological distance. It is almost as if Eva's desire to create or to will by words a happy life were so strong that disruptive political, social, and psychological forces were necessarily relegated to the back room of her imagination. If toward the end of the novel, Mimí looks at Eva and says, "All you've ever done is work, work, work. You were born a bastard with blood of every color in your veins, you never had a family, no one sent you to school or had you vaccinated or gave you vitamins" (*EL*, 266), this is barely the sense of Eva's life that she has communicated to the reader throughout her narration. Her life is continually presented in such a seductively interesting manner that Allende's readers may even feel dull by comparison. Similarly, aside from one brief allusion to Eva's "dark skin" (*EL*, 51) and her sporadic interest in the Indians with whom she interacts, there is never any acknowledgment of her Indian blood. This detachment is justified in great measure by the strong sense of the mother-daughter relationship that unites Eva and Consuelo even after the latter's death and by Eva's feeling that "[f]rom my father I inherited stamina. . . . Everything else I owe to my mother" (*EL*, 21). An important piece of this maternal legacy is Consuelo's love of storytelling and her belief that "reality is not only what we see on the surface; it has a magical dimension as well and, if we so desire, it is legitimate to enhance it and color it to make our journey through life less trying" (*EL*, 22). While Eva clearly follows her mother's model of substituting imagination for reality, this characteristic also responds to her concerted decision not to let politicized ethnic identities take precedence over the celebratory tone of self creation that imbues her life. *Eva Luna* is clearly a bildungsroman that reflects the individual's ability to use adverse social conditions to prosper rather than to be defeated.

Fiercely determined to survive and to make the best of her meager circumstances even at an early age, the seven-year-old Eva befriends her first *patrón*, Professor Jones, and is his sole companion when he dies. Sold by her *madrina* (godmother) as a domestic servant to her new masters, she rebels against the spinster sister but gracefully accepts in exchange for money the caresses of the bachelor brother. Happy and secure with her next *patrona*, the Yugoslavian widow who creates objects out of the doughlike Universal Matter and with whom she listens to the radio every day, Eva bounces back once more when the widow returns to Europe and she is charged with emptying the plush bed pan of a cabinet minister. Inevitably, she rebels and empties the bed pan on the minister's head. Resistance and adaptation, rather than bitterness and frustration, thus form the core of Eva's upbringing as she learns to navigate the human comedy while protecting herself from hurt and despair. Her *madrina* beats her to a pulp when she runs away from the spinster's house, but Eva registers not one word of rage in her narration and in later years consciously obliges herself to develop "a tolerable image" of her godmother (*EL,* 157) to feel at peace with the past. Even her anger toward her spinster *patrona* is mediated by their weekly trips to the market place, where her imagination runs wild with the smells and sounds of the lively city, providing her with countless tidbits that constitute the tales she tells her adopted grandmother, Elvira. That is, Eva the storyteller and the future adult writer is born and created through the process of careful selection and suppression of experiences that Eva the child lives.

Eva's transition from orality to writing and from childhood to adulthood is facilitated by the Turkish immigrant, Riad Halabí, her last *patrón,* more appropriately called a gentle mentor and guide. Riad finds Eva alone and dirty in the city streets following the Revolt of the Whores and the subsequent police raid on a neighborhood brothel where Eva had been living under the protection of the brothel's madam, La Señora, and her friends, Melesio and Huberto Naranjo. He takes the adolescent Eva to the village of Agua Santa, an hour from the capital, where over the course of several years he bequeaths her companionship, the ability to read and to write, the love of books, and the awakening of her sexuality. This last topic is of considerable importance in the novel and functions as one of the most clearly defined, though often contradictory, political issues that Eva confronts and articulates in her narrative of maturation.

By her own account, Eva's sexual evolution passes through several stages in the novel and is mediated by various influences of a diverse nature: the model of sensuality suggested by her mother; the affirmation of compliance with patriarchy articulated by her *madrina,* La Señora, and by Huberto Naranjo; the mixed message of resistance and conformity realized daily in Mimí's creation of a feminine self; and the concern for sexual pleasure expressed by Riad Halabí and Rolf Carlé. The theoretical, the experiential, and the oneiric blend together with the fictional and the voyeuristic to create a complex package of sexual initiation that alternately reveals Eva's control over her body and her subservience to social codes of female behavior. Her theoretical introduction to sexuality emanates from two different sources, one verbal and the other pictorial. Her *madrina,* suffering from the trauma of giving birth to a two-headed biracial baby[16] and reneging so completely on sexuality that she has her vagina stitched up, threatens to do the same to Eva and informs her, "As long as you're untouched, you're worth something. . . . but when you lose it, you're nobody" (*EL,* 106). Eva's reaction crystallizes the web of duplicity that surrounds female virginity in a patriarchal society. She does not understand why the part of her body "that was so sinful and forbidden could at the same time be so valuable" (*EL*, 106).

Eva's entry into the realm of the forbidden is facilitated through the world of books, most notably the French books on sexual positions "beyond anatomical possibilities" (*EL*, 125) furtively stashed away in La Señora's brothel for the edification of her girls and the *Thousand and One Nights* that blew "eroticism and fantasy" into her life "with the force of a typhoon" (*EL*, 153). But it is not until she secretly witnesses, at age 15, the lovemaking between Riad Halabí's wife, Zulema, and Riad's cousin, Kamal, that Eva experiences in her own body the erotic impulses found in her readings. Confronted with the "great, dark sex" of Kamal (*EL*, 165) directly pointed at her, Eva is filled with both a desire and a fear that she will not release from her psyche until many years later, long after she has known sexual pleasure at the hands of Riad Halabí.

It is not surprising that Riad is Eva's first lover; infinitely gentle, loving, and sensitive to human vulnerabilities because he bears the mark of a cleft lip that he knows brings others discomfort, he is Eva's mentor in every sense. As Eva herself acknowledges, "I . . . loved him deeply . . . I owed him everything" (*EL*, 200). This is no exaggeration. Riad teaches her how to cook and how to belly dance; he arranges private classes with the village teacher so she can learn to read and write; and he buys her the *Thousand and One Nights*, reads to her from Arabic poets, and talks to her about a myriad of topics. He also obtains a birth certificate for her so that she legally exists. And he introduces her to the pleasures of her body. Longing for someone to feel passion for him despite his cleft lip, Riad is healed through Eva's love from the shame of Zulema's suicide and his knowledge that his wife betrayed him much as Eva is healed through his gentleness from the ignominious treatment she received by the police who accused her of Zulema's death. Thus, their lovemaking is celebratory as well as cathartic. In Eva's own words:

> His hands, and all the rest of his solid body, had been refined into a single sensitive instrument tuned to giving pleasure to a woman who wanted to be fulfilled. . . . Riad Halabí was wise and tender, and that night he gave me such pleasure that many years and more than one man would pass through my life before I again felt so complete. He taught me the multiple possibilities of my womanhood, so I would never compromise for less. I gratefully received the splendid gift of my own sensuality; I came to know my body; I learned that I had been born for that enjoyment—and I could not imagine life without Riad Halabí. (*EL*, 201)

This affirmation aside, Eva, does in fact, settle for less in her subsequent relationship with Huberto Naranjo, her boyhood friend turned guerrilla fighter. Despite Eva's ability to resist norms of female beauty imposed by a rigidly gendered society and to declare, "I decided I was beautiful—for the simple reason that I wanted to be. And then never gave the matter a second thought" (*EL*, 187), her passion for Huberto reveals her compliance with patriarchal conventions. Instead of assuming the difficult and delicate role of instructing him about woman's sexuality, Eva molds her sexual passion to suit his psychological needs and re-creates herself in the image of purity that Naranjo seems to demand of her (Karrer, 161). As she relates, "In order not to upset him, I sometimes feigned a satisfaction I was far from experiencing. My need to make him love me and stay with me was so great that I had decided to follow Mimí's advice and not practice any of the tricks I had learned from La Señora's books, or teach him Riad Halabí's knowing caresses. I never spoke of my fantasies, or indicated the precise chords Riad had struck, because I sensed he would hound me with questions—Where? Who with? When did you do it?" (*EL*, 229).

Her projection of a subdued erotic self extends so far that she even creates for Naranjo a story about the loss of her virginity, a story with far greater political implications than Eva herself realizes. Recognizing that the truth about her first lovemaking with a man old enough to be her father would disrupt his view of her innocence, Eva tells him she was raped by the police who arrested her for Zulema's death. The utilization of such a fiction to manipulate Huberto's feelings of rage and pity curiously corresponds to the manipulation of the reader regarding this same episode and provides a telling comment about the relationship between fiction and politics in this book. In the early pages of the novel, Eva describes herself as follows, "I have no marks on my skin, only a few cigarette burns . . ." (*EL*, 22). This comment is fraught with meaning for a reader of contemporary Latin American literature and creates a sense of anticipation in the text. However, the expectation of torture and abuse is not explained until chapter 8, when Eva is arrested and accused of Zulema's death. Stripped of her dress, tied to a chair, punched, interrogated, and deprived of water, she recalls the feeling of pain she experienced: "I tried to move, but my body hurt all over, especially my legs, which were pocked with cigarette burns" (*EL*, 194). Yet, despite being tortured, if not raped, Eva does not view this experience in a broader political context and professes no dislike for the police in general. It would thus seem that her fictionalization of her deflowerment, an account that actually corresponds to the reality of many women in Latin America and that is suggested in both *The House of the Spirits* and *Of Love and Shadows,* reveals a calculated exploitation—for narrative effect and psychological manipulation—of an explosive political topic that, in fact, appears to have little political meaning for Eva herself.

Curiously, the explicit sexual violence of her fictionalized account lurks to some degree in her subconscious and is finally exorcized at the end of the novel when Eva begins a relationship with Rolf Carlé, the filmmaker and television personality whose life, like her own, has been devoted to apprehending images through art and presenting them to the viewing public as semblances of reality. Joined together with both him and Naranjo in a daring plan to rescue guerrillas from the Santa Maria penal colony, Eva releases through two successive dreams the demons that have suppressed her menstrual cycle for almost a decade. Both dreams represent an oneiric version of the fusion of opposites that characterize the entire novel; this time, fear and excitement, pain and pleasure, passivity and control coexist,[17] revealing the degree to which Eva feels empowered to create sexual fantasies while dreaming about herself as a woman "impaled" by the "powerful sex of a man" and "in the arms of a lover whose face was covered with a mask of Universal Matter and who thrust deep inside [her] with every swell of the waves, leaving [her] bruised, swollen, thirsty, and happy" (*EL,* 284). By orchestrating in her subconscious a violent penetration responding to both the fictional version of her rape and her confusion over seeing Kamal's "great, dark sex" pointed at her, but by controlling this fantasy, Eva reinstates her right to fully create her own sexuality and be freed of the demons of the past. Her menstrual cycle resumes, and she begins a passionate amorous relationship with Rolf, who has been duly initiated into woman's "capacity for pleasure" (*EL,* 98) by his delightfully sensuous cousins with whom he was joined in a playful and voluptuous ménage-à-trois for several years.

The fact that one of the two endings of the novel celebrates a lovemaking characterized by "such ardor that all the wood in the house glowed like polished gold" (*EL,* 307) is a tribute to the way in which this female bildungsroman can also be read as a tale of romance (Diamond-Nigh, 40).[18] In a certain sense, Rolf Carlé is Eva's kindred soul, her other half, although they differ in that Eva actively participates in life, while Rolf actively observes it (Allende, 1988). Like Eva, Rolf has suppressed unpleasant memories from his past: his father's abuse of his mother and his siblings, his participation in burying bodies of concentration camp victims during World War II, his father's violent death at the hands of his students, the lonely death of his developmentally disabled sister, Katharina.[19] Like Eva, he, too, discovered the world of books as a teenager and voraciously consumed everything he could find in his uncle's small Venezuelan village, La Colonia. Like Eva, he, too, is an "incorrigible dreamer" (*EL,* 92) moved by sympathy and compassion for those in need. He, too, awakened as a youth to the world of unbridled and guilt-free sexuality. He, too, is drawn to Huberto Naranjo's idealism and political struggle while recognizing the impossibility of its success in Venezuela. Finally, like Eva, he, too, dreams in the jungle as they await the beginning of the guerrilla rescue, a dream that haunts him in days to come. It is nothing less than the other half of the dream that released Eva's menstrual cycle. For if Eva dreams of herself "in a flutter of lace and yellow taffeta petticoats" penetrated by the "powerful sex of a man waiting below" her swing (*EL,* 284), Rolf dreams of a "ghost in yellow petticoats . . . teasing him, eluding him, inflaming him, lifting him to glory" (*EL,* 305).

Their romance, however, is ultimately converted into still another fiction at the novel's close when Eva's script, *Bolero,* coincides with the novel *Eva Luna,* creating a literary hall of mirrors composed of words, stories, and images that mutually reflect one another. As Eva herself narrates at the novel's close referring to Rolf: "He strode forward, and kissed me exactly as it happens in romantic novels, exactly as I had been wanting him to do for a century, and exactly as I had been describing moments before in a scene between the protagonists of my *Bolero*" (*EL,* 306). Yet, if Eva's television script evokes the heightened passion of soap operas or Latin American *telenovelas,* Allende immediately disrupts this mode and casts the reader into the postmodern world of uncertainty that ultimately defines her text. Eva suggests that her story of kindred souls united is just one version of a tale that may have a different ending, an ending where "that love wore thin and nothing was left but shreds" (*EL,* 307). Acknowledging this as a possibility, she nonetheless adds, "Or maybe, that isn't how it happened. Perhaps we had the good fortune to stumble into an exceptional love, a love I did not have to invent, only clothe in all its glory so it could endure in memory" (*EL,* 307). In the novel's concluding sentence, Eva seems to opt for the happy ending, adding that Rolf "was able to exorcise his nightmares" and that she at last was able to perform the belly dance that Riad taught her and to regale her lover with many stories (*EL,* 307).

A novel of this nature that places such a premium on the creative and imaginative process necessarily sustains a somewhat difficult relationship with external reality and political forces. But because Isabel Allende is a novelist for whom fiction is inextricably connected to social and political events, her characters' lives become immersed in a complex web of Venezuelan politics that spans several decades. While not occupying the same prominent role they had in her previous novels, political concerns are nonetheless clearly articulated and presented from varied perspectives. Characters who appear in a somewhat anecdotal capacity at the beginning of the work—most notably, Huberto Naranjo—assume greater stature and depth as they become spokespersons for political causes, and Eva develops still further as she becomes politicized to social realities that previously meant little to her. Similarly, Rolf Carlé, who arrives in Venezuela carrying a complicated psychological package of guilt and despair over his role in his village during World War II, is able to alleviate his horror of injustice by contributing to political change in his adopted country. The inclusion of political concerns thus not only adds texture to the characters' lives, but more significantly perhaps, adds a markedly human and personal dimension to abstract ideological principles and historical events.

Although Allende allows herself a certain amount of chronological imprecision in her description of Venezuelan politics and never names her tropical country as Venezuela per se, her references are clear enough to enable the reader to reconstruct 60 years of a shifting political climate marked by dictatorships with their concomitant police brutality, corruption, and censorship; a presumably democratic rule characterized by betrayal of its supporters and the suspension of constitutional rights;[20] the birth of the guerrilla movement as a response to state-sanctioned violence and injustice; and the legalization of the Communist Party and dismantlement of the guerrila movement. Without directly mentioning the leaders in charge, Allende alludes to the dictatorships of General Juan Vicente Gómez (1908–1935), called El Benefactor in the novel, and General Marco Pérez Jiménez (1948–1958); the presidency of Rómulo Betancourt (1959–1964); and the election of Rafael Caldera in 1969.[21] Since Eva herself was born in 1943, several years after the birth of Huberto Naranjo and eight years after the death of General Gómez and the birth of Rolf Carlé, her coming of age coincides primarily with the Betancourt presidency. As she herself states with regard to the popular uprising that led to the overthrow and subsequent exile of General Pérez Jiménez, "In many places people did not learn of the overthrow of the dictatorship because, among other things, they had not known that the General was in power all those years. They lived on the periphery of current events. . . . The details of the news did not reach Agua Santa, so I did not learn what had happened until many years later when, out of curiosity, I was scanning the newspapers of the period" (*EL*, 177–78).

If this comment makes it abundantly clear that Eva's literary and sexual awakening precedes her political awakening, her arrival in the capital city during the Betancourt presidency—a historical period that coincides with Fidel Castro's revolution in Cuba and the birth of the guerrilla movement in Venezuela—ushers her into a political climate that contrasts dramatically with the marginal concern given to political realities in Agua Santa. While Riad Halabí is responsible for the development of Eva's sense of herself as a potential writer and a sensual woman, the birth of her political self owes much to Huberto Naranjo. Allende's portrayal of this character strikes a delicate balance between respect for his commitment to combating injustice and criticism of his inbred machismo. To this degree, she reveals the conflicts between leftist politics and sexual politics and points out the shortcomings of a revolutionary agenda that excludes on the basis of gender.

Naranjo himself does not correspond to the typical guerrilla fighter. Raised in the streets as a boy with little formal schooling but with a hatred of injustice and an acute awareness of the privileges enjoyed by the rich at the hands of a corrupt government, he is unable to articulate his rage in a broader political context until he meets a group of university students committed to guerrilla warfare. As Eva tells us:

> That night Naranjo heard a young man put into words the confusion he had carried in his heart for years. It was a revelation. At first he felt incapable of understanding much of their impassioned rhetoric—even less repeating it—but he knew instinctively that his private war against the Country Club *señoritos* and his defiance of police authority were child's play in the light of these ideas he was hearing for the first time. Contact with the guerrillas changed his life. . . . They made him see clearly the schisms that determine men's lives from birth, and he vowed to put all his rage, ineffectual until then, to the service of their cause. (*EL*, 181)

The transformation of Huberto Naranjo into *Comandante* Rogelio is given psychological depth as Eva narrates his love and compassion for his young recruits, his loneliness and longing for human contact, and his struggle against physical pain, hunger, and fatigue. His political commitment is similarly given credibility as Eva speaks of his unwavering belief that "violence originated with the government" and that "unemployment, poverty, corruption, and social injustice" were also "forms of violence" (*EL*, 232) that legitimized the acts of violence practiced by the guerrillas. Naranjo's words and deeds clearly affect Eva in many ways and enable her to read national politics with the same subtlety with which she reads texts. Increasingly aware of the censorship imposed on the media's reporting of any kind of dissident or guerrilla activity, Eva tells Rolf, "You know what kind of democracy this is . . . They use the excuse they're fighting Communism, but there's really no more freedom than we had in the General's time" (*EL*, 295). Yet, despite the fact that she helps him in his outrageous plan to rescue fellow comrades from the Santa María penal colony, Eva is ultimately as skeptical of Naranjo's ideology as she is of the government's false claim to democracy. Acutely aware of the gender-based fallacy in his conviction that he was waging a "man's war" (*EL*, 232) that would, nonetheless, make them all equal and free in the future, she issues a disheartening judgment that has many political implications of its own: "For Naranjo, and others like him, 'the people' seemed to be composed exclusively of men; we women should contribute to the struggle but were excluded from decision-making and power. His revolution would not change my fate in any fundamental way; under any circumstances, as long as I lived I would still have to make my own way. Perhaps it was at that moment I realized that mine is a war with no end in view; I might as well fight it cheerfully or I would spend my life waiting for some distant victory in order to be happy" (*EL*, 233).

Eva's realization, similar to that of countless other women equally marginalized from revolutionary struggles by their male companions, leads to a conclusion firmly rooted in an individualistic philosophy. Failing to articulate her sense of exclusion within a feminist framework that would allow her to unite with other women to combat injustice and patriarchal oppression, she seems to discard the possibility of any revolutionary change and clings to personal determination and will as a means of finding happiness. Although she subsequently tells Mimí that more important than changing their personal situation is changing "that of society as a whole" (*EL*, 267), neither she nor Allende articulate such changes within an identifiable political structure. Clearly, Allende is not promoting any concrete ideology of political transformation in *Eva Luna*. Further, despite her documentation of certain activities that correspond to real events in the history of the Venezuelan guerrilla movement—strikes, attacks against oil pipelines (Cott, 168), the legalization of the Communist Party in 1969[22]—Allende closes her rendition of this movement with an episode so profoundly fictitious in nature that it raises serious questions about the subordination of political concerns to narrative craft. By this I am referring to the daring raid on the Santa María penal colony organized by Huberto Naranjo with the assistance of Eva, Rolf, and the Indians who live in the region.

This episode brings together, in fact, many narrative strands previously explored in earlier sections of the novel. Confronted with the impossibility of smuggling weapons into the prison for the guerrillas to use in their escape, Eva comes up with the ingenious solution of molding false grenades out of the Universal Matter, or dough, utilized by her Yugoslavian *patrona* with great success decades before. Mimí, previously imprisoned in Santa María because of her homosexual activities during the Pérez Jiménez dictatorship, similarly provides a floor plan of the penal colony, whereas the Indians whom Eva met while living in the nearby village of Santa Agua function as guides and liaisons with the prison in order to seek revenge against the military for its oppression of the indigenous people. That is, earlier episodes of Eva's narrative fuel this successful concluding chapter of the guerrilla movement. The guerrilla fighters, armed with grenades that appear as real as life itself, are rescued from jail. No one is injured, and the government is at a loss to explain the inefficacy of their soldiers to halt the attack. Clearly one may argue that the absurdity of this amateurish political endeavor is the best weapon to deflate a hollow and inflationary government rhetoric that describes the raid as a major plot of international Communists threatening the entire "peace of the continent" (*EL*, 293). But I wonder if the sheer fictitiousness of the episode doesn't make a mockery of a guerrilla movement that even as late as the mid 1960s was functioning as a group with a much more substantial core of members than that articulated in *Eva Luna* (Cott, 203).

Perhaps both observations hold true; satire and mockery somehow join hands in this section of the novel as Allende makes blatantly clear, with specific regard to Venezuela in the late 1960s, that the guerrilla movement does not present any viable option for radically restructuring political and social practices. Certainly, the state-controlled television offers no opportunity for dissident ideologies to be considered by the viewing public. Rolf Carlé's extensive footage documenting guerrilla activities in the mountains is censored by national television; Naranjo's appearance on television following the guerrilla raid is immediately cut off; and the elections for the new president—presumably Rafael Caldera in 1969—take place in a climate characterized by freedom of speech within the limited confines of respect for "standards of morality, good conduct, and patriotism" (*EL*, 297).

Further, as Eva considers writing the guerrilla raid into her television serial for the purpose of using fiction to uncover a reality censored by the State, Allende introduces additional considerations about the relationship between the mass media and an agenda of political and social change. Eva's *Bolero* situates itself in a somewhat ambivalent space of compliance and resistance with regard to mainstream ideology. The very fact that it is a *telenovela* and that it is called *Bolero* is in itself significant.[23] The *telenovela*, "the particular Latin American style of television serial," considered "the leading edge of the cultural industry's penetration into everyday life,"[24] has enjoyed, since the 1960s, a vast viewing public that surpasses "the total copies of all García Márquez's work sold in Spanish" in the space of one episode alone (Rowe and Schelling, 232). By choosing to frame her autobiography in terms of this mass-produced form of entertainment designed for a wide viewing audience and broadcast at prime time,[25] Eva Luna is clearly situating herself within mainstream culture and commercial success. Significantly, in a somewhat ironic twist, Eva's inspiration for quitting her job as a secretary and devoting herself exclusively to writing is fueled in great measure by the commercial success of García Márquez himself. Mimí regales Eva with notebooks, pencils, dictionaries, and finally a typewriter, convinced that she can be as famous as that "thickly mustached Colombian writer on a triumphal tour" flocked by "a line of people outside a bookstore waiting to have their books signed" (*EL*, 225). Eva's success, in fact, and by implication, Allende's, seems to surpass that of the Colombian master. Attempting to connect viscerally with her public and to engage her viewers in the conscious act of sharing a familiar collective memory,[26] she entitles her series, *Bolero*, "as homage to the songs that had nurtured [her] girlhood hours" (*EL*, 296) and those of her public as well. Yet, within this complicity that she establishes with the demands of the mass media, there is a marked note of resistance and a genuine attempt— characteristic of post-Boom Latin American literature—to replace traditional codes with new configurations.

Although the reader is never provided with a totally coherent idea of the content of *Bolero*, Eva provides sufficient information to enable us to view it as the story of her life and Rolf Carlé's complete with such portrayals as a virgin's passionate union with a snake-bitten Indian, a professor who embalms cadavers, a minister of State who defecates in a plush receptacle instead of a toilet, a street urchin who turns into a guerrilla

commander, a beautiful woman who is born male, a gentle Arab, and an
Austrian teacher hung by his students. The introduction of such characters and thematic elements serves to radically restructure the simplistic
concept of good versus evil and the notion of family romance plots central to Latin American *telenovelas* in general (Rowe and Schelling, 232)
and to the particular series in which Mimí stars as the evil Alejandra.
Similarly, the rendition of such a baroque plot with complicated twists
and turns defies the highly formulaic structure of the classic *telenovela*.[27]
Despite this deviation from the norm, *Bolero* penetrates the public sphere
with meteoric success. By Eva's own account, "I doubt that anyone
understood that eccentric story, habituated as they were to jealousy,
scorn, ambition, or at least virginity, but none of these appeared on their
screens; and they went off to bed every night with their heads spinning
from . . . atrocities that would not bear logical analysis and that defied all
laws of the commercial television romance" (*EL*, 296).

It is not difficult to wonder what it is about *Bolero* that seizes the public imagination—its novelty, its subversion of conventional norms, its
sheer eccentricity? Since in fact Eva does not give the reader enough
details to understand how the public receives her series—a crucial component in evaluating the ways in which the media can serve as vehicles
for social change (Rowe and Schelling, 7)—it is not easy to assess its
political impact in a broader sense. Further, the limits on subversion in a
state-controlled industry are made blatantly clear when Eva is told in no
uncertain terms by the general in charge of the Armed Forces not to
mention the guerrilla raid in her series and to censor some of her more
controversial episodes, among them La Señora's somewhat kinky ideas
for business ventures and the politically inspired origin of the Revolt of
the Whores. Thus, although *Bolero* adds texture to the conventional
happy ending of the *telenovela* and introduces subversive elements that
may lead the public to rethink sexual issues, gender roles, and family
structures, it upholds the national ideal of patriotism by censoring political dissidence. Suppression, a psychological force that governs Eva's
memory of the past and her physiological functions, applies to political
life as well; hence, we may conclude that Eva Luna's television serial,
Bolero, achieves a modicum of "emancipatory potential" (Yúdice, 12) but
necessarily falls short of delivering a coherent package of ideological
weight. Rhythmically skirting the minefields of convention but ultimately targeted by the forces of censorship, it stretches the limits of
what has been considered mass or low art but is allowed to go no further
than officially sanctioned boundaries.

However, the novel in which *Bolero* is inserted, Allende's *Eva Luna*—
the uncensored version that re-creates in detail the guerrilla raid, the
Revolt of the Whores, and La Senora's kinky business ventures—erases
boundaries, disrupts hierarchies, and suggests the galvanizing role of literature in dismantling codified notions of truth. Imagination and the
sheer power of the word to transform reality are the creative forces that
Allende brings to center stage in her novel, as countless layers of myths,
narrative modes, high and low art, political accounts, gender crossing,
and celebrations of human dignity are blended together in an original
hybrid stew as distinctive as the one Rolf's aunt makes for her nephew.
While clearly one more construct, one more artifice more elaborate than
its individual components, Allende's novel with its emphasis on hybrid-
ness ultimately recalls the tremendous diversity of Latin America itself
that Allende pays homage to in *Eva Luna*. Continually voicing through
her protagonist a vision of Latin America where "all ages of history coexist in this immoderate geography" (*EL*, 178) and where in the
Venezuelan tropics and city that shape her tale "everything was jumbled
together" (*EL*, 210), Allende does not imply, however, that this jum-
bling produces uniformly felicitous results. The magical "Palace of the
Poor floating some fifteen centimeters above the rich humus of the jungle soil" (*EL*, 286) is ultimately an illusion momentarily apprehended by
some, which disappears in a haze of social injustice; the Indians who participate in the guerrilla raid know they will be forced to relocate when
the Army comes to pursue them as they have done countless times in
the past.

Yet, as General Tolomeo Rodríguez receives Eva Luna in his office
framed by a stained-glass window portraying Christopher Columbus
and speaks to her about her *telenovela* and the imminent legalization of
the Communist Party by the new president, Allende's readers may sense
that she is offering her rendition of a continent marked by violent con-
quests and social injustice in the past but with the potential for political
and social change in the future. In the meanwhile, in that somewhat
undefined space of the present, the best means for passing the time, she
suggests, is to tell a good story filled with humor, wit, pointed touches
of irreverence, and an imaginative spirit strong enough to free the
human spirit, play havoc with consecrated myths, and bring forth a new
version of Eve, Eva Luna.

Chapter Five

The Stories of Eva Luna

While each of Isabel Allende's books seems to emerge almost organically from the one that immediately precedes it, as well as from the particular conditions of the author's life, the relationship between Allende's 1987 novel, *Eva Luna,* and her 1989 *Cuentos de Eva Luna (Stories of Eva Luna,* 1991) is singularly and understandably intense. Adding texture and breadth to Eva's role as storyteller, Allende completes in her short story collection the unfinished agenda of her novel; by her own account, she eliminated six or seven of Eva's stories from *Eva Luna* because the novel was simply too lengthy (Allende, 1988). Significantly, two of the stories that she left intact prefigured in theme and subversive flair the collection of 23 stories and a prologue that she published two years later. The first one, told to Huberto Naranjo as a gesture of friendship and gratitude when Eva is a mere nine years old, is an extravagantly absurd tale with feminist overtones drawn from radio episodes, ballads, and Eva's active imagination. It concerns a bandit's girlfriend who tires of playing the role of the angelical and suffering sweetheart and decides to have some fun of her own; she buys a red dress and "the most delicious ice cream and the best malted milks," (*EL,* 65), dons a fruit-adorned turban, and dances the mambo on a tabletop, much to the chagrin of the outlaw who is no longer able to terrorize either her or all the children he has rendered orphans through his violence. While this delightful tale clearly responds to the fantasies of the young (and hungry) Eva, it also reveals Allende's satirical deflation of male dominance.

Eva's second story, told to Rolf Carlé when Eva is an adult and mentioned in chapter 4, is much more sophisticated and suggestive, crystallizing in one long paragraph the complex dynamics of storytelling and the fusion of lives through the power of the word. The protagonist of the tale, a storyteller herself, is asked by a warrior to sell him a past that will fill in the spaces of his life left bare by years of violence and blood. As the storyteller weaves her tale for the lonely warrior and calls upon the strands of her own life to compose the story, she discovers that "their pasts had been woven into a single strand. . . . and she surrendered herself to the pleasure of blending with him into a single story. . . ." (*EL,* 281). The seamless process of storytelling and story sharing thus erases the distinction between the teller and the listener, refashions experience into words, and becomes a vehicle and metaphor for union on multiple levels. As Walter Benjamin has succinctly described, "The storyteller takes what he tells from the experience—his own or that reported by others. And he in turn makes it the experience of those who are listening to his tale."[1]

For Allende, who was brought up in the oral tradition of storytelling,[2] has spent her entire life telling stories to her loved ones, and ultimately pictures herself as "one of those storytellers in Latin America and Africa who go from one village to another and sit in the middle of the plaza and tell a story,"[3] *The Stories of Eva Luna* provides a narrative framework for giving free reign to a genre that is an integral part of her creative and personal self. Belisa Crepusculario, the storyteller protagonist of Eva Luna's story "Two Words," does, in fact, sit in the middle of the plaza selling her words and providing solace for those in need. Yet, while the storyteller reconfigures mundane reality through her stories and "experiences through them a kind of freedom,"[4] the craft of writing a story, and most notably a story about storytelling, requires tremendous restraint.

Allende, acutely aware of the challenge involved in mastering this genre that she compares to poetry,[5] recognizes that while "novels can be written intermittently and rehashed endlessly because the complexity of their structure allows numerous errors and false starts to slip by undetected . . . the short story has to be handled very carefully so as to achieve the firmness and transparency of a watercolor (Allende, 1990, 5)." Indeed, she concludes, "the development and culmination of the story can leave no loose ends" (Allende, 1990, 5). If Allende's theory of short story writing bears significant resemblance to Edgar Allan Poe's— both speak of the importance of "a certain unique or singular effect" in the story communicated by the "very first sentence"[6]—her feminist twists, penchant for tales of love, underlying political concerns, and overriding belief in the imagination as "the supreme instrument of human realization" (Alter, 18) distinguish her writings from the lugubrious tales of the master of horror.

Allende's stories also bear little resemblance to the short stories of such eminent Latin American authors as Jorge Luis Borges and Julio Cortázar, whose writing Allende greatly admires.[7] Whereas Borges perfects a style of metaphysical fiction marked by "a series of hallucinatory, although hauntingly real, visions of the absurd human experience,"[8] and Cortázar delves into a surrealistic realm that sustains "an awareness of the precarious balance between the rational consciousness and the unconscious" (McMurray, 113), Allende's stories are primarily anchored in social and political realities. Reflecting on Latin American women's writing and her own body of work, Allende observes that they are "characterized by a subversive kind of happiness" that derives from "a newfound power of expression and the sheer joy of exercising it to denounce ancient injustices and to clamor for changes" (Allende, 1990, 6).

The Stories of Eva Luna not only springs from Allende's felicitous blending of theory and ideology and the unfinished agenda of her previous novel, the conditions in her life in 1988 were also singularly propitious for the creation of a short story collection. Divorced from her first husband, Miguel Frías, and engaged in a new relationship with William Gordon, whom she married that same year, Allende found herself living in a California household she humorously describes as mildly dysfunctional. With the television blasting, Willie's children fighting, the dog barking, and no initial space of her own, it was impossible for her to contemplate an endeavor as lengthy and demanding as a novel (Correas Zapata, 105). Instead, retrieving from memory and countless newspaper clippings actual people and events, Allende wrote in the space of a year most of the 23 tales and the prologue of *The Stories of Eva Luna.*

While Allende has stated that the theme of love unites all the stories (Correas Zapata, 106), I would venture to say that more than love, the straining for union—a union crystallized in Eva's story to Rolf about the lonely warrior—is the underlying premise of the majority of these stories. By this, I mean the coming together of human beings, the blending of lives, based on the sharing of such diverse elements as love, desire, cultural affinity, art, fear, nightmares, memory, words, the past, and the need for illusions. Allende forcefully demonstrates in story after story that the ties that bond people together far surpass those that divide them. Her desire to expand the boundaries of communication and interrelationships through the power of words, the joys of sensuality, the capacity for forgiveness, and the recognition of human dignity gives this collection a utopian quality as mundane reality is transformed by both Allende and Eva's fertile imagination. Within this context, it is not surprising that Allende once again calls upon Scheherazade's eloquence for her collection's epigraph. Unlike the Argentinean short story master, Jorge Luis Borges, who found in the *Thousand and One Nights* inspiration for his metaphysical themes, complex "labyrinthine structures and paradoxes . . . of circularity and infinity,"[9] Allende's relationship to *The Arabian Nights* evokes, instead, a feminist connection and woman's right to

appropriate words. Sidestepping issues of political power and the control
of discourse in patriarchal societies, Allende, as well as her characters
Eva Luna, Consuelo, and Belisa Crepusculario, passionately declares:
"Words . . . are in the air, carried by the wind. I can seize the one I want,
they are all free. . . . Infinite words . . . to be used a thousand times
without fear of wearing them out. They are there, within my grasp."[10]

The Stories of Eva Luna puts words to use in a multitude of engaging
social and personal settings. Some stories spring directly from *Eva Luna*
and reintroduce such familiar places as Agua Santa, La Colonia, the prostitutes' neighborhood around Calle República, and the Palace of the Poor,
and such familiar characters as Rolf Carlé; Riad Halabí; the school-
teacher, Inés; Eva's *madrina;* La Señora; Don Rupert; Doña Burgel; El
Benefactor; and the members of the tribe of the Children of the Moon.
Others examine the lives and dreams of prostitutes, doctors, priests,
criminals, the powerful, the exiled, and the dispossessed. Some are little
jewels, perfectly realized; others reveal the excesses of Allende's imagination and surpass the limits of the credible. Some offer thoughtful analyses
of social and political issues; others provide disconcerting views of sexual
politics and gender roles. As Eva herself succinctly reflects in the first sentence of "Interminable Life," "There are all kinds of stories" (*SEL,* 12). In
an attempt to provide a wide range of Allende's style and concerns in this
collection and to pay proper tribute to those stories that are the most textured and suggestive, I concentrate my analysis on the prologue of the
text and six of the stories: "Two Words," "Toad's Mouth," "Tosca," "Simple Maria," "Our Secret," and "And of Clay Are We Created."

The brief prologue, narrated in first person by Rolf Carlé to Eva
Luna, is a condensed and lyrical introduction to many of the stories in
the collection and the view of art that infuses Allende's writings. Evoking a moment of their shared past—a past that forms part of the end of
Eva Luna—Rolf retrieves from his memory his first lovemaking experience with Eva beneath the white mosquito netting in his aunt and
uncle's mountain village, La Colonia. A television reporter and filmmaker, Rolf fixes the image of intimacy of Eva and himself "in the frozen
images of a photograph" (*SEL,* 4), similar to a Renaissance painting.
Aware that he is both spectator of the portrait he has engraved in his
mind and protagonist of the same portrait, he creates a marked sense of
distance between the aesthetic object he contemplates and the subjective reality of himself as observer. He needs to keep the mental painting
congealed in time, fixed in space to make it "immune to the fading of
memory" (*SEL,* 5): "always the same peaceful smile on the man's face,

always the woman's languor . . . and always the silk shawl and the dark hair fall with the same delicacy" (*SEL,* 4). Yet, at the same time, he knows that the timeless frame surrounding art can be broken; the frozen image can come alive. Eva's writing is a tribute to that process; engaging in an implicit dialogue with her, he notes, "You think in words; for you, language is an inexhaustible thread you weave as if life were created as you tell it" (*SEL,* 4).

Ceding to the desire to emerge from art into life, a life that is created in the process of telling, Rolf slowly abandons his role of observer and becomes full participant in the painting. Celebrating the breaking of the "quiet symmetry of the painting" (*SEL,* 5) and acknowledging the power of words, he asks Eva to tell him a story, a story she has never told anyone, a request he similarly made in *Eva Luna* and that produced Eva's story of the lonely warrior. With this request, Allende justifies *The Stories of Eva Luna:* they are the gift of a talented storyteller to the man she loves who fulfills the dual role of spectator—that is, listener and receiver of her tales—and protagonist of one of her stories. Indeed, the last story in the collection, "And of Clay Are We Created" is about Rolf and his struggle to reclaim his past and his memory from behind the camera lens. The framing prologue and the concluding story thus shape the entire collection, creating, in fact, a "quiet symmetry" that palpitates with life and the importance of forging a union with others. Thus, although "And of Clay Are We Created" corresponds to the end of the volume, I discuss it now to uncover the subtle threads that are carefully woven together throughout Allende's stories. Like many of the stories in this collection, "And of Clay Are We Created" corresponds to a real event, one that Allende witnessed on television from Caracas: the eruption of the Nevado Ruiz volcano in Colombia in 1985 and the particular agony of a young girl, Omayra Sánchez, who was trapped in the mud for three days before she died. Omayra's anguish, "her dark eyes full of resignation and wisdom" (Correas Zapata, 111), affected Allende so profoundly that she wrote her story as a means of exorcizing the girl's phantom from her mind. If Allende was the spectator of this event in real life, she refracts this perspective in multiple ways as the reader observes Eva Luna, the narrator of the story, observing Rolf on television, as he, in turn, observes and films the 13-year-old Azucena—the fictional Omayra—until he can no longer be a spectator of her agony and sets his camera aside to experience her suffering and with it, his own.

The volcanic quagmire that traps Azucena and the image of her legs fixed and immobilized by the hands of her dead brothers and sisters clinging to her tiny body beneath the mud become a powerful metaphor for the torrent of memories that erupts and flows through Rolf as he confronts his past, equally buried behind his camera, yet exercising a firm grasp on his life. Much more than a metaphor, the dead bodies buried in the mud evoke for Rolf the bodies of the concentration victims he was forced to bury as a youth in Austria. Similarly, Azucena's entrapment re-creates the "visceral terror" (*SEL,* 363) he felt while locked up in an armoire by his abusive father. Further, Azucena's pain at seeing her dead siblings rekindles his love for his sister, Katharina, whose death he never mourned. Rolf not only shares Azucena's pain, "he *was* Azucena" (*SEL,* 364), reliving his life through hers and experiencing a powerful epiphany as he realizes that the tears he sheds are for himself and his years of buried hurt. Instead of Rolf consoling Azucena, she, in fact, consoles him by giving him the opportunity to find the most vulnerable part of his being.

The extremely moving and tender tone of this story is given extra texture as Eva shares Azucena and Rolf's anguish and serves as a powerful human lens that provides the reader access to their tale. She records the moment when Rolf lets go of his "fictive distance" (*SEL,* 355) and with it, his camera, and she understands that all his exploits and skills in reporting "were merely an attempt to keep his most ancient fears at bay, a stratagem for taking refuge behind a lens to test whether reality was more tolerable from that perspective" (*SEL,* 364). In essence, her narration provides the script for the external gestures and scenes she watches on television and that must have been filmed by still another reporter, thus multiplying further the play of perspectives Allende creates here. Eva's presence in this human drama is not merely one of spectator; as Rolf seeks to console the dying girl and keep her distracted while waiting for help, he tells her the stories that Eva had told him "in a thousand and one nights beneath the white mosquito netting" of their bed (*SEL,* 362). Thus, Rolf, transformed in part by Eva's stories and the force of his own emotions, becomes a male Scheherazade of sorts, using Eva's inspiration and words to delay death.

The sophistication of the technological age complete with satellites that transmit Azucena's image throughout the world is, ironically, not sufficient to rescue the girl, who dies after three days, accompanied by Rolf. As Eva writes Rolf's story and observes him upon his return, much as he observes her in the prologue of the work, she notes his cameras "forgotten in a closet" (*SEL,* 367) and the inner voyage he must complete before he is able to return to her with his wounds healed and his nightmares exorcised. This is the solitary path of healing, Allende implies, one that she herself will experience years later following the death of her daughter, Paula.[11]

The bond that unites Rolf and Azucena in "And of Clay Are We Created," a bond based on Rolf's powerful evocation of his past, forms much of the thematic force behind the story "Our Secret." Curiously, the theoretical justification for this story is suggested in the first paragraph of still another story previously mentioned, "Interminable Life." In this story, Eva describes the many kinds of stories that exist in life, among them those manifested whole, those taken from reality and then transformed by imagination, and those forged from inspiration that acquire reality in the telling. And then, she adds, "there are secret stories that remain hidden in the shadows of the mind; they are like living organisms, they grow roots and tentacles, they become covered with excrescences and parasites, and with time are transformed into the matter of nightmares. To exorcise the demons of memory, it is sometimes necessary to tell them as a story" (*SEL,* 261). "Our Secret" pays tribute to the role that cathartic sharing has in exorcising the demons of memory. It also provides an interesting link with Allende's first novels and reintroduces the theme of political torture that played such a predominant role in *The House of the Spirits* and *Of Love and Shadows.*[12]

"Our Secret" is a story marked by silences, physical and psychological scars, the fear of memory, and "the terrible vacuum of unspoken words" (*SEL,* 184). Narrated in third person from the perspective of the unnamed male protagonist, it focuses on two Chileans who initiate a casual encounter in a country that bears resemblance to Venezuela. Establishing the boundaries of safe conversation, they share topical and nostalgic impressions of growing up in the same neighborhood and attempt to keep at bay what they know they cannot share. As they try to solidify their relationship through lovemaking, the pressing reality of their lives as exiles and victims of persecution becomes increasingly palpable. The woman's sordid apartment is marked by the presence of a suitcase, the sign of impermanence, transition, and lack of roots. The poster of Chile on the wall—the mother country who has rendered her children "frightened orphans" (*SEL,* 187)—is a visible reminder of a reality that cannot be obscured, much like the bracelets the woman wears that, once removed, reveal white scars circling her wrists. The man's self-consciousness about the scars on his body, his fear of darkness, and his inability to reach climax or to find his voice "buried somewhere in his gut" (*SEL,* 186) create a tone of disquiet and tension in the story that dissipates the sense of "urgent anticipation" (*SEL,* 184) that had united the two until they find themselves physically and metaphorically naked in bed.

As with "And of Clay Are We Created," "Our Secret" reaches a point where the characters must either recede and solidify silence or painfully confront the demons of memory. The presence of absence is so strong in the story that the text abounds in synonyms for silence and muteness and images of crucifixion and martyrdom as the man pictures his body stretched out on the bed, "crucified" (*SEL,* 187), with a "bandage pressing upon on his head like a crown of nails" (*SEL,* 185). The protagonist's retreat into silence, a silence that plunges him into "an endless precipice" (*SEL,* 187), is paradoxically accompanied by screams and the cries of the tortured as well as by his own wrenching sobs as he confronts his guilt and betrayal. Significantly, the only character given a name in this story is Ana Díaz, a haunting image from the man's past who also appears as the committed activist and friend of Alba Trueba in *The House of the Spirits.*

The protagonist's nightmare, though never articulated at any point in the story, is discerned by his companion who absolves him of "his most deeply hidden wound" (*SEL,* 187) and his guilt over having betrayed his comrades. Acknowledging that "fear is stronger than desire, than love or hatred or guilt or rage, stronger than loyalty" (*SEL,* 187), and sharing his pain, if not the exact experience of treachery that he has kept hidden in his sealed box of memory, she provides him with the chance to begin to tell the story that is not told here. That story, about his "most hidden secret" and "forbidden words," is, in fact, the one that will exorcise the demons of his past and suggest the hope for the "promises of tomorrow" (*SEL,* 188). To this degree, "Our Secret" is a story about the sharing of a past and the release of silence, which can lead, in turn, to the sharing of words and the transformation of grief and guilt.

Following the publication of *The Stories of Eva Luna* and the death of her daughter, Paula, Allende pointedly stated that she believes that love is greater than fear (Correas Zapata, 106). Many of the stories in this collection pay tribute to the force of love, and even more, to the power the individual has to create the illusion of love and to sustain that illusion in the face of a contrary reality. Allende's most complex and successful rendition of this theme is the story "Tosca," a title that also suggests the role that art, representation, and, specifically, opera, plays in the individual's construction of an imaginary self. The story, narrated in third person by Eva Luna, centers on Maruzia Rugieri, a woman who fashions a life for herself based on pure representation and fantasy. She abandons the piano, for which she has a gift, to study opera, for which she has no talent. She marries an architect, Ezio Longo, who is madly in love with her but for whom she feels very little. She falls in love with a medical student, Leonardo Gómez, whom she meets on a streetcar and who is quietly whistling an aria from the opera "Tosca." Immediately seduced by Leonardo or his bel canto and projecting onto him the role of the lover, Mario, while appropriating for herself the role of Tosca, Maurizia becomes fixed in the world of art, a world as artificial as the structures her husband-architect builds.

The relationship between Maurizia and Leonardo is a classic case of misreading or misappropriation of roles. Maurizia Rugieri bears little resemblance to the famous singer, Floria Tosca; Leonardo, a timid and frail man, is quite different from the painter, Mario, who was executed by a firing squad; and Ezio Longo, a generous and sentimental soul, has tender qualities unlike those of the villainous chief of police, Scarpia, who intervenes between the two lovers and who is killed by Tosca. Maurizia is so blinded by her identification with her artistic and amorous role that all vestige of reality disappears from her life, and she abandons her husband and young son to join Leonardo in the hot provinces of what appear to be Venezuela. Attempting to appropriate for herself the genius of Puccini and Verdi, she converts Leonardo Gómez into "the hero of her personal opera, investing him with utopian virtues, and exalting to the point of mania the quality of his love, never pausing to measure her lover's response or gauge whether he was keeping pace with her in their grand passion" (*SEL,* 130). Fiction upon fiction consumes and constructs her life as she uses words to embellish a reality that is harsh and lonely and re-creates herself as Florence Nightingale helping her doctor-lover in the jungle. The one word she chooses never to mention is the name of her young son, left in the care of her husband as part of the terms of their separation.

Maurizia and Leonardo's move to Agua Santa in the mid 1950s provides Allende with the opportunity to add a parodic and Cervantine dimension to the theme of the fusion of art and life. Much as Cervantes reveals the degree to which the boundaries between reality and representation become eclipsed as Don Quixote so-called heroically intervenes in a staged puppet show and attempts to rescue Melisendra and Don Gaiferos from the Moorish troops pursuing them, Allende demonstrates how the inhabitants of Agua Santa confuse opera and life in their reactions to the performances that Maurizia and Leonardo present to the small town.

Confronted with Maurizia, whom they call Tosca, transformed into Madame Butterfly and "decked out in an outlandish bathrobe, with knitting needles in her hair" (*SEL,* 132), they are immediately seduced by the force of her tragic fate although they fail to understand a word of what she is singing. Their total submersion in the fictional world of the theater is so intense that when Maurizia–Madame Butterfly prepares to plunge a kitchen knife into her stomach, "the audience cried out with horror and a spectator rushed to the stage to dissuade her, grabbing the weapon from her hands and pulling her to her feet" (*SEL,* 133).

Yet despite the passionate reaction the townspeople have toward this opera and their intense dislike of the North American sailor, whose callous treatment of Madame Butterfly leads to her disaster, their relationship to art is still ultimately formulaic and very Caribbean. Every performance thereafter is consigned to a set script: "song, death, explication of the opera's plot by the soprano, public discussion, and closing party" (*SEL,* 133), complete with merrymaking and tropical *cumbias.* That is, in contrast to Maurizia, who lives the role at every moment and for whom the "habit of theater" is "deeply ingrained" (*SEL,* 134), the townspeople live it as entertainment, a pause from reality but not reality itself. Unlike Don Quixote, who was able to transform his fascination with knight errantry and books of chivalry into a quest that was bigger than himself, Maurizia's obsession is confined to the narrow boundaries of self.

Evoking the dilemma of her characters in "And of Clay Are We Created" and "Our Secret," Allende provides Maurizia with a similar opportunity to emerge from behind the metaphoric lens that distances her from life and to open the sealed box that contains the memory of her past prior to her transformation into Tosca and Madame Butterfly. Leonardo Gómez dies, and with his death, he acquires the materiality of art he enjoyed metaphorically in life: a bronze bust of his image is commissioned by the town and installed in the main square facing the statue of Simon Bolivar, the country's liberator. While the positioning of his bust may be read ironically, since Leonardo in life helped to entrap Maurizia in a world of fantasy rather than free her, his death provides her with the possibility to either construct a new role, "the legend of her despair" (*SEL,* 134), or shed all artifice and confront her former self and the genuine loss of her son. The highway that comes through Agua Santa—a bridge with Maurizia's past since it is constructed by Ezio Longo and their son—crystallizes the journey the 51-year-old woman must take as she prepares to reintroduce herself to her husband and son, who is now 28 years old.

The end of the story finds Maurizia simultaneously in the world of artistic representation as she pictures herself "on a stage playing out the most dramatic moment of the long theater of her life" (*SEL*, 136) and in the realm of reality as she painfully realizes that "the true hero of the drama was Ezio Longo" (*SEL*, 137) and not Leonardo Gómez. Yet, at the exact "infinite moment" when she must decide "between reality and dream" (*SEL*, 137), she senses the bond that exists between father and son and knows that she can never be part of their lives. The new script she has fashioned from the fabric of reality, the one of forgiveness by husband and son, can never be realized; thus, "under the protection of Leonardo Gómez's umbrella" (*SEL*, 136), that is, the safety of the past, she retreats anew into the realm of fantasy. The solitary macaw that hovers above her head like a "bizarre archangel" (*SEL*, 137) with a cacophonous song suggests a brutal parody of Maurizia's failed operatic career and her inability to find redemption. While imagination may be an indispensable instrument in the realization of dreams, Allende implies that it may also be "the eternal snare of delusion of a creature doomed to futility" (Alter, 18).

The subtly defined borderline between empowerment and entrapment created by imagination and illusions is a theme that Allende explores in several stories of her collection and that acquires additional levels of meaning when inserted in the complex terrain of sexual politics. "Simple María" offers a provocative rendition of the creation of love and female sexual desire at the same time that it offers new ways of reading male sexuality. From the very title of this story, Allende casts the reader into a world where certainty is undermined by ambiguity, gender stereotypes are dismantled, and social conventions are replaced by the law of desire. One of the five stories of the collection in which Eva refers to herself in first person, "Simple María" is about a prostitute who has just died. As her friends gather around her coffin on the Calle República to mourn her loss, they fulfill the same role that Allende and Eva play throughout the volume as they re-create or create Maria's life and her past: "one by one, her friends uncovered scraps of information about her life and pieced them together patiently, filling in the blank spaces with fantasy, until they had reconstructed a past for her" (*SEL*, 168).

Given the fact that Maria's friends are prostitutes whose lives have been marked by "poverty and accumulated injustice . . . [and] every form of violence" (*SEL*, 167), the reader can easily surmise that their fantasies about her will generate a different kind of script, one in which they project onto her—and the blank pages of her life—all they have never known in their own lives. Eva, who joins them in mourning the prostitute's death, thus becomes the storyteller who tells the story of Maria invented by others. The potential unreliability of the narrator is thus a product of the ultimate uncertainty of the original sources, providing a revealing comment about the nature of storytelling for Allende herself. If for Allende, the freedom she experiences in writing fiction is inextricably related to the freedom to lie (Allende, 1992b, 290), her fictional storytellers, in turn, share this ability to fabricate arbitrary worlds that spring from a seemingly utopian desire to right social wrongs and glorify the individual as creator of his or her own destiny.

Simple María's life is a case in point: born to a comfortable family of Spanish émigrés and struck by a freight train at the age of 12, she is left with little ability for reasoning but with "the impatience of her senses" intact (*SEL,* 171). Married to an elderly doctor whose death leaves her free to explore her sexual desires, she and her young son are promptly sent off on a sea voyage to Spain by a family eager to harness her erotic desires. Tragedy and pleasure—Thanatos and Eros—await her at sea as her son is ludicrously killed in a bizarre accident, and María seeks consolation in the arms of a Greek sailor, discovering in the process her potential for endless sexual pleasure. This experience, in fact, marks her life and determines her decision to jump ship with the sailor and break free of the "inescapable guardianship of her parents and brothers, free of social pressures and veils at mass, free finally to savor the torrent of emotions that originated on her skin and sank through every pore to her innermost grottoes, where she was tossed and tumbled in roaring cataracts that left her exhausted and happy" (*SEL,* 177). Eventually exhausting her Greek lover, who finds himself threatened by the "moist, tumid, inflamed woman" (*SEL,* 177) whose desire he cannot match, María seeks to re-create with countless other men her experience with the sailor, earning her the status of the "most famous prostitute in the port" (*SEL,* 178) and freezing her life in a photo of the past. Ultimately forced by time, disillusion, and plain wear and tear to make her way to the capital and the Calle República, she persists in creating the illusion of love for herself and her lovers until she finally gives in to despair and wills her own death.

Within this narrative framework that stretches the limits of verisimilitude and credibility, Allende causes several disruptions in conventional beliefs that add texture to this story and make Simple María more complex than her name warrants. If, as Julia Kristeva has noted, in "Western societies, sexual pleasure . . . is granted to women provided that it isn't discussed,"[13] Allende rewrites this concept by creating a character—or by having her characters create a character—whose life is based on the attempt to fulfill desire and who names those parts of her body—"innermost grottoes"—most susceptible to the experience of pleasure. While initially there seems to be a basic contradiction between Maria's profession as prostitute and her experience of sexual pleasure, since as Luce Irigaray has acutely noted, a woman who sells her body to a male economy has little "right to her own sexual pleasure,"[14] Allende radically redefines the notion of prostitution as it applies to María. Money is merely the vehicle that enables her to live; pleasure is what she seeks, and men are simultaneously portrayed as mere objects for the realization of her desire, and subjects for whom love is, in fact, more important than a transitory sexual act. That is, just as María's fantasies are fueled by a "sincere passion" (*SEL*, 178) and a singular ability to anticipate "the other's desires" (*SEL*, 179), the sailors who travel from all over the globe to be with her ultimately want to experience the "illusion of love" (*SEL*, 178) that she feels and sells to each one in handcrafted packets.

Differences between the sexes are significantly erased as Allende provides a utopian view of sexual politics in which sex as a business or a purely physical act is converted into a shared momentary illusion for the two parties involved. While social realities clearly intrude on the lives of the other prostitutes, creating a more realistic view of a denigrated female profession, María lives "protected by the armor of her invented love" (*SEL*, 168), and thus her story, unlike the others, "had a glow of elegance that gave wing to the imagination" (*SEL*, 167). Her death similarly offers a different twist to the typical Allende scenario of entrapment in the frozen experience of the past or progression to a different dimension where revelation replaces stagnation. Seeking to escape from the impossibility of finding "that ancient illusion in every passing man" (*SEL*, 180), María simply decides to die, a fate that the protagonist also chooses in the story "Clarisa." But in accordance with the playful ambiguity and undermining of truth that permeate this story and much of Allende's fiction in general, Eva suggests that the jug of thick chocolate María drinks before dying may, in fact, be poison. This rational explanation reduces the fantastic tone of this story delicately poised on the threshold between social reality and imaginative spirit.

If Simple María's sexuality is shaped by an obsessive desire to re-create a moment of the past, Allende provides an even more daring and playful portrait of female pleasure in the short story "Toad's Mouth," which by her own account, "is prohibited in Mormon schools and heads the black list of many Christian fundamentalist sects" (Correas Zapata, 109). The first paragraph of this story, as well as the end, appears in *Eva Luna* and is apparently one of the stories Allende eliminated from her novel (*EL*, 255). Based on the true legend of a woman who earned her living in Patagonia by opening her legs and inviting men to throw money at her private parts (Correas Zapata, 110), as well as on a popular game in the Hispanic world that involves tossing coins into the mouth of a fake toad,[15] Allende adds a number of personal flourishes to these suggestive games of chance.

The protagonist of this story is Hermelinda, a good-natured, sensuous woman who earns her living in the harsh climate of Tierra del Fuego by selling "games of fantasy" (*SEL*, 60). While in reality Hermelinda is an inventive prostitute with a liking for men, a distaste for conventional life, and a sense of pride in the "sparks of pleasure she afforded the drovers" (*SEL*, 64) who work for the British Sheepbreeders, Ltd, nowhere in the story does Allende actually mention the word *prostitute*. Hermelinda is simply presented as a feisty and independent woman with sharp business skills who entertains the drovers in numerous ways. Thus, the revolutionary potential of such a character is dramatically reduced because there is no body of opposition that calls into question her activities. The British are barely present in the story, isolating themselves from their workers through fences and shrubs and creating the "illusion of a gentle English countryside" (*SEL*, 60), much as Hermelinda creates in her men the illusion of sexual fantasies and desires.

If feminist critics such as Jane Gallop distinguish between the prostitute who works for money and the prostitute "as subversive force" who "does it . . . for pleasure,"[16] the implication is that subversion is resistance against a social system that does not acknowledge the existence of female libertines or even women as the "subject of desire."[17] By presenting Hermelinda in an isolated setting where societal forces and institutions of patriarchy are minimized—despite the presence of a British industry—Allende once again highlights individual rather than collective acts of resistance at the same time that she acknowledges and celebrates woman's autonomous sexual desire. That is, Allende writes against the current of convention as she did in "Simple María" but does not bestow broader meaning to individual acts of nonconformity.

Similarly, by implicitly playing havoc with psychoanalytical views of woman as the metonymic "hole" rather than the "whole" (Gallop, 22), Allende demonstrates that woman can be both the hole, that is, the object of the coin toss, and the whole, or the subject of desire. As narrated in third person by Eva, Hermelinda's "ancient love secrets" (*SEL,* 63) are so potent that men travel hundreds of kilometers to be with her. While clearly creating herself to correspond to male fantasies of women, Hermelinda still maintains control of the rules of the game at every minute and reigns among the men of the pampas "like a queen bee" (*SEL,* 61). In essence, she is an erotic version of the storyteller who creates desire in her listeners through her words. Here, the emphasis on orality, characteristic of storytelling, is textured with suggestive and colliding images of women's genitalia. Hermelinda's private parts are alternately described as "the dark center of her body . . . as open as a fruit," "a merry toad's mouth," "the gate of heaven," and "a sultan's treasure" (*SEL,* 63), images that simultaneously evoke in the midst of the Argentinean pampas the sensuality of the *Thousand and One Nights,* poetic metaphors of standard use, and the frog's orifice that graces the story's title. The combination of such diverse metaphors to describe female genitalia has the delightful effect of situating the story in both the sublime celestial sphere and the comical terrain of amphibian eroticism. That is, Allende's penchant for humor and hybrid images functions in this sexual context to prevent any monolithic mythologizing of the female body by the male fantasy.

The sense of union created between Hermelinda and the drovers is radically disrupted when the newcomer, Pablo, arrives, enticed by her fame and his desire to flee his own solitary nature and find the woman "who could change the way the wind blew" (*SEL,* 65). Immediately seduced and inflamed by the young woman in yellow petticoats and no underwear whose legs are spread wide on the floor, he sees her as a beautiful and wild puma that he, the hunter, must conquer. This becomes the crucial moment of the story when Allende, even more than her protagonist, must come to terms with the complex issue of the relationship between the sexes and the concept of power. If she allows Hermelinda to be subdued, she negates much of the celebration of woman's autonomy. Choosing a solution that evokes the ambiguity concerning Simple María's death and that similarly characterizes the end of *Eva Luna* with its two versions of the relationship between Eva and Rolf, Allende does not let the reader know who conquers whom. As Pablo prepares to toss his coin into the slot and win the prize of the seductive Hermelinda, Eva narrates that "he transfixed Hermelinda with a knifelike gaze, forcing her to abandon her contortionist's tricks" (*SEL,* 66). But then, she adds, "Or that may not be how it was; it may be that she chose him from among the others to honor with her company" (*SEL,* 66). Creating a postmodern script for a tale set far from twentieth-century civilization, Allende skillfully casts the vote into the hands of her reader-voyeur, although she does clarify that the story ends with the two lovers riding off in the distance with a bag of coins tied to Hermelinda's waist, "a new expression in her eyes and a satisfied swish to her memorable rump" (*SEL*, 66). While this rather conventional and stereotypical description pays tribute to both female and male power—she holds the money, he holds the key to her heart—Allende's final nod at irony and play is restored when the British, seeking to distract the distraught drovers, purchase for them a huge ceramic toad. Artifice clearly does not work for the drovers as it did for Maurizia in "Tosca," or for Rolf Carlé, and the integrity of woman's body as sensual reality and not construct or illusion is maintained throughout this unusual tale.

The blending or union of lives in *The Stories of Eva Luna* is achieved not only through illusions, memories, fears, art, hidden secrets, and sexual intimacy, but also through words. Allende's most compelling rendition of the power of words in transforming and uniting human beings is her story "Two Words," which focuses on Belisa Crepusculario, a storyteller and seller of words. Nowhere is Allende's debt to Scheherazade more evident than in this deceptively simple tale about a woman whose family was "so poor they did not even have names to give their children" (*SEL*, 10). If, as Allende suggests, a significant form of deprivation is the absence of language, "the terrible vacuum of unspoken words" (*SEL*, 184), Belisa Crepusculario compensates for her deficient birthright by claiming for herself the power of naming. Entering into a terrain traditionally reserved for either the supreme creator or male representatives on earth, she simultaneously names herself and "cloaks herself" in the "poetry of 'beauty' [Belisa] and 'twilight' [Crepusculario]" (*SEL*, 9) and thus fashions the first set of the two words that will ultimately change her life. Not content to remain in the world of orality, her transition from illiteracy to writing arrives in the form of a newspaper she finds one day that so entices her curiosity that she pays "a priest twenty pesos to teach her to read and write" (*SEL*, 12) and hence launches herself in the honorable profession of selling words.

Belisa Crepusulario's decision to enter the marketplace of words is fraught with implications of a vast social and political nature. Realizing that for a woman of her social class, survival is integrally related to selling her body (prostitution), selling her soul (working as a servant), or selling her gift for words in the form of factual stories, legal arguments, invented insults for enemies, or verses, she rejects the profession reserved for such women as Simple María and Hermelinda and enters the public arena traditionally occupied by men. As in many of the stories of this collection, issues of power and political concerns are initially simplified, and individual will triumphs over a vast social machinery. Belisa naively concludes that "words make their way in the world without a master and that anyone with a little cleverness can appropriate them and do business with them" (*SEL*, 12). This statement is open to countless speculations: Is Allende voicing through her character a glorification of the emancipatory potential of the subaltern classes who have been isolated from spheres of verbal power, or is she providing, instead, a less-politicized version of what Robert Alter has termed "the double function of language as magical conjuration and radical probing" (Alter, 186)?

Both interpretations simultaneously collide and coalesce when Belisa is kidnapped by El Mulato, the henchman of the famous Colonel, and asked to write a speech for him that will put an end to violence and tyranny and enable him to win the presidential elections. The so-called master needs to appropriate the correct words to seduce his public; the subaltern's role is to create them for him and, much like Doña Marina with regard to Hernando Cortés, translate his will to the people. Words thus enter the political arena and function as a substitute for physical force. Simultaneously playing the role of speech writer, spin doctor, and media consultant for the lonely and attractive warrior, Belisa Crepusulario discards "harsh, cold words, words that were too flowery, words worn from abuse, words that offered improbable promises, untruthful and confusing words, until all she had left were words sure to touch the minds of men and women's intuition" (*SEL*, 15–16). Once again, Allende's colliding ideologies surface in the text. Belisa has the power of naming and the ability to create a political platform of "radical probing" that will presumably enable the colonel to win the race. Yet the language she uses is one that stereotypically assigns to men the process of reason and to women the process of feeling. While this strategy may be read as a conscious and realistic attempt to facilitate the colonel's success by appealing to each of the sexes, it may also be viewed as an elitist and sexist mechanism ironically created by a woman of the lower class who fails to attribute to other women the analytical skills she herself enjoys.

While some readers, including myself, are intrigued by the socio-political implications of this story, Allende seems more interested in developing the theme of the magic of words[18] and their power to unite human beings. Much as the public is seduced by the utopian discourse of the colonel, he, too has been seduced, hypnotized, and transformed

by the "magical conjuration" of the two words Belisa Crepusculario
gives him "for his exclusive use" (*SEL*, 17) as a bonus for his payment of
her services. In a desperate attempt to dispel the potency of Belisa's
magic, El Mulato seeks her out once again and urges the colonel to give
her back her words. Instead, he gives her his heart, thus completing his
transformation from warrior to gentle lover, a metamorphosis that
evokes the radical change in the King after 1,001 nights of stories by
Scheherazade. If, as Robert Alter has noted, "in primitive cultures, the
word is magical, exerting power over the physical world" (Alter, 11),
Allende provides a compelling fictionalization of this concept in "Two
Words," where language, in fact, transforms the political arena and the
physical world, as well as the individual who falls prey to its spell. Significantly, although Allende provides details concerning the colonel's
public speech, at no point in the story does she reveal what the two
words are, believing that "they are different for everyone"[19] and suggesting to her readers that they create their own version.

The search for union that unites the six stories and the prologue discussed in this chapter appears in other tales as well. "Walimai" is a lyrical rendition of the union of the body of a warrior of the Children of the
Moon and the spirit of a dead Indian of the Ila tribe, a union designed to
provide peace to the Ila woman who was raped by white men and saved
from further ignominy by the warrior who kills her, nurtures her spirit
within his own, and then sets it free. "Interminable Life" fictionalizes the
true story of an elderly doctor and his wife who attempt to die together
to achieve a dignity in death that corresponds to their life (Correas Zapata, 111). "Phantom Palace" explores the cultural ties between a white
woman, Marcia Lieberman—the name of Allende's photographer—and
the Indians who live in the jungle and who occupy the palace of El
Benefactor, the dictator Juan Vicente Gómez, after his death. "The Gold
of Tomas Vargas" features the complicity between two women who
band together to empower themselves against their abusive husband
and lover. And "Revenge," one of the most polemical stories of the collection, explores the intimate relationship between a rapist and his victim, a bond created by the obsessive memory each one harbors of the
other and the dissolution of their hatred after 25 years. Other stories
present heightened scenarios of betrayal, sexual obsession, unrequited
love, justice, and the abuse of human rights.

While *The Stories of Eva Luna* are uneven in quality and are frequently
characterized by conflicting ideological messages and instantaneous love
as a means to conclude the tale, they provide snapshots of complex

human beings who replace hatred and discord with the utopian belief in the sharing and blending of lives. There is no better messenger of this idealistic social and cultural endeavor than the storyteller herself, who "joins the ranks of the teachers and sages" and who "has counsel—not for a few situations, as the proverb does, but for many, like the sage" (Benjamin, 108). By empowering her readers to join in the process of deciphering ambiguous meanings and filling in the blank spaces with their own imaginations, Allende creates in the process countless verbal magicians, countless Scheherazades of both sexes for whom stories gracefully enrich reality.

Chapter Six
The Infinite Plan

Isabel Allende's move to the United States in December 1987 and her marriage to San Francisco lawyer William Gordon dramatically affected her literary production and, most notably, her fourth novel, *El plan infinito* (1991) (*The Infinite Plan,* 1993). It is, without a doubt, a book that poses numerous challenges for its Latin American author. If *The House of the Spirits* marks Allende's incursion into Latin America's male literary club, *The Infinite Plan* marks her foray into a terrain occupied by countless authors and books that have found a place in the North American literary imagination. It is a new rendition of the compelling American dream fictionalized by such giants as Theodore Dreiser, F. Scott Fitzgerald, and Arthur Miller; a powerful contribution to the literature that describes the reality of those who live in the borderland of two cultures; and a haunting addition to the fiction written about the Vietnam War. *The Infinite Plan* also has the distinction of being the first novel Allende has written that focuses on a male protagonist, Gregory Reeves, whose first-person narration is interspersed throughout the predominantly third-person narrative perspective. To this degree, it is a complex novel that obliges Allende to enter a psychological and cultural context vastly different from that of her previous fiction and own life experiences. It is not surprising that she spent several years completing this work as she assimilated and researched the California reality that forms the backdrop of her text (Correas Zapata, 212).

This is not to suggest that Allende's distance from the world she describes was a barrier to her literary endeavor. To the contrary, it was precisely her experience of being an outsider that attracted her to those who were also marginal in California and enabled her to fictionalize the complexities of Chicano life and the relationship between whites and Latinos in an east Los Angeles barrio (Allende, 1994a, 370–71). Allende's husband, Gordon, proved indispensable in familiarizing her with the cultural clashes and reverse racism that figure so predominantly in the first part of the novel (Allende, 1993a, 53).[1] In fact, Gordon's life prior to his encounter with Allende—his upbringing as a gringo in east Los Angeles, his failed marriages, his chaotic existence, and his legal problems—forms the basis of Gregory Reeves's biography (Correas Zapata, 139). Carmen Morales, another major character in the work, who subsequently changes her name to Tamar, similarly owes her existence to a composite of two real people: Carmen Alvarez, Gordon's childhood friend, and Tabra Tunoa, a well-known California jewelry designer and personal friend of Allende, who went from street vendor in Berkeley to owner of a lucrative jewelry business (Correas Zapata, 139; Fussell, 53). That is, Allende continues in *The Infinite Plan* a trademark of her literary style: characters are frequently taken from real life and transformed according to the exigencies of fiction. As opposed to such authors as Alice Walker for whom the "crowning moment" of the artistic process occurs when characters she has created "walk through the door," Isabel Allende pointedly fictionalizes people who have already "walked through the door."[2] In the particular case of *The Infinite Plan*, Allende has candidly stated that she actually had to tone down and eliminate aspects of Gordon's story to make Gregory Reeves's life more believable to the reader (Correas Zapata, 114).

Although Allende's previous novels have been characterized by strong doses of psychological penetration, I would venture to say that *The Infinite Plan* reveals the full range of Allende's ability to capture the complexities of the human soul. Gregory Reeves is, without a doubt, Allende's most tormented character. His long odyssey through a Los Angeles barrio in the 1940s and 1950s, Berkeley and Vietnam in the 1960s, and San Francisco in the 1970s and 1980s highlights the degree to which he cannot escape his inner demons despite radical changes in location. His submersion in intense social and political issues of his time enables Allende to create a broad tapestry of American life in which "events and social upheaval are not seen as mere historical conditions of a certain time frame but become personalized experiences in terms of individual characters."[3]

Although the presence of historical events from World War II to Vietnam looms large in this novel and the personal and the political are frequently entwined, the union of the two has a different tenor than in Allende's previous novels. Unlike *The House of the Spirits*, *Of Love and Shadows*, and *Eva Luna*, where commitment to political change shapes the actions and lives of many of the characters, *The Infinite Plan*—set in the United States rather than in Latin America and clearly inflected with American values—is more concerned with the transformation of self than with the transformation of society. Allende's utopian design for a better world is suggested through her characters' attempts to erase cultural, ethnic, and gender-based boundaries, but none of the characters confront structures of power as do Miguel from *The House of the Spirits,* Irene and Francisco from *Of Love and Shadows,* and Huberto Naranjo from *Eva Luna.* Nonetheless, as Allende herself recognizes, there is an epic quality about her characters that ultimately defines the force and appeal of her narrative. Gregory Reeves, Carmen Morales, and others "resound with the sounds of the world and the time and the places where they live" and their stories acquire broader meaning when viewed as part of their "collective history."[4]

The Infinite Plan is divided into four parts, each of which corresponds to a specific time in the life of Gregory Reeves. A more extensive bildungsroman than *Eva Luna,* Allende's previous incursion in this genre, *The Infinite Plan* is also a confession told to a third party who is none less than the author herself. Allende clearly situates herself as recipient of Gregory's story and implied narrator in the first paragraph of the novel where she states: "Forty-some years later, during a long confession in which he reviewed his life and drew up an accounting of his errors and achievements, Gregory Reeves told me of his earliest memory."[5] If her presence in the work is further suggested in part 3, when she introduces herself as a friend of Carmen Morales's son, Dai, her role in the novel is not completely clarified until the last pages. It is here that Allende the narrator, witness, and friend merges with Allende the author, and Gregory Reeve's biography merges in kind with that of Allende's husband, William Gordon, who received for his fiftieth birthday a copy of her second novel, *Of Love and Shadows* (Fussell, 80), thus providing the initial bond that would lead to their meeting and subsequent marriage. As Reeves himself narrates at the novel's close:

> In the solitude of the countryside, I recaptured the silence of my childhood, the silence the soul finds in the peace of nature. . . . Did you know that it was in that wild country I learned about you? Carmen had given me your second novel, and I read it during that vacation, never imagining that one day I would meet you and make this long confession. . . . The night we met, you asked me to tell you my story. It's very long, I warned you. That's all right, I have a lot of time, you said, not suspecting what you were getting into when you walked into this infinite plan. (*IP,* 378, 379, 382)

The relationship between author and character thus spills over from the text into life itself or vice versa and from orality to writing, creating a

complex narrative perspective in which Reeves's first-person narration—
approximately 70 pages of this 377-page novel—adds a quality of dramatic urgency to the author's third-person omniscient narration that is
simultaneously "objective" in its portrayal of "approximately fifty years of
social history" and "subjective" in its rendition of Gregory's life (Perricone, 1994, 57). A lengthy quotation from Reeves's confession that precedes the beginning of the novel introduces the reader to the dark world
of shadows that lurk in the protagonist's consciousness and that are gradually clarified and confronted throughout his long journey into self:

> I am alone, at dawn, on the mountaintop. Below, through the milky
> mist, I see the bodies of my friends. Some that have rolled down the
> slopes lie like disjointed red dolls; others are ashen statues surprised by
> the eternity of death. Stealthy shadows are climbing toward me. Silence.
> I wait. They approach. I fire against dark silhouettes in black pajamas,
> faceless ghosts. I feel the recoil of the machine gun; I grip it so tightly my
> hands burn as incandescent lines of fire cross through the sky, but there is
> no sound. The attackers have become transparent; they are not stopped
> by the bullets that pass right through them, they continue their implaca-
> ble advance. I am surrounded. . . . Silence. . . .
> My own scream wakes me, and I keep screaming, screaming . . . (*IP*)

While the actual events described in this passage refer concretely to
Reeves's experience in Vietnam and an attack that occurred on a mountaintop, the images transcend their literal meaning and become a
metaphorical representation of the protagonist's existential anguish. Isolated in a space that no one shares, continually observing life from a distance, pursued by ghosts of the past who surround him with their silent
claims and by enemies both external and internal, his screams or ability
to break the silence constitute the power behind his first-person narrative. Though occupying less than one-fifth of the novel, his haunting
rendition of personal loss, betrayal, fear, abandonment, and death in the
first three parts of the novel is gradually transformed in the fourth part
into a tale of aliveness and peace in which the dead are finally laid to rest
and Reeves descends delivered and healed from the solitary mountain.

Part 1 of the novel captures aspects of Gregory Reeves's life from the
age of four through to his high school years. The early years of his life
are characterized by an unconventional upbringing shaped by his father,
the Australian immigrant, Charles Reeves, Doctor in Divine Sciences,
who travels in a truck throughout the dusty roads of the West with his

family—his wife, Nora, and their children, Judy and Gregory, and
Nora's girlhood friend from Russia, Olga—predicating the word of the
"Infinite Plan" and offering "the rules of a good life" (*IP,* 28) to those
who sign up for his classes and buy his books. Based on the firm belief
that everything in the universe has a reason or purpose for being, the
Infinite Plan not only shapes the livelihood of the Reeves family, but the
entire course of Gregory's life as he seeks to understand and experience
the meaning behind his own existence.

If the Reeveses appear in some initial way to resemble other characters in Allende's work who similarly sell "hope" (*IP,* 5), it soon becomes
clear that this is not merely an unconventional family, but a dsyfunc-
tional one.[6] When Charles Reeves becomes ill with a stomach ulcer, the
family is forced to give up the vagabond life that Gregory cherishes and
settle in a Los Angeles barrio, where one of Reeves's followers, Pedro
Morales, helps them find a place to live. The sense of power Charles
Reeves experiences as a man chosen to impart a mission by a higher
order gradually deteriorates, together with his mind. He engages in an
affair with the family's traveling companion, Olga; he beats Gregory
with his belt and burns his palm with a match to discourage him from
stealing; he sexually abuses his daughter, Judy; and he masturbates in
public and in the presence of his wife, Nora. Nora, in turn, retreats into
a world of coldness and indifference and detaches herself from both
everyday realities and the emotional needs of her young son.

The loss of freedom and family unity that Gregory experiences at age
six upon his father's illness and subsequent death is coupled with the
radical sense of displacement he feels at being a blonde-haired, blue-
eyed gringo in a Chicano barrio where the sounds of Spanish add lin-
guistic fuel to his psychological estrangement. Forced to survive in the
midst of abject poverty and neglect, he develops complex mechanisms of
denial and repression. He continues to idealize his father despite his
bouts of alcoholism and abuse and chooses to ignore the oppressive and
secretive air of mystery that penetrates his family life. Silence, or the
muffled scream, becomes his way of dealing with events too painful to
process or articulate. If at the tender age of five he is the inadvertent
witness to the rape of a young black girl by two white men, his response
to that situation—a combination of terror, impotence, and rage—reproduces itself in different scenarios throughout his life as he is alternately
the victim and the protector of the defenseless.

Gregory's own rape by a school mate, Martínez—an event painfully
narrated in first person—not only intensifies his sense of powerlessness

and desire to silence shame and humiliation, but also symbolically marks his social status. In a neighborhood where the dominant model of ethnicity and race has been inverted, Gregory's sexual violation provides a graphic representation of this phenomenon. He becomes the quintessential *other,* the black girl, the victim, whose bodily integrity is penetrated. The degree to which Martínez has penetrated his being is crystallized in Gregory's rendition of the rape, which contains not only his own words, but those of Martínez as well. As he recounts: "I still feel the knife blade against my throat, but I don't think I'm bleeding anymore. If you move I'll kill you, you fucking sonofabitch gringo, and I had no way to defend myself, all I could do was cry and curse while he was doing it to me. . . . He walked away laughing. If anyone finds out, I'm fucked; they'll call me a pansy for the rest of my life. No one must ever find out!" (*IP,* 82–83).

Gregory's refuge from pain becomes the Morales household dominated by the patriarch, Pedro Morales; nurtured by the matriarch, Inmaculada Morales; and enlivened by the irrepressible spirit of their daughter Carmen, who becomes Gregory's soul mate and best friend. Artfully weaving together sociology and psychology, Allende creates a textured portrait of barrio life that echoes passages from the writings of Gloria Anzaldúa and Sandra Cisneros and presents the complex borderland separating two cultures from the perspective of the outsider who, in this case, is not Chicano, but a white male. Gregory Reeves would no doubt agree with Gloria Anzaldúa's assessment that "the psychological borderlands, the sexual borderlands and the spiritual borderlands are not particular to the Southwest. In fact, the Borderlands are physically present wherever two or more cultures edge each other, where people of different races occupy the same territory, where under, lower, middle and upper classes touch, where the space between two individuals shrinks with intimacy. . . . It's not a comfortable territory to live in, this place of contradictions. Hatred, anger and exploitation are the prominent features of this landscape."[7]

Despite Allende's endeavor to erase borderlands and to transform hatred and anger into love and compassion through the particular bond she establishes between the Reeves and the Morales families (Castillo de Berchenko, 162), *The Infinite Plan* does not make light of problematic race relations in the barrio, nor does it obscure the ultimately privileged place that whites enjoy in the society at large. If Gregory is made to feel like an outcast because of the color of his skin, if he is at the bottom of the hierarchy in a social setting where, despite the attempts of the school system to officiate English only, Spanish is blatantly spoken as an act of resistance, Allende suggests that barrio life provides an enclave of Chicano supremacy that disappears on the other side of the borderland. Revealing a level of political awareness that corresponds more to the adult Reeves than to the youth who is victimized, Gregory reflects on the destructive cycle of racism: "In that Latino ghetto I experienced the unpleasantness of being different, I did not fit in; I wanted to be like everyone else, to blend into the crowd, to be invisible, so I could walk through the streets or play in the schoolyard unharmed by the gangs of dark-skinned boys who vented on me the aggression they themselves received from whites the minute they stepped outside the barrio" (*IP,* 54).

Allende's portrait of gang life is particularly informative and written in a journalistic style that evokes the analyses of barrio gangs' "multiple marginality" offered by such anthropologists as James Diego Vigil.[8] If Vigil's main thesis is that "the gang subcultural style is a response to the pressures of street life and serves to give certain barrio youth a source of familial support, goals and directives, and sanctions and guides" (Diego Vigil, 2), *The Infinite Plan* provides countless examples of this concept. Allende describes in vivid detail the rituals and codes that distinguish gangs—from dress to hand gestures to colors, signs, and wall graffiti— and she documents the sense of identity gangs give to barrio youths who drop out of school and have no job or home. This topic becomes most powerful when personalized in the form of Gregory's confrontation with Los Carniceros, a gang ruled over by the Martínez boys and characterized by their "vaselined hair, leather jackets, studs and chains . . . cocky walk . . . [and] stacked heels" (*IP,* 102).

The challenge that develops between Gregory and the youth who raped him years before is one that transcends the terms of their duel; for Gregory, the enemy is not Martínez, but his own sense of male pride and virility, his desire to conquer his fear of death. The fact that he chooses as the test of manhood a race against a train that is described as "an awesome, enormous snake of iron and thunder" (*IP,* 101) only intensifies the sexual overtones of this episode. Cultural differences also intervene in this final clash as Martínez, fixed in his role of the "absolute macho" (*IP,* 101), is obliged to feign an "indifference to danger" (*IP,* 101) that results in his donning pachuco-style clothes for a race that requires the sneakers and casual clothes worn by Greg. Armed with the spiritual protection afforded by the scapulary of the Virgin of Guadalupe that Carmen gives him and filled with a terror that is articulated in a "single terrible bellow" (*IP,* 103) loud enough to make up for all the silences of his past,

Gregory is "suspended above a bottomless abyss, floating in front of the locomotive, a bird petrified in mid-flight," his body preparing for "the last leap forward . . . focused on the certainty of death" (*IP*, 104). Finding himself on the other side of the tracks triumphant over the "the enormous beast clacking by" (*IP*, 104), his success and realization that "pieces of Martínez were scattered across the landscape" (*IP*, 104) serve to reconfigure the struggle for authority that marks part 1 of the novel.

The dismemberment of Martínez or the Chicano body and the supremacy of the Anglo body reconstituted as a whole have subtle political implications that initiate the next part of the novel where Gregory "was more assured and for the first time in years felt good about himself and finally stopped wishing he were dark-skinned like everyone else in the barrio—in fact, he began to evaluate the advantages of not being like them" (*IP*, 107). Retaining his love of Latin music and storytelling and his interest in the Spanish language, which he learns to speak, he increasingly identifies with his whiteness and the power it commands in society at large. His personal odyssey to reclaim and fortify a sense of self provides an interesting fictionalization of the thesis of the Italian Marxist, Antonio Gramsci, for whom "consciousness is 'strangely composite'" and "always contains contradictions between hegemonic ideology and critical 'good sense.'"[9] That is, despite—or perhaps because of—Gregory's experience of marginality and his critical awareness of social hierarchies, he is seduced by the dominant ideological model and the promise of freedom on the other side of the barrio.

Gregory is assisted in his journey by skillful mentors and friends who initially appear in part 1 of the novel and help him transgress physical, sexual, and intellectual borders, thus marking his future in countless ways. Foremost among these is Carmen Morales, Gregory's best friend, who is able to envision a reality beyond the barrio with its restrictive cultural and gender-encoded rules. Born of parents who enter the country illegally from Zacatecas, Mexico, as "'wire-cuttin' wetbacks" (*IP*, 41) and who try to hold on to their heritage by isolating themselves from the "crazy" gringos (*IP*, 43), Carmen's rich imagination, vitality, and dislike of social conventions implicitly clash with her restrictive family life. Even at a young age, before her subsequent departure from the barrio, she might well have uttered the words of Sandra Cisneros's Esperanza in *The House on Mango Street*: ". . . I have decided not to grow up tame like the others who lay their necks on the threshold waiting for the ball and chain."[10] Yet, Allende makes it clear that Carmen's revolt is of a silent nature and that "she had a strong practical sense that allowed her to

escape rigid family traditions without confrontation with her father"
(*IP*, 73). Her ease in negotiating the spheres of two cultures—a characteristic that will earn her success in the future—is apparent when she
teaches Gregory North American dances and more significantly, when
she takes him to Pershing Square beyond "the invisible frontier that
people of his status never crossed" (*IP*, 88). Submerged in the world of
whiteness, he makes more money shining shoes there than in the barrio
and performs with Carmen a juggling act complete with burning candles, sharp knives, and music. This literal act of juggling will be
repeated metaphorically in later years when he juggles multiple respon-
sibilities and psychological burdens.

If Carmen gives Gregory the courage to cross physical borders—an
act that reproduces in miniature the travels of their two sets of immigrant parents—Cyrus, the elderly elevator operator and bibliophile at
the local library, infuses the adolescent Reeves with the desire to cross
intellectual borders. Mentor, friend, and father figure, he shares with
Gregory his secret of belonging to the Communist Party, gives him lists
of books to read, instructs him about "the dangers of individualism,"
imparts to him the belief that those who rise high have the power to
effect changes in "this damned capitalistic society" (*IP*, 123), and leaves
him $800 in his will to pay for a university education. Although Cyrus
dies at the beginning of part 2, his words continually reverberate in
Gregory's head in subsequent sections, frequently producing enormous
guilt for the adult Reeves who betrays his mentor and embarks on the
American dream of money and self-interest. Allende's view of the contradictory forces that constitute human consciousness surfaces once
more as Gregory discards critical thinking in order to satisfy the
demands of his impoverished childhood only to return to his mentor's
teachings at the novel's close. While some critics have noted that "there
is nothing comparable for male readers to the spectrum of female to
female relationships in Allende's writing,"[11] the extremely touching
relationship between Gregory and Cyrus, crowned by Gregory's gesture
of using the $800 to give his friend a memorable funeral, is a notable
exception and a further indication of how arbitrary boundaries, in this
case of age, can be torn down.

Gregory's last mentor in the first part of the novel is his parents'
friend and traveling companion, Olga. A flamboyant and adventurous
woman who is a quintessential Allende character complete with bright
red hair, a crystal ball, an indomitable will, and skills as a healer and
midwife, she has a central role in the Reeves's family life and is alter-

nately Nora Reeves's friend, head of the Reeves family when Charles Reeves gets ill, Charles's nursemaid and lover, and finally, Gregory's sexual mentor. Settled in a rented room in the barrio where she earns a living through her fortune telling, therapeutic massages, abortions, homeopathic remedies, spiritualist sessions, and doses of "magic and hope" (*IP,* 60), she rescues Gregory from his "unconfessable doubts concerning his virility" (*IP,* 92) that besiege him since his rape by Martínez. He turns to her at age 17, filled with an unnamed desperation and contradictory views about sex gleaned from the Morales brothers, Hollywood movies, the gospel of the Catholic Church, and his own research and fantasies, and she responds in turn with the full generosity of her nature. Teaching him the fine art of being attuned to woman's sexuality at the same time that she satisfies his own needs, she ushers him into manhood with a tenderness and wisdom that he will recall countless times in his future. Their passionate and satisfying lovemaking evokes Riad Halabí's relationship with Eva Luna, thus affirming once more Allende's belief that sexual pleasure belongs to women and men of all ages and follows no formulaic script dictated by social conventions.

These mentors compensate in great degree for the physical absence of Gregory's father and the emotional absence of his mother that mark him profoundly and will be a recurring theme in his adult life. Although Gregory intellectually appreciates his mother's legacy—her belief in the equality of all people, her high regard for education, her love of opera, her sense of dignity and honor—he cannot forgive her for her inability to deal with reality or to provide him with a loving home after his father's death. Forced from the age of seven to supplement through countless odd jobs the meager household income and sent by his mother to a foster home from which he escapes, his complex feelings of anger and neediness never have the opportunity to be voiced. Hence, he develops a resilient exterior that together with his innate good humor enables him to survive and prosper yet not experience the fears that shaped his childhood.

Gregory's departure from the barrio in part 2 following Cyrus's death and his decision to enroll at Berkeley mark the beginning of a new stage in his life. Acutely aware, as Sandra Cisneros poignantly documents in *Woman Hollering Creek,* that pursuing an education to better his life was a betrayal to his community, he nonetheless recognizes the dead-end life of the wetback or factory worker and the stultifying limits of barrio existence. Taking with him $90 and "very few good memories" (*IP,* 125), he arrives at Berkeley, "the Mecca of godless pilgrims, the far extreme of the continent, where people came to escape old delusions or to find a utopia" (*IP,* 126), and immediately experiences a sense of freedom. New mentors and friends fill the void left by Cyrus and Carmen, and Gregory's personal horizons expand as Timothy Duane teaches him to navigate Berkeley, Joan and Susan teach him to cook, and Balcescu teaches him to garden and cultivate roses in wine barrels. The political consciousness that Cyrus assiduously nurtured in his disciple now becomes part of a collective endeavor as the seeds of revolutionary zeal flourish and Gregory participates in protests and civil rights issues.

Carefully blending once again social history and attention to individual psychology, Allende captures in sweeping strokes a unique moment in American life and Gregory's reaction to such diverse phenomena as protests against the Vietnam War, parties adorned with Ho Chi Minh and Che Guevara posters, the hippie movement, the Black Panthers, transcendental meditation, aquatic childbirth techniques, primal scream therapy, free love, and open marriage. Initially seduced by the continual barrage of new ideas and experiences that permeate Berkeley in the 1960s, Gregory's disenchantment grows as he recognizes that "his romantic ideas about student life had been buried under meaningless routine" (*IP,* 152). Weary of politicized street skirmishes, hippie ethics, unchallenging professors, and the continual burden of working several jobs to stay afloat, he is increasingly besieged with a relentless need to find the love that eluded him during his childhood. He graduates with honorable mention in literature, enrolls in law school in San Francisco, and pursues the refined and distant Samantha Ernst. As Allende narrates: "All his life he had wanted to be part of a real family, like the Moraleses, and he was so in love with the dream of domesticity that he was determined to carry it out with the first available woman, without bothering to ask whether she shared the same plans" (*IP,* 147).

The articulation of his "secret hope for a patriarchal existence" (*IP,* 149) in the midst of a social milieu characterized by the continual upheaval of traditions and the concerted disavowal of monogamy creates a series of internal tensions for Gregory that ultimately result in his failed marriage to Samantha. Unable to perceive that he is pursued by incomplete business from the past, he falls in love with a cold woman with little ability to navigate everyday life and thus reproduces the web of protectiveness and distance that marked his relationship with his mother years before. Like Pedro Morales, Reeves works day and night to support his wife and daughter but without the benefit of a loving wife who creates a home for her family. If to some degree, Gregory marries an upper-class but less intellectual or spiritual version of his mother, he is also haunted by his father's ghost and fears cuddling his daughter, Margaret, after his sister Judy warns him about the incestuous paternal curse. His complex inner family drama is also tinged with cultural politics when, Samantha, in a display of ethnocentrism that reveals her profound disregard for her husband's needs and her manipulation of trendy fads to mask her inability to love, classifies his objection to collective masturbation as "a typical remark of an underdeveloped foreign culture," and adds: "You're like those Latinos you grew up with. You should have stayed in the barrio" (*IP,* 171).

Confronted with Samantha's infidelity, a betrayal that similarly reactivates insecurities from the past, Gregory finds himself once again the outsider, estranged from his family life and the sexual trends of his times, as rootless as the roses he learns to cultivate in wine barrels. Brought up in a family where secrets were buried and communication was minimal, Reeves processes Samantha's betrayal in characteristically solitary fashion: he stays with friends, takes the bar exam, and reports to the army, prepared to go to Vietnam after having taken Reserve Officer's Training Corps (R.O.T.C.) classes during his undergraduate years. His decision to enlist is fraught with the same contradictions that mark other aspects of his life. While his enrollment in R.O.T.C. and subsequent enlistment are justified by the financial aid R.O.T.C. students receive and by the superficial interest he displays in "the adventure of the war" (*IP,* 148), his political commitments suggest an aversion to a military venture actively condemned in the streets of Berkeley.[12] Allende seems to justify this decision in terms of Gregory's ultimate need to escape. No longer able to disappear into the shed where he spent hours alone crying as a child, no longer able to race the train in a fearless battle against death, he confesses, "I left for Vietnam harboring the secret fantasy of dying so I would not have to face the drudgery and pain of living" (*IP,* 179). The possibility of military bravado as a salvation for his damaged male ego perhaps lurks in his subconscious as well. Carefully introducing into this section of her novel the reflection of the 50-year-old Reeves who looks back on this stage of his life, she records his comment, "I believe that period was the worst; something fundamental in my soul was forever twisted, and I was never again the same. . . . I grew up as a street fighter. I should have been tough from the beginning, but it wasn't that way" (*IP,* 177).

At the same time that Allende captures in minute detail Gregory's evolution in Berkeley, she implicitly contrasts it with Carmen Morales's

development and her own experience of marginality. Allende brings to
bear the full force of gender politics—national and personal—as she
traces the complexities of Carmen's need to separate herself from her
culture's "double standard that made prisoners of women but granted a
hunting license to men" (*IP,* 136). At exactly the same moment in time
when Gregory idealizes the Morales's family life and longs to fashion
himself after its patriarch, Carmen is more suspect of her parents' "wed-
ded bliss" (*IP,* 136) and notes that they never embrace in public and that
her father is rumored to have a son by another woman. Lacking the
physical mobility of her friend whose only barriers to success are his
inner demons and social class, Carmen is hindered by the additional limitations of gender and ethnicity. Unable to harness the courage to leave
home despite her fiery nature, her salvation ironically appears in the
form of an unwanted pregnancy and a subsequent abortion by Olga
that results in her father's disavowal of his favorite daughter, Gregory's
interrogation by the police, and Olga's departure to Puerto Rico to
escape possible persecution.

Detailing with equal skill the repressive national climate of pre–Roe v.
Wade abortion politics and the tension generated in the Morales household by the daughter's transgression, Allende poignantly describes Carmen's departure from home with her mother's support and savings. Like
Gloria Anzaldúa in *Borderlands,* Carmen, too, might declare, "I had to
leave home so I could find myself, find my own intrinsic nature buried
under the personality that had been imposed on me" (Anzaldúa, 16). The
question of Carmen's nature, however, is enmeshed in identity politics
when she finds herself labeled a gringa by the Indian and mestiza women
she meets in Mexico City while working in a silver workshop. Allende
patently makes the point that postmodernist feminists have passionately
argued: identity is ultimately relational and fluid rather than fixed and
immobile; "the configuration of the gendered self cannot be enclosed in
time or space."[13] While Carmen's subsequent creation of a new self will
be accompanied by travels throughout the world that add texture to the
complex relationship between identity and place, the initial impetus for
her growth begins in Mexico City where she, like Gregory before her, is
surrounded by skillful mentors, "silent Indians with magic hands, who
rarely spoke to her but taught her the secret of their art" (*IP,* 166).

As Allende follows in part 3 of the novel Carmen's journey from
Mexico City to Barcelona before her return to California seven years
after her departure, she demonstrates that at the same time Carmen's
creative abilities as a jewelry designer expand dramatically and earn her

a recognition that will eventually make her rich and famous, her emotional life and view of herself as a woman remain tied to the barrio mentality and the gender role imposed on her. Prepared to serve her Mexican lover-anthropologist in exchange for the benefits of his gifted mind, she not only attends to all his personal needs, but turns over her earnings to him and tolerates his physical abuses when he is drunk; she repeats a similar pattern in Spain with her Japanese lover, a fellow student and craftsman, whose "ancestral customs" dictated that "he came first, and he expected to be served" (*IP*, 218). Rejecting the official role of housewife sanctified by her culture yet living the conditions implicit in the role, Carmen's willingness to conform to stultifying patriarchal expectations attests to the ponderous weight of gender and ethnicity in identity formation. Skilled in assimilating gypsy, Moorish, and North African influences into her craft, she is unable to transcend her place of origin in her personal life, thus demonstrating that the "capacity to resist and to understand is limited and influenced by class, race, and gender position" (Weiler, 51).

Carmen's return to the barrio—dressed in full regalia of colored skirts and bracelets galore—seven years after her departure to comfort her ailing father and her subsequent decision to follow Olga's suggestion and move to Berkeley inaugurate her full emergence into selfhood. Similar to Gregory, she, too, experiences an exhilarating sense of freedom in Berkeley, as well as the full explosion of her creative talents. Dedicating herself to designing jewelry and clothes and gradually gaining recognition for her work, she renames herself Tamar, an act that marks her "private christening into a second self."[14] Cultural politics and the desire to authorize a new and exotic self clearly intervene in this decision; had Carmen arrived in Berkeley in the 1980s instead of the end of the 1960s, she might have worn with pride the name Carmen Morales. Acutely aware of the low regard a humble Chicana would have in a market place crazed with a fever for the "ethnic . . . no one could locate on the map" (*IP*, 242), she negates her place of origin, advertises herself as "TAMAR, ETHNIC JEWELRY" (*IP*, 242), and tells her customers that she is a gypsy. Unwilling to separate her life into the private and the public, she assumes in every sense her new identity and even demands that Gregory call her by her adopted name.

Once again, Anzaldúa's words frame Carmen's odyssey. If the Chicana author declares, "I want the freedom to carve and chisel my own face" (Anzaldúa, 22), by carving and chiseling both her jewelry and name, Carmen also writes the script of her own life and becomes, as

Gregory perceptively notes, "the protagonist of her own novel" (*IP*, 242). The text she authors draws upon her Latin American heritage in her designs but transcends its place of origin to include other continents as well, thus suggesting the concept of pluralistic cultures, a theme that will increasingly define Carmen's approach to her life and work. Significantly, Carmen's emotional life during this period is not centered on subservient relationships with men—a part of her past that she has laid to rest—but on her adopted son, Dai, the offspring of her brother, Juan José, who died in Vietnam, and his Vietnamese lover, Thui Nguyen. Carmen's relationship with her son, based on "an indestructible bond. . . . [of] mutual acceptance and good humor" (*IP*, 274), cannot help but remind the reader of mother-daughter relationships in other novels by Allende, thus adding a different dimension to the intense bonds among women that characterize her fiction.

Much as Carmen's links to Berkeley and Vietnam alter the course of her life in part 3, Gregory's experience in Vietnam marks his life during the next two decades. By Allende's own account, this part of the novel was provided to her by a Vietnam veteran whom she interviewed at great length and whose story she transcribed (Correas Zapata, 114). While there is one basic inconsistency here between fiction and reality worthy of note—Gregory's enrollment in R.O.T.C. while at Berkeley would have qualified him to be an officer instead of a common soldier—this section of the novel is one of the most powerfully narrated and captures the complexities and contradictions of the Vietnam War for those who fought in the front lines. Tim O'Brien, Vietnam veteran and author of the acclaimed book, *The Things They Carried,* describes the effect of Vietnam like a "powerful drug: that mix of unnamed terror and unnamed pleasure that comes as the needle slips in and you know you're missing something."[15] Defining in detail an experience that can scarcely be understood by those who have not lived it, O'Brien suggests that war is "mystery and terror and adventure and courage and discovery and holiness and pity and despair and longing and love. War is nasty; war is fun. War is thrilling; war is drudgery. War makes you a man; war makes you dead. The truths are contradictory. . . . Almost everything is true. Almost nothing is true . . . You can't tell where you are, or why you're there, and the only certainty is overwhelming ambiguity" (O'Brien, 87, 88).

Gregory Reeves lives all of the contradictory emotions described by O'Brien and dissects in microscopic detail both his reasons for fighting in the war and his reactions to its horrors and beauties. Simultaneously seeking to escape from guilt and failure, to throw himself into "something exhilarating" (*IP*, 184), and to find his manhood, he, too, speaks of the "strange fascination of violence" (*IP*, 190), the atrocious pleasure of the proximity of death and the experience of aliveness, the "overwhelming compassion . . . for all the accumulated pain" (*IP*, 186), and the "absolute power" (*IP*, 198) he feels in defying death and saving 11 infantrymen on a mountaintop. Sketchy political analyses and perceptive sociological comments coexist with Gregory's personal reflections as he notes the divisions in race and ethnicity that separate the soldiers in the camps and points to the reality of a classist and racist America that doesn't send the rich or powerful to war. Voices from the past ring in his ears as the comments made by his mother and Cyrus on race and class injustice acquire special meaning when he realizes that "we're not even equal when we go war" (*IP*, 192).

Eventually sent to a village to teach English and monitor the sympathies of the villagers toward the Vietcong—an appropriate utilization of the skills in Vietnamese he acquired at the Language Institute in Monterrey before his departure—Reeves finds a sense of acceptance and belonging that he had never experienced in his life. Touched by the gentle ways of the villagers, fascinated by their wonderful gift for storytelling, disarmed by the physical expressions of friendship shown by the men, "he stopped seeing himself as a white giant, he forgot differences in size, culture, race, language, and goals, and allowed himself the pleasure of being like everyone else" (*IP*, 210). His three-month stay is crowned by his realization "that in almost thirty years of life, this remote village in Asia was the only place where he had felt accepted as a part of a community" (*IP*, 210).

This sense of belonging and the erasing of borders ultimately fade in Reeves's mental scrapbook of his Vietnam experience. Infected with an ailment that lands him in a hospital; pained at the death of his close friend, Juan José Morales; seized with a feeling of rage against both the politicians who propagated the war and the draft evaders safe at home, he resolves never to feel again like a "hunted animal" (*IP*, 210). Instead, he is determined to milk the system dry and acquire the prestige, money, and power that would compensate for both his impoverished childhood and the psychological distress he experiences at age 28 in this "late rite of passage" (*IP*, 184). While Allende makes no extensive political claims about the Vietnam War, she documents the uncomfortable silences that greet the veterans upon their return, their sense of displacement in society, and the lack of "moral resolution" to a war ultimately considered "an unholy debacle" (*IP*, 245). More importantly, from a narrative perspective, she makes abundantly clear the damage it causes her protagonist. Hardened, cynical, closed down to the moral and ethical truths he was exposed to as a youth, and immune to the sense of humanity he experienced in the village, Reeves engages in a mad dance against death in the coming years as his thirst for women, money, success, and prestige drives him further and further away from the ability to love and find his center.

Part 4 of the novel follows Reeves in the decades of the 1970s and 1980s as he relentlessly pursues his goals and marches to the beat of an increasingly materialistic society intent on recovering its pride after the Vietnam failure. The lack of collective spirit of the nation thus merges with the personal aspirations of Allende's protagonist as she traces a new era characterized by the burgeoning of the women's movement, "the 'me' generation, the reliance on psychotherapy, the frequency of divorce, the 'yuppies' syndrome, the rise of drug use . . . the health food craze" (Perricone, 1994, 55). Instructed in this stage of his life by the head of the San Francisco law firm that hires him, "the perfect master for a laborious apprenticeship in greed" (*IP*, 283), Reeves lives on the edge, assiduously silencing the voices of Cyrus and "a host of questioning spirits" (*IP*, 320), and juggling complex legal cases, long working hours, little sleep, trips, debts, wild parties, and countless women. Falling in love again with a woman half his age as ill equipped to deal with reality as his mother and previous wife, he finds himself once more in the role of protector for a woman unable to give him the affection he craves.

Reeves recovers a piece of his former self when he quits his lucrative job and sets up his own practice devoted to the poor, but his life falls apart when his marriage to Shannon deteriorates in a manner similar to his first one. He finds himself betrayed by his wife's infidelity and left in charge of a hyperactive son, David, whose unruly manner, innumerable pets, and insatiable emotional demands wreck havoc on his already fragile life and increasing sense of failure over the disappearances of his daughter, Margaret. His emotional breakdown or dark night of the soul is dramatically triggered by his mother's death, which brings back a flood of memories from the past and confronts him with his complete sense of aloneness and abandonment. In one of the most moving passages of the novel, which reveals Allende's tremendous skill in capturing the complex textures of the human soul, Reeves begins to face the beast within him that he has spent his entire life trying to elude:

> He broke into tears, weeping as he had not wept since the war, a visceral wail that came from the most remote past. . . . He wept for neglect in his

childhood, for battles and defeats he had vainly hoped to transform into victories, for unpaid debts and the betrayals of a lifetime, for the loss of his mother and his tardy recognition of her affection. . . . He wept for the sum of his errors and for the perfect love he dreamed of but believed impossible to find, for his father . . . for his sister . . . for Olga . . . and his many unfortunate brethren, the blacks, Latins, and illegal immigrants, poor, deprived, and humble . . . for the memories of the war . . . Juan José Morales . . . the hundred dead on the mountain. And when he realized that in fact he was crying for himself, he opened his eyes and at last faced the beast, looked at its face and thus learned that the animal always crouching behind him . . . was the tenacious fear of being alone that had afflicted him since as a trembling boy he had hidden in the shed. (335)

Reeves's painful process of healing involves the destruction of countless myths of masculinity that have shaped his life since his childhood in the barrio. Allende provides in *The Infinite Plan* not only a feminist agenda, clearly manifested in Carmen Morales's creation of an autonomous self, but also a compelling portrait of the reconstruction of the male self and the stripping away of crippling social norms—real men don't cry, real men don't talk about their problems—that impede aliveness. As Gregory opens himself up first to Carmen, and then to his therapist, Ming O'Brien, he meets head on his internal enemy, the transparent shadows of his recurring nightmare on the mountain, and slowly lays to rest the ghosts of his tormented past.

Stripping away, barrier after barrier, the roadblocks to finding his personal truth and acknowledging his fear of failure and the "terror of being alone" (*IP,* 381), Reeves reaches an epiphany that is laced with spiritual significance as the mountain of despair that has pursued him becomes transformed into one of deliverance. Re-creating with his son, David, the sense of happiness he experienced as a child with his father in the solitude of nature, he shouts his name into the dusk-filled sky, and as he recounts, "the echo from the mountains returned it to me, purified" (*IP,* 379). This personal and cosmic affirmation of self brings peace and acceptance, and Reeves's final encounter with truth leads him to the realization that "the most important thing was not, as I had imagined, to survive or be successful; the most important thing was the search for my soul, which I had left behind in the quicksand of my childhood. When I found it, I learned that the power I had wasted such desperate energy to gain had always been inside me. I was reconciled with myself, I accepted myself with a touch of kindness, and then, and only then, was rewarded with my first glimpse of peace" (*IP,* 381).

This ability to distinguish between material values and human worth ultimately distinguishes Gregory Reeves from the Jay Gatsbys and Willie Lomans who have also sought the American dream only to wind up dead and defeated by illusions impossible to sustain. Pragmatic idealism seems to be the social philosophy Allende ultimately ascribes to as she describes Reeves's passionate commitment to illegal immigrants and the disenfranchised in his legal practice and Carmen's humane commitment to her workers in her vast enterprise consisting of Tamar branches throughout the world. Pointedly noting that for Carmen "there was no conflict between a good eye for business and compassion" (*IP*, 313), Allende provides an interesting model on how to "juggle cultures" (Anzaldúa, 79) in a capitalist marketplace. As Carmen travels to Thailand, Bali, India, and North Africa in search of new materials for her designs, she reaffirms a message she and Gregory gleaned in their barrio days: "the world is not white and never will be" (*IP*, 313). The personal and the political merge together as Allende reveals how Carmen becomes empowered by such a realization. She proudly flaunts "her brown skin and Latin features" (*IP*, 313) and employs in her expanding operations "so many poor Latins, Asian and Central American refugees, and physically disabled . . . that Greg called his friend's business 'Tamar's Hospice'" (*IP*, 313). Her ability to open her life and work to multiple influences and people is perhaps the best example Allende provides in *The Infinite Plan* of crossing cultural borders and decentering conventional associations between race and power.

In a typical Allende scenario, it is Carmen who rescues Greg from bankruptcy, thus repaying all the acts of kindness and bankrolling that he had shown her since they were six years old and providing a female version of the Chicana success story. Significantly, while Allende takes care to underline Carmen's success as designer and mother, she leaves the issue of her emotional life on a more ambiguous and open note. Recreating in part through this character her own dramatic proposal to Willie Gordon shortly after meeting him in California, she sends Carmen off on a journey to Rome to propose marriage to her former lover, Leo Galupi. While describing the passion and comfort the two feel after more than a decade apart, she never tells us if Leo accepts Carmen's offer, thus suggesting that fiction, like life, is often an inconclusive affair.

Such a premise does not apply, however, to Gregory Reeves, whose life comes together at the novel's close. Assisted by his skilled accountant and his secretary, his legal practice continues. Aware of the need for providing stability, love, and discipline for David, his parenting skills—

like Carmen's—produce notable changes and reconfigure traditional notions about the importance of biology for "mothering."[16] Most significantly, loved and supported by the implied narrator of his tale, he finds companionship when he had finally accepted solitude. Implicitly criticizing the vacuous American dream of success without soul and capturing the way in which human life is constructed "step by step" (Allende, 1993c, 44) by negotiating the unfinished business of the past and present, Allende completes her protagonist's journey through self and society and offers it to her readers as a mirror of life.

Yet, to confuse life and art in Allende's fiction would be a grave mistake. The critic Robert Alter has noted that "all serious novelists must confront the arbitrariness, the necessary falsification, of the worlds they invent through words."[17] This comment acquires special meaning in Allende's case. Skillfully employing a series of literary techniques and conventions that add a markedly fictitious note to her novel—continual foreshadowings, multiple use of narrative persons, textured symbolism, felicitous as well as strained coincidences, unexplained encounters—she situates such narrative strategies in a context inspired by real people and events. Acutely aware of the dynamics between fiction and reality, Allende provides her own version of Alter's comment by suggesting that "a writer is a liar, basically" and that "the craft . . . is to make it believable" (Allende, 1993c, 50). This is without a doubt one of the most salient and successful aspects of her narrative talent—her tremendous ability to make the reader believe in the world she invents and to use art to fashion the complex story of individuals who transcend borderlands of race, gender, and ethnicity, and inhabit new spaces of freedom. Defining her novel as a "window open to an infinite landscape,"[18] she ultimately makes us contemplate and even hope that there is a purpose behind each individual act in the infinite plan of all our lives.[19]

Chapter Seven
Paula

Isabel Allende was in Spain on a promotional tour of *The Infinite Plan* in December 1991 when her agent interrupted her lecture to tell her that her 28-year-old daughter, Paula, had been taken to a Madrid hospital. She was diagnosed as suffering from porphyria, a hereditary disease characterized by a metabolic disorder and enzyme deficiency that, if properly treated, is curable. Unfortunately, Paula was administered the wrong drugs and as a result fell into a coma. Allende's yearlong struggle in Madrid and California to save her daughter's life and ultimately accept the inevitability of her death is documented in moving detail in her 1994 book, *Paula* (*P*, 1995). Considered by many critics to be Allende's best work to date, it is a complex book that weaves together several narrative strands and is at once the fascinating autobiography of Isabel Allende, a joyful and elegiac memoir of her daughter, Paula, and a vivid testimony of the Chilean military coup of 1973 and the repressive Pinochet regime. *Paula* is also a homage to the role of words in salvaging the past and retrieving loss. Confronted with a situation beyond her control, Allende could do nothing but write to distract herself. Her reams of yellow paper—a body of writing that unlike her daughter moves with agility and grace—provided the space where the events of a year fused with the events of a lifetime and where personal and political loss were implicitly juxtaposed with one another. In this sense, *Paula* is a tightly crafted rendition of many themes and life experiences that have appeared fictionalized in Allende's previous works but that acquire new meaning in the context of her autobiographical endeavor and struggle against death.

Precisely because *Paula* is written with such a sense of urgency and in such a confessional tone, it invites the reader to view it as a reflection of reality and not as a literary construct forged from the fragile domain of memory. Critics have praised its "authentic" voice (Mujica, 38) and "verisimilitude."[1] Yet, autobiographical writing is a complex process in which words and memories are used to capture and transform the texture of a human life. That is, rather than a mimetic exercise in which art reproduces life, autobiography creates and reconstructs a life from the dual threads of fact and fantasy. Acutely aware that her journey through the inner self is a voyage through both the archive of experience and the terrain of imagination, Allende implicitly informs her readers of this creative blend while paying tribute to her daughter's role in facilitating her odyssey: "You, Paula, have given me this silence in which to examine my path through the world, to return to the true and the fantastic paths, to recover memories others have forgotten, to remember what never happened and what still may happen. Absent, mute, paralyzed, you are my guide" (*P,* 162).

By suggesting that the processes of memory involve not only retrieving what has happened, but also inventing what never happened, Allende confirms the theory that "'the unreliability' of autobiography is . . . 'an unescapable condition.'"[2] Hence, the final result of her autobiographical enterprise is not the true story of Isabel Allende but the text in which Allende remembers and reads Allende, and the reader, in turn, reads the author reading herself.[3] As Allende attempts "to fix the fleeting images of an imperfect memory" (*P,* 238), she inevitably engages in the process of "transformative remembering," that is, the recollection of past events that acquire special meaning in the context of her present emotional stress and that serve the necessary function of contributing to the redefinition of her self.[4] Faced with the overwhelming need to rescue her daughter from the possibility of death, Allende recalls, narrates, or reconstructs those events in her past that project her as Allende the brave, Allende the daring, Allende the rebel, Allende the risk taker. That is not to suggest, however, that images of fear, psychological paralysis, or resignation do not permeate these pages because they certainly do, providing in their own way a counterpart to Paula's physical paralysis. But ultimately if autobiography may be viewed as each person's "metaphor" of his or her self,[5] or what Allende has called the creation of one's "own legend,"[6] the image Allende projects of herself is jointly that of a Chilean Demeter who defies the gods of the underworld and their military counterparts and a commanding heir to Lot's wife who looks behind to find strength and meaning in a past both invented and real.

Allende's discovery of "particles of truth, small crystals that fit in the palm of one hand and justify [her] passage through this world" (*P,* 9) is one that is mediated not only by memory, but by gender, class, language, and culture. *Paula,* in fact, bears a marked similarity to the autobiographical endeavor in Spanish-America meticulously described by the Argentinean writer, Sylvia Molloy. If, according to Molloy, Spanish-

American autobiography or "self-writing" is characterized by the presence of a "documentary imperative"[7] and a "strong testimonial stance"
(Molloy, 8) that transforms autobiographers into witnesses of social and
political realities of the past, if it is marked by the combined strands of
personal memory and "collective memory" (Molloy, 165) and by "the
vacillation between public persona and private self" (Molloy, 4),
Allende's *Paula* provides a richly crafted version of these concerns. Continually intertwined with Allende's personal journey and that of her
ancestors is the plight of her native country, Chile, whose loss of freedom
following the military coup offers a highly politicized and factual rendition of a theme that lyrically permeates the entire text. Yet, if as Molloy
also observes, Spanish-American autobiographers are prone to self-
censorship (Molloy, 6), Allende—in her "personal mythos" (Jelinek, 4)
of the nonconformist who rejects cultural norms of silence and compliance ordained for her gender—brings forth recovered memories of
childhood seduction that fill the spaces of the unspeakable and pose
numerous questions about the writing of self.

Paula's narrative structure responds in great measure to the author's
view of memory as "a Mexican mural in which all times are simultane-
ous" (*P,* 23). Hence, it is carefully constructed as a seamless voyage
between past and present with few of the foreshadowings that characterize Allende's style. The slippage in time is often achieved by a simple
phrase or image: the recollection of an adolescent Paula showing her
somewhat naive mother a condom triggers an image of the eight-year-
old Allende attracted to the seductive lure of a young fisherman; the
description of the lively Aurelia dancing in Paula's hospital ward
reminds Allende of her own stint as a follies dancer in Chile; the electric
stimuli Paula receives in the hospital to measure her reactions catapults
the author back in time to the torture of political prisoners in Pinochet's
Chile; and the re-creation of Allende's painful exile in 1975 and beginning of a new life in Venezuela ushers in a description of the birth of her
granddaughter, Andrea, in 1992 in California. Yet, despite the apparent
ease with which disparate events are linked together, and despite
Allende's comment that "memory, like fiction, moves from revelation to
revelation" (Correas Zapata, 131), there is a strong ordering consciousness apparent in the text and the sense that Allende's tight control over
the narrative material is a humble compensation for her loss of control
over her daughter's fate.

Paula is divided into two parts and an epilogue that capture in
chronological sequence the progression of Paula's disease and Allende's

life from childhood to the present. Referring specifically to the year of Paula's illness, part 1 narrates her stay in a Madrid hospital from December 1991 to May 1992; part 2 describes her stay in her mother's home in San Rafael, California, from May to December 1992; and the epilogue, entitled Christmas 1992, recounts her death several weeks earlier on 6 December. From a narrative point of view, what is of particular interest is the dialogue that Allende sustains with her daughter and refashions in each section in accordance with the deterioration of Paula's condition. Allende has noted in a 1993 interview that the first sentence of a book establishes its tone (Allende, 1993c, 42); in this context, the first brief sentence of *Paula,* followed by a more lengthy one, jointly communicates the author's longing and purpose: "Listen, Paula. I am going to tell you a story, so that when you wake up you will not feel so lost" (*P,* 3). The direct, but gentle command that constitutes her first address to her daughter is joined in subsequent pages by others such as: "Wake up, Paula, please wake up . . ." (*P,* 35), "Breathe, Paula, you must breathe . . ." (*P,* 94), "Don't be afraid, Paula" (*P,* 158). Exhortations blend with questions that are never answered as Allende tries to probe a soul that is beyond communication: "Where are you wandering, Paula? How will you be when you wake up?" (*P,* 7); "Will you get well, Paula? . . . Do you want to live, Paula?" (*P,* 34). Finally, introspective and hypothetical statements complete her mute conversation as she painfully wonders "how things might have been if you had fallen into more capable hands, if they had not immobilized you with drugs, if . . . , if. . . . How can I shake this guilt?" (*P,* 22).

The tone of urgency, intimacy, and hope that characterizes part 1 notably disappears from much of part 2 as the graceful "you" Allende conversed with is replaced with the most distant "she," and speaking and writing become an exercise no longer destined for Paula but for Allende herself. The first sentence of part 2 shapes the narrative of this new stage as the author both resists and recognizes a painful truth: "I am no longer writing so when my daughter wakes up she will not feel so lost, because she is not going to wake up. These are pages Paula will never read. . . ." (*P,* 205). As Paula recedes from Allende's conscious mind as the recipient of her words, she penetrates her subconscious with increasing depth and appears in her mother's dreams to articulate her own desires and fears. Here the tight sense of structural unity in the text's composition is apparent: Allende's dream in part 2 pointedly addresses and rewrites both her dream in part 1 and the directives and questions she previously asked her daughter. If, in the first section,

Allende dreams that she and a 12-year-old Paula are floating through the sky and she is desperately trying to hold on to her daughter and not let her disappear through the small opening of a hollow tower, in part 2, Paula begs her mother not to hold her back any longer. Echoing the first words of the text (Perricone, 1998, 46), she gently commands, "Listen, Mama," and then adds, "Help me one more time, Mama" (P, 315); "Look at my wasted body, think of how my soul wants to escape and the terrible bonds holding it back, (P, 315–16); "Don't torture yourself thinking about what could have been, things you wish you had done differently, omissions, mistakes. . . . Get all that out of your head!" (P, 316).

Raising in turn her own questions, Paula asks, "Why is this happening?" (P, 315) and suggests that while it is painful to let go of a world she has loved, she needs her mother to help her "cross to the other side" because she is "eager to be free" but fears "the infinite loneliness of death" (P, 315). Precisely because Paula responds so soothingly to her mother's wishes, fears, and infinite feelings of guilt, and because her thoughts are articulated in parallel fashion to Allende's, it is tempting to view her words as part of a refined literary construct and as a projection of the author's needs rather than as the expression of an autonomous subject. This interpretation is set aside, however, when Allende introduces in the final pages of part 2 fragments of a letter that Paula wrote during her honeymoon to be opened after her death but that Allende in fact reads in California before her death. The presence of Paula's own words or "own story" (Perricone, 1998, 46)—a document whose existence Allende has attested to both in interviews and the televised BBC program "Listen, Paula"—reinforces, in fact, the poignant message of her mother's dream and gives it a note of authenticity that transcends its literary function within the text. As if anticipating her future fate, Paula tells her loved ones that she does not want "to remain trapped" in her body (P, 321) and that she knows she "will be closer to those she loves" (P, 322) once she is freed from it. Issuing her last gentle commands: "Please don't be sad. . . . Don't forget me, and . . . let's see a smile on those faces! Remember that we spirits can best help, accompany, and protect, those who are happy" (P, 322), she gives her mother the strength to accompany her to the other side and to let her go. The last pages of the book thus reinstate the dialogue Allende sustained with Paula in the first section; but, instead of telling her daughter to listen, to wake up, to breathe, she says: "Forgive me for having made you wait so long, Paula. . . . I've been too slow, but now I have no doubt, your letter is so revealing!" (P, 322). The union of mother and daughter, in words and spirit, is achieved both in Allende's final dream where she and Paula ascend together hand in hand through the hollow tower and in the last lines of the book where Allende assumes within herself the "I" and "you" previously separately and powerfully proclaims, "I am Paula and I am also Isabel, I am nothing and all other things in this life and other lives, immortal" (*P,* 330). Finalizing her last exhortations to the daughter she has finally freed but harbors within, she gives credence to Paula's view of death and writes, "Godspeed, Paula, woman. Welcome, Paula, spirit" (*P,* 330).

This harmonious blending of voices, much like a symphony whose different movements and tones come together at the end, fulfills a dual narrative and psychological function, and further, reinforces the degree to which *Paula* is much more than a spontaneous exercise in writing initiated in a hospital corner. Allende has carefully recounted the evolution of her text from the letter she began to her daughter in the hospital to her eventual decision to turn the reams of yellow paper into a book destined not only for Paula's immediate family, but also for others who had experienced a similar pain.[8] Using her initial notes, the 190 letters she wrote to her mother during the year of Paula's illness, and countless letters that Paula and Ernesto wrote to each other, Allende fashioned a literary text that reads at once like fiction and nonfiction. While framing her narrative in a linear sequence that captures events in her life and Chilean history, Allende's finely tuned sense of how to tell a good story ultimately determines her rendition of events. Thus, her most tantalizing story—the tale of her seduction at age eight—is notably not narrated in continuous fashion but almost teasingly presented in parts, such as when she suggestively introduces the fisherman who takes her into the woods but then abruptly changes the topic and says, "This is the moment, however, to focus on . . ." (*P,* 46). Similarly, as she catches herself alluding to Salvador Allende's political success in 1970 while relating the events of 1966, she immediately backtracks and adds, "But I don't want to get ahead of myself" (*P,* 137). Further, subjugating narrative demands to the implicit psychological desires of her daughter, she tells Paula: "I imagine that you would prefer to hear about the happiest part of your childhood, the days when Granny was still alive, and your parents loved each other, and Chile was your country, but this notebook is coming to the seventies, when things began to change" (*P,* 163). That is, narrative flow is often deemed more important than psychological gratification at the same time that literary form imitates life. Much as Paula's disease has an unrelenting progression from beginning to end,

Allende's narrative and its "documentary imperative" is shaped by a similar design and in this sense differs from the "nonlinear and nonprogressive" narrative that has so often characterized autobiographies by women (Jelinek, 171).

Reflecting in 1995 on the experience of writing *Paula,* Allende commented, "I feel that I prepared my whole life without knowing it to be able to write this book" (Mujica, 39). The gifted writer who creates a life for such complex characters as Alba Trueba, Clara del Valle, and Eva Luna is now called upon to re-create her own life for her daughter as she indicates in the first pages of her book: "My life is created as I narrate, and my memory grows stronger with writing; what I do not put in words on a page will be erased by time" (*P,* 8). The novelist who gives a sense of meaning and order to her husband's past in *The Infinite Plan* must now find purpose in her own past that she sees as having "little meaning . . . no order . . . no clarity . . . or path, only a blind journey guided by instinct and detours" (*P,* 23). The courageous woman whose life has been marked by constant goodbyes to loved ones and homeland must now face the most difficult farewell of her lifetime. Finally, the spiritual person whose grandmother accompanies her through life must try to envision her daughter fulfilling a similar role. In its poignant attempt to re-create personal and political losses and to find meaning in life beyond death, *Paula* provides a particularly rich view of modern autobiography, which "can be said to occupy a place between losing and finding, a liminal space where what has been lost can only be recalled and what might be possible, only anticipated" (Gunn, 137).

Allende's autobiographical account of this liminal space spans the 50 years of her own life and countless decades before as she re-creates her family history from the time of her grandfather's parents through to the present, complete with her birth in Peru; her childhood in Chile; her two-year stay in Bolivia and three-year stay in Beirut, where she attends an English school for girls; her return to Chile at age 15; her marriage in 1962 to Michael Frías; her work in journalism and television; the birth of her children, Paula and Nicolás; the Chilean coup of 1973 and her clandestine political activities; her exile to Venezuela with her family in 1975 and her subsequent feelings of paralysis and rootlessness; her marital crisis and three-month love affair in Madrid; her return to her husband and her work as a school administrator in Caracas; the illness of her grandfather in Chile in 1981 and the farewell letter she writes to him that becomes *The House of the Spirits;* her affirmation of herself as writer; her divorce from her husband in 1987; her move to California in

December 1987 and her marriage to William Gordon in 1988; her return to Chile in 1988 to vote in the national plebiscite; and her speaking engagement in Madrid in 1991 when her daughter takes ill. Carefully dividing her life into two parts that correspond in some measure to the external division of her narrative between Madrid and California, part 1 re-creates her life until the first days after the Chilean coup, whereas part 2 resumes with Pablo Neruda's death on 23 September 1973 and Allende's subsequent exile to Venezuela.

Regardless of the topic—childhood, adolescence, marriage, politics, exile, writing—*Paula* reads like a good novel. In fact, the German edition of *Paula* billed it as a novel and not as a memoir, and it was on the best-seller list for fiction in Germany and the Netherlands.[9] A self-deprecating sense of humor and a dazzling display of metaphors and similes worthy of Allende's best pages continually appear in this text. She comically describes her first experience of love at first sight and the object of her desire: two "enormous, protruding ears" that give her tall, skinny idol "the air of a Greek amphora" (*P*, 60). She humorously relates her audition for a follies girl position clad in woolen knickers and "two-sizes-too large gold shoes" that make her shuffle "like a wooden duck" (*P*, 177). And in a pointed barb at North American popular culture, she vividly relates her first experience in the movies with Gordon: "The first time we went to the movies and I found myself sitting in the dark beside a lover wearing a checkered shirt and cowboy boots and holding a liter of soda and bucket of popcorn in his lap, while on the screen a madman ripped a girl's breasts with an ice pick, I thought I had come to the end of my rope" (*P*, 305–6). These delightful anecdotes and others sprinkled throughout the text, not only about herself, but also about her grandfather, Tío Ramón, and the cast of warm individuals she meets in the hospital ward reveal Allende's bent for humor and contribute to create a text that, although painfully sad, never loses sight of the importance of laughter.

While certain episodes recounted in *Paula* have not appeared fictionalized in her previous work, others form part of her literary canon. In fact, as I read the author's description of her childhood years in her grandfather's house, I wasn't quite sure if the subject in question was Isabel Allende or Alba Trueba. The big house with its secret corners, tantalizing cellar, and eccentric family members who live inside—her authoritarian and stoic grandfather, Tata; her grandmother, Memé, who teaches the young Isabel Esperanto and introduces her to spiritist sessions at the three-legged table; her mother, Pancha, whose bedtime stories excite her daughter's imagination; her father, Tomás Allende, who mysteriously disappears when his daughter is very small; her uncles, who delight in teasing her with their outrageous exploits—recall in different ways the oddities of the Trueba–del Valle clan and their house of the spirits. As Allende's narrative progresses to include her years interviewing prostitutes, seers, and quasi saints for her magazine articles and gathering information on the disappeared, the image of Irene Beltrán from *Of Love and Shadows* comes to mind, while the portrait of the writer who affirms her creativity, sensuality, and love of words evokes her literary soul mate, *Eva Luna*. To this degree, reading *Paula* in the light of Allende's previous works reveals the way in which "autobiography is not so much a mode of literature as literature is a mode of autobiography" (Olney qtd in Smith, 3). Ultimately, the two genres intersect to such a point that it is not clear if art imitates life or if the author draws from her fiction in her shaping of self.

Allende's portrayal of herself as a solitary and shy child whose unusual family, unconditional maternal love, varied experiences and travels, and creative imagination help her blossom into a self-confident, energetic, and courageous adult is continually marked by reflections on gender that evoke those made by several of her female characters, among them Eva Luna and Carmen Morales from *The Infinite Plan*. Acutely aware from an early age of the multiple restrictions she suffered because of gender, she models herself after her strong and independent grandfather, takes lessons in verbal self-defense from her stepfather, Tío Ramón, gets her first job when she is 17 in order to be self-sufficient, finds articulation for her "mute rage" (*P,* 142) in feminist literature by North American and European women writers, and pointedly states that "forty years had to go by before I accepted my condition and realized that, with twice the effort and half the recognition, I had achieved what some men sometimes achieve" (*P,* 142).

What is particularly interesting about Allende's account of gender roles in a rigid Chilean society characterized by defined boundaries of class and sex is the noticeable split between her private and public self. Working full-time in television and journalism and authoring on the side children's books and plays, she spends much of her married life in Chile engaged in a wifely indulgence of all her husband's wants and needs. By her own account: "My feminism did not include sharing household duties, in fact, the idea never entered my mind; I thought liberation had to do with going out into the world and assuming male duties, not with delegating part of my load. The result was a terrible fatigue . . ." (*P,* 146). It is perhaps for this reason that following her divorce in 1987 she was so attracted to her future husband, Willie Gordon, who not only regaled her with a home-cooked meal on their second date, but did several loads of wash, bathed his son, and fed numerous pets during the course of the evening, much to the amazement of the fascinated Allende, who had never seen a man perform so many domestic functions.

This duality between resistance and compliance is given a much more unusual twist in Allende's rendition of a childhood incident in which gender norms and moral codes are drastically disrupted, producing a dramatic narration that highlights several aspects of the author's autobiographical endeavor in *Paula.* As previously suggested, this episode refers to her sexual encounter with a young fisherman during her family's summer vacation in 1950, a story that is first introduced in the book on page 45, mentioned again on page 60, related in great detail on pages 103–109, concluded on pages 151–155, and given an afterward on pages 227–228. As recounted by the author, on Christmas day in 1950, while alone on the beach, she meets a fisherman who gives her a sea urchin to taste, tells her that it has the smell "of the bottom of the ocean and of women when they are hot" (*P,* 104), places her hand on his bathing suit where she feels something moving, "like a piece of garden hose" (*P,* 105), and invites her to return to the woods with him later in the day to see "how your Papa and Mama do it" (*P,* 106). Ignoring all the mandates of her social upbringing engraved on her soul by her stern housekeeper, Margara—"Don't talk to strangers, Don't let anyone touch you, If someone touches you between your legs it's not just a mortal sin, you'll be pregnant besides, your belly will swell up like a balloon, bigger and bigger until it explodes and you will die" (*P,* 107)—she cedes to curiosity and "a fascination more powerful than terror" (*P,* 107). She follows the fisherman deep into the woods where he removes her dress, caresses her nipples, presses his fingers between her legs, kisses her face, and rubs his body hard against her "in an incomprehensible paroxysm of moans and rasping breath" (*P,* 108). Stroking her hair and commanding her not to tell her grandfather, he tells her to return the next day.

The young Allende spends Christmas night wide awake reliving the events of the afternoon, "confused by the mingling of repugnance and dark pleasure" (*P,* 152) she feels as she recalls the fisherman's fingers on her body. Ignoring the word *dirty* that keeps echoing in her head and believing that her pact of silence will keep the fisherman alive, she slips out of her house the next day only to discover in town a circle of people and two policemen gathered around the body of the fisherman who had received a deadly blow on the head. Convinced that he had paid for their "mutual crime" (P, 154), fearful that her grandfather had ordered him killed, and filled with a great sense of relief at having regained her freedom, she guards the episode in a "separate compartment" of her mind (P, 109), only to resurrect it 25 years later, in 1975. Shortly before leaving Chile for exile in Venezuela she asks her grandfather if he ever killed a man and is infinitely gratified on more than one level when he replies, "this country is filled with murderers, but I'm not one of them" (P, 228).

While reading Allende's narration of this episode, I could not help but ask myself why she included it in *Paula*. I wondered how she could possibly recall in such detail the events of the day including the color of the sundress she was wearing. I questioned whether the episode actually happened or if it responded instead to her desire "to remember what never happened" (P, 162). Even though I accepted the premise that autobiographical writing is inevitably unreliable and also acknowledged Allende's view that "the mind selects, enhances, and betrays" (P, 23), I still felt the need "to expect 'truth' of some kind" (Smith, 46). Yet, as recent studies of "autobiographical memory" have revealed, the concept of truth becomes enmeshed in the act of narration, creating an intimate relationship between the recall of events and "imaginative processes" (Haaken, 52). That is, as individuals relate forgotten or discarded memories, "there is a certain social license for elaboration and dramatic emphasis in transforming personal experience into an emotionally compelling tale" (Haaken, 53). This is certainly the process Allende engages in as she creates and re-creates a tale that has special meaning for her childhood, her adult life, and her present state of caring for her sick daughter.

Daring to defy social conventions and gender norms and to engage in an experience that leaves her with "a vague tenderness for the little girl" she was and "for the man who did not rape" her (P, 109), Allende radically rewrites the classic script of child seduction and victimization. Reflecting on this episode 40 years later as she writes *Paula*, she concludes: "At other times in my life, I have experienced that same moral vertigo when facing danger, and have yielded to it because I couldn't resist the urgent call to adventure. At times that temptation has been detrimental—for example, during the military dictatorship—and at others it has been enriching—as when I met Willie, and the thrill of the gamble impelled me to follow him" (P, 107). It is tempting to challenge this somewhat strange conflation of a childhood experience, a political commitment, and an adult romantic involvement under the broad category of a "call to adventure," which robs each episode of its individual flavor and almost trivializes Allende's political activism during the Pinochet regime. For some, such a statement may respond to Allende's rhetorical flourishes or "overblown romanticism."[10] I suspect, however, that this homogenizing of diverse experiences responds instead to the "impulse governing the autobiographical venture": the creation of "a self image" that is an "individual construct" but also a "social artifact, as revealing of a psyche as it is of a culture" (Molloy, 8). That is, when Allende is confronted with a patriarchal culture that issues more dictates to girls than to boys, when she experiences firsthand the profound disregard for human rights of the Pinochet regime, and when she is later given the opportunity to uproot her life again and experience love with a man who does "a mother's work" (*P,* 301), she fearlessly swims against the current of conformity, cedes to danger and risk, and subsequently finds a connection among these three different events. In this way, she constructs a powerful self-image needed in the present as she contemplates heroic efforts to save her daughter. In this context, the issue of the truth or invention of the fisherman episode seems irrelevant. A fascinating story in its own right, it functions in conjunction with Allende's other daring acts to invest her past with a meaning that applies to the present and makes credible her declaration: "I am not defeated, there is still much I can do. Western medicine is not the only alternative in these cases, I shall knock at other doors and resort to other methods, including the most improbable, to save my daughter" (*P,* 234).

Allende has commented in a 1998 interview that during one of her speaking engagements, a student asked her if she didn't feel vulnerable for having told all her secrets. She replied that to the contrary, she felt stronger because "secrets make one weaker and truth makes one stronger" (Correas Zapata, 130). She has also mentioned that her mother urged her to leave the fisherman episode out because it did not make her "look good."[11] Precisely because "conventions about the 'private' as well as conventions about propriety in self-revelation are culturally determined" (Smith, 17),[12] Allende's decision to tell a story that raises many questions about propriety is a further indication of her willingness to rewrite gender norms and cast off cultural taboos concerning woman's self expression. The fisherman episode also has ramifications for another piece of the self-image that Allende constructs in the text, that of Allende the writer. Attributing certain scenarios of child seduction that appear in her work to her experience as a little girl (Allende,

1995, 443), she suggests that her fiction is born in part out of personal memories buried in regions of the mind until they are ready to emerge transformed on the written page.

For the reader in search of the genesis of a writer, *Paula* is a rich source of insight and information and reveals the intricate bond that unites life experience, reading, storytelling, and writing. Describing the impact that fiction and books have had on Latin American writers, Sylvia Molloy comments that the Argentinean authors Domingo Faustino Sarmiento and Victoria Ocampo favor "the Hamlet-like position—the younger reader with a book in hand" (Molloy, 56). In Allende's case, it might be more appropriate to talk about the young reader with a book in one hand and the other surreptitiously concealed under bed covers or in wardrobes, thus highlighting the nature of her childhood and adolescent readings, both forbidden and allowed. Rejoicing in the complete works of Shakespeare that Tío Ramón gives her when she is nine years old, she also devours the "forbidden books" of her absent father and delights in "the voraciousness inspired by secrecy" (*P,* 51). Years later she experiences in Beirut the same pleasure when she discovers four leather-bound volumes of the *Thousand and One Nights* zealously guarded in Tío Ramón's wardrobe. Armed with her trusty flashlight and impelled by her pressing desire to find the "dirty parts" (*P,* 71), she spends three years reading pieces of the tales and relishing the "orgy of exotic words, eroticism, and fantasy" (*P,* 71) that feeds her imagination. Similar to Victoria Ocampo for whom "books were a new world in which freedom reigned" (Molloy, 58), Allende's assimilation of the sensuality of her adolescent readings is mediated, however, by the puritanism of her British school for girls. By her own account, "For decades I wavered between those two tendencies, torn apart inside and awash in a sea of intermingled desires and sins, until finally in the heat of Venezuela, when I was nearly forty years old, I at last freed myself from Miss St. John's rigid precepts" (*P,* 71). Allende's creative spirit is not only fueled by her readings, but also by the encouragement she receives from her mother to paint the walls of her room with murals to her liking—an act imitated by Alba in *The House of the Spirits*—and to record her thoughts in notebooks. The transition from the suspenseful childhood tales she tells her terrified brothers and the notebooks she fills in Bolivia to her best-selling novels is a slow but continual one marked by the daily letters she writes to her mother upon their first separation when she was 15; her translations of popular novels from English to Spanish complete with original touches "to better the heroine's image" (*P,* 98); magazine writing; television script writing;

and the authoring of horoscopes, love-lorn columns, recipes, children's books, and plays. What seems to define the early Allende "on the periphery of literature" (*P,* 275)—and the current Allende as well—is her unabashed and unbridled ability to add personal flourishes and twists that convert factual material into fiction. Acknowledging that as a journalist she was "incapable of being objective," she ultimately followed Pablo Neruda's suggestion that she turn to fiction instead because "in literature those defects are virtues" (*P,* 182). His judgment, of course, proved correct and the blurring of "the limits between truth and invention" (*P,* 275) is, indeed, the trademark of Allende's style, even perhaps in *Paula,* as this chapter has suggested.

The beginning of Allende's career as a novelist is recounted in moving detail in the pages of *Paula* where she describes the yearlong process of writing *The House of the Spirits* and bringing to life characters who inhabit her dreams and waking hours and free her from the "long period of paralysis and muteness" (*P,* 277) that had characterized her exile in Caracas. The joy with which Allende describes the creative process and her affirmation of herself as a writer are comparable to the joy she expresses about "the process of engendering a child" (*P,* 231); both are viewed as "voyages into one's inner self, during which body, mind, and soul shift course and turn toward the very center of existence" (*P,* 231). In this context, her experience witnessing the birth of her granddaughter, Andrea, and cutting her umbilical cord becomes paradigmatic of countless experiences in her life where she has participated in rites of joyful celebration and painful separation. Birth and death, in fact, are continually interwoven in *Paula.* The death of Allende's grandfather contributes to the birth of Allende as novelist; the birth of her granddaughter, Andrea, takes place in the same room where Paula dies; and the death of Paula the woman ushers in the birth of Paula the spirit. Moreover, the demise of Chilean democracy and the short-lived hope for an end to social injustice is implicitly juxtaposed to the early death of Paula and the promise she had of making the world a better place. To this degree, in its continual fusion of the personal and the political, *Paula* provides depth and texture to Sylvia Molloy's observation that "true rememoration . . . is an ever renewed merging of . . . two memories: the communal and the individual" (Molloy, 165).

Summoning Allende's finely honed skills as journalist, *Paula* recreates in solid Latin American testimonial fashion the birth and death of Marxism in Chile complete with a thoughtful and measured evaluation of Salvador Allende, a detailed account of the social and economic reforms of the Allende government, the protest of food shortages by the upper class, the role of the United States in sabotaging the Marxist government, the creation of the black market, the truck drivers' strike, the general "climate of insecurity and latent violence" (P, 184) in the months before the coup, and the "apparent economic miracle" of the Pinochet regime (P, 221). This "documentary imperative" so characteristic of Latin American autobiographical writing becomes increasingly personalized as Allende inserts her own family history in the context of her nation's history. The result is a sustained 65-page narrative only occasionally interrupted by other reflections that reads like a chapter from *The House of the Spirits* or *Of Love and Shadows*.

From the beginning of her lengthy account, Allende makes it abundantly clear that she is not a radical but a political independent whose family life is divided but never undermined by her parents' allegiance to the Marxist reforms of their friend and relative Salvador Allende and the conservative and even reactionary ideology of her grandfather and in-laws. Her evolution from enthusiastic supporter of her uncle's policies to underground activist is one that is realized almost unconsciously and without premeditation. Believing up to the last minute that a military coup could never occur in Chile, the Switzerland of Latin America, her awakening to political reality is marked by the bombing of La Moneda Presidential Palace; the death of her uncle; the moving and symbolic funeral procession for Pablo Neruda in which she participates; the presence of corpses in the Mapocho River in Santiago; the disappearance and torture of friends; the assassination of her parents' close friend in exile, General Prats; and tight government censorship that results in the loss of her magazine position. As Allende narrates her involvement in a wide range of clandestine activities that involve sheltering leftist extremists, assisting them in reaching asylum, taping interviews for publication in Germany, and raising funds for food for the needy, a portrait emerges of her blend of courage, naïveté, and candidness. Making no claim to heroism of any nature, she describes how her initial sense of invulnerability rapidly changes to terror when she receives death threats by phone, is told that she is on the government's blacklist, and warned via her children that her "days are numbered" (P, 227).

Choosing exile in Venezuela as the best option available, she reflects on this decision that impacted so strongly on her life and her family's and that has been the focus of many of early interviews: "I, like thousands of other Chileans, have often asked myself whether I did the right thing in leaving my country during the dictatorship, whether I had the right to uproot my children and drag my husband to an uncertain future in a strange country, or whether it would have been better to stay where we were, trying to pass unnoticed—these are questions than cannot be answered. Events developed inexorably, as in Greek tragedies; disaster lay before my eyes, but I could not avoid taking the steps that led to it" (*P,* 213). It would be difficult to imagine Isabel Allende passing unnoticed, especially in a country where her television programs had given her a celebrity status. Her willingness to open herself to difficult and risky situations and her genuine concern for the victims of oppression inevitably swept her along a fast-paced political path that had innumerable consequences for her future.

Allende's thoughtful meditation on the complexities of life's drama is given its most poignant rendition as she attempts to harness the energy and courage that marked her political work and channel them to save her daughter's life. Her textured descriptions of her daughter that appear interlaced with recollections about herself bring life to a young woman whose name graces the title of the work. Interestingly, several critics have expressed disappointment with what they perceive as the sketchy and unsubstantial portrait of Paula that emerges in the text (DiBattista, 105). It has even been suggested that a more appropriate title for this book would be "Isabel."[13] Significantly, Allende has commented that the logical title was "Listen, Paula," the first words of her memoir. But since that sounded too harsh in other languages and even like a military order in German, she simply named it "Paula" (Allende, 2000b). While Allende's self-portrait is infinitely more elaborate than the portrait of her daughter, Paula's life is indeed given form and substance in her mother's touching and often humorous account of her deeds. In fact, despite the most obvious difference between Allende and Paula—the mother's love of adornment versus the daughter's cultivation of simplicity—it is not difficult to see a marked resemblance between these two strong women.

As fiercely independent, resourceful, and motivated as her mother and seemingly needing little outside approval or incentive for her actions, Paula hides her Granny's liquor bottles at a young age to salvage her dignity. She takes care of her younger brother when Allende follows her lover to Madrid, informs her mother at age 16 that she wants to go to a gynecologist and find out about contraceptives, does volunteer work in the roughest slums of Caracas despite concerns for her safety, and teaches herself Italian and French after having mastered English. Seemingly unintimidated by a mother whose energy and vitality could easily have overshadowed her children, Paula's relationship with Allende is characterized by a delightful sense of irreverence, a strong sense of solidarity and support, and a healthy disagreement about important topics. Allende makes it very clear that it is Paula who helps her organize her first course on creative writing in the States and who urges her to focus in on the big issues instead of small concerns as she contemplates her living arrangements with Gordon. It is Paula who gently mocks her mother's sexual naïveté about condoms and who criticizes her belief that a church wedding is a "nuisance" (*P,* 124). It is Paula who seeks her mother's advice on how best to combine her graduate studies in psychology and her romantic involvement with Ernesto and who tells her of her innermost struggle to find God without success.

While the relationship between Allende and Paula recalls the intense mother-daughter bonding that appears in many of Allende's novels, I would add that there is a touch of reality present in *Paula* that is often missing from her fiction where disagreements and harsh judgments are notably absent. Thus, when Allende returns from her three-month fling in Madrid with her Argentinean lover during Paula's adolescence, she significantly notes that Paula greets "her with a forced hug and hard eyes" (*P,* 206); she similarly records that Paula shed abundant tears of compassion for her father "whom she always protected" (*P,* 296–97) when her parents decided to divorce in 1987. Above all, however, Allende's admiration for her brilliant and caring daughter marks the pages of this book. Recalling tender deeds both past and present, she recounts Paula's involvement with old people at a geriatric home in Santiago for whom she knitted sweaters and brought gifts and to whom she wrote letters from Venezuela. She describes her and Nicolás's decision to give their bicycles to the children of their teacher whose husband had been disappeared by the military regime. She notes her volunteer work in a school in Spain, the countless lives she touched through her gentleness and intelligence, and her desire to found a home for the elderly as a way of giving them the care and love she wasn't able to give her Granny when she moved to Caracas. Paula's own letter to her family, written during her honeymoon, bears further tribute to her generosity as she asks that her savings be used to help needy children. Never sanctifying this bright young woman who was obsessed with knowledge and learning, who was by far the smartest person in the family, who received the best grades in her class, and who was capable of memorizing the smallest detail, Allende humanizes her daughter with her humorous rendition of how she fainted when vaccinated, was terrified in horror movies, and threw a "comic fit of jealousy when Celia and Nicolás were married" (*P,* 328).

A tone of elegiac lament also permeates this book (Perricone, 1998, 43) as Allende crystallizes the qualities of her first-born child—"Oh, your grace, Paula! Your sweetness, your unpredictable intensity, your fierce intellectual discipline, your generosity, your insane tenderness" (*P,* 77)— and ultimately longs to be "erased" and "dissolved" so that Paula's "inexhaustible and joyful goodness may completely replace" her own "lifelong fears . . . paltry ambitions . . . depleted vanity" (*P,* 323). Unable to realize her wish, she instead incorporates within herself the essence of Paula's spirit. Her very moving and detailed description of Paula's death in the epilogue seamlessly brings together countless aspects of everything Allende had written and lived up to that moment. Much as Allende attended to Granny in death and returned to her all the kindness she had given to her children (*P,* 252–53), and much as Clara and Eva Luna bathed and dressed Férula and Zulema following their respective deaths in *The House of the Spirits* and *Eva Luna,* Allende and her family gently accompany Paula in her passage from this world and bid her farewell with music and prayers and with keepsakes and photos placed on her breast. As Allende describes:

> We celebrated the gifts she had given us in life, and all of us said goodbye and prayed in each our way. As the hours went by, something solemn and sacred filled the room, just as on the occasion of Andrea's birth. The two moments are much alike: birth and death are made of the same fabric. The air became more and more still; we moved slowly, in order not to disturb our hearts' repose. We were filled with Paula's spirit, as if we were all one being and there was no separation among us: life and death were joined. For a few hours, we experienced that reality the soul knows, absent time or space.
> I slipped into bed beside my daughter, cradling her against my bosom, as I had when she was young. . . . All during the slow night, we waited, remembering the difficult moments, but especially the happy ones, telling stories, crying a little and smiling a lot, honoring the light of Paula as she sank deeper and deeper into the final sleep, her breast barely rising at slower and slower intervals. Her mission in this world was to unite all those who passed through her life, and that night we all felt sheltered beneath her starry wings, immersed in that pure silence where perhaps angels reign. (*P,* 328)

Retracing with great candor the period following Paula's death, Allende has movingly written in recent years about the hours when the family left her body untouched so that her husband, Ernesto, who had

been in China when she died, could see her one more time. She has spoken about the paralyzing sadness and pain she felt for months afterward
and that only the act of writing *Paula*, rather than a vacation, therapy, or
antidepressants, was able to relieve (Correas Zapata, 121). She has discussed the difficulty involved in writing an autobiographical book and
"attempting to be honest without betraying too much the people who
appear in the book with their real names" (Correas Zapata, 214). She
has also recounted the innumerable letters her readers have written to
her sharing her pain and reflecting on their own experiences; in characteristic fashion she has answered each one, spending more than two
years on this correspondence (Correas Zapata, 217). Her speaking
engagements have attracted crowds throughout the United States,
where *Paula* has been on the *New York Times* best sellers list, and the
public is often visibly moved by her story. In both public and private,
she has commented on the invaluable life lesson she learned from her
daughter's death. In a 1993 interview, Allende offered the following
reflection that may be considered an additional epilogue to the one
included in *Paula:*

> . . . I'm not a religious person. I'm not into any of the traditional reli-
> gions, but I believe in the power of the spirit. And I do believe that we all
> belong to something that is one and whole, and our souls are just parti-
> cles of that wholeness that for a while inhabit these bodies. We have to
> go through life, but that is only one part of life's journey. And more and
> more I'm convinced that is so. That's why I don't fear death and I'm not
> afraid of many things that people usually fear. And I'm quite detached
> from this world because I have the strong feeling that this is only part of
> what my spirit or this particle of spirit has to do.[14]

Reaffirming her daughter's presence in her life and her writing,
where she fulfills the role of Sybil, or guide, Allende pays no better tribute to a person whose inspirational spirit more than justifies the title
Paula (Cortínez, 64). If autobiography does indeed occupy the liminal
space between losing and finding, the reader concludes *Paula* with the
intimate sense that despite all of Allende's losses, and most significantly,
the loss of her daughter, she has found, in the process, a renewed source
of spirituality, a sober sense of her ultimate inability to distract death
and protect her loved ones, and a companion and "guardian angel"
(Allende, 1994c, 393) whom she carries with her, "like a second skin"
(Correas Zapata, 204). Allende's ability to relate the story of her difficult

year with humor, flair, and obvious attachment toward living despite her pain is the most telling indication that what she has not lost is her boundless sense of vitality and gift for loving. A poignant tale about letting go, *Paula* also celebrates the joys of tenaciously holding on in the difficult struggle of living and dying.

Chapter Eight
Daughter of Fortune

While the process of writing *Paula* did a great deal to alleviate the tremendous sadness that Allende experienced following her daughter's death in 1992, it was not sufficient to unleash her creative muse that remained silent and seemingly blocked for several years thereafter. "Those years were three centuries filled with the sensation that the world had lost its colors and that a universal grayness had spread inexorably over every surface," she tells us, three years of attempting to "exorcise" her sadness with "futile rituals" that bore no result (*A*, 24).[1] Slowly, however, Allende recovered her passion for living and writing as delicious dreams of swimming in a pool of rice pudding and wrapping a naked Antonio Banderas in a Mexican tortilla began penetrating her nightly slumbers. As Allende herself humorously relates in the introduction to her 1997 book, *Afrodita: Cuentos, recetas y otros afrodisíacos* (*Aphrodite: A Memoir of the Senses*, 1998): "I cannot pinpoint the moment when I saw the first brush strokes of color, but when my dreams about food began, I knew that I was reaching the end of a long tunnel of mourning and finally coming out the other end, into the light, with a tremendous desire to eat and cuddle once again. And so, little by little, pound after pound and kiss after kiss, this project was born" (*A*, 25).

"This project"—*Aphrodite*—is nothing less than a delightful work of nonfiction, which, as one critic has noted, is "virtually unclassifiable."[2] Simultaneously a history of aphrodisiacs, an assortment of short stories, a cookbook filled with tantalizing recipes and illustrations designed to induce states of passion, a "mapless journey through the regions of sensual memory" (*A*, 11), and an autobiographical account of Allende's own relationship with food and, occasionally, eros, it is also a good-natured critique of patriarchal norms. Releasing with full force her bent for humor and social commentary, Allende makes it abundantly clear that while aphrodisiacs are an important component of phallocratic societies obsessed with virility, the symbol or "prized possession" of patriarchy "is rather insignificant compared to an arm or a leg and . . . can comfortably be fitted into a sardine can" (*A*, 27). If this tongue-in-cheek tone reminds the reader of Allende's earlier demythification of patriarchy in *Civilice a su troglodita* (Civilize your troglodyte), *Aphrodite* is also a book that serves "as a literary aphrodisiac for Allende's dormant literary powers" (Rodden, 25) or future writings. In fact, shortly after she completed it, she began writing what would become her sixth work of fiction, *Hija de la fortuna* (*Daughter of Fortune*), published in Spanish and English in 1999.[3]

Allende's debt to *Aphrodite* is apparent in countless pages of *Daughter of Fortune,* thus revealing the degree to which each of her texts builds upon previous ones, forming a tight-knit universe where themes, characters, and passions are woven together in familiar and unexpected patterns. After celebrating in *Aphrodite* the joys of food and singing the praises of her mother and collaborator, Panchita Llona, whose fine nose can detect every possible ingredient and aroma, it is not surprising that Allende's female protagonist in *Daughter of Fortune,* Eliza Sommers, is a young woman whose two special talents are "a good sense of smell and a good memory" (*DF,* 3), both of which she uses to create her extraordinary recipes. Similarly, after spending countless paragraphs extolling the virtues of the Chinese pillow books—the ancient erotic manual of the Orient—it is fitting that her male protagonist in *Daughter of Fortune,* Tao Chi'en, is conversant in the 222 positions outlined in the pillow books, while also believing, as does Allende herself, that "the best aphrodisiac is love" (*A,* 183). In this sense, Eliza and Tao Chi'en spring whole from the pages of *Aphrodite,* at the same time that *Daughter of Fortune* bears no resemblance to a mapless journey through the senses, but is, instead, a clearly demarcated expedition through the historical past of the California gold rush.

Allende's fascination with California has emerged as a constant in her writings since her move to the San Francisco area in December 1987. While social issues related to east Los Angeles, Berkeley, and San Francisco are fictionalized in *The Infinite Plan,* and health-crazed Californians are gently satirized in *Aphrodite, Daughter of Fortune* removes itself from twentieth-century reality and returns to the tumultuous era of the nineteenth century when legends were created, passion and greed were unleashed, and diverse ethnic groups struggled to shape a new life for themselves in America. It is not surprising that Allende chose the gold rush as the central theme for her novel given her interest in complex political and historical moments when human motivation is revealed in all its raw complexity. By her own account, she was particularly interested in the gold rush because "it's a time of extremes . . . a time when all the human vices and the human virtues appear enlarged, magnified."[4] Allende's investigative skills, which have played such an important role in creating an accurate historical context in virtually all her works of fiction, as well as in *Aphrodite,* are summoned in great measure here as she duplicates historical accounts of the experiences of Chileans and Chinese during the gold rush period.

Crisscrossing diverse continents, Allende takes her readers on a voyage from Chile, China, and Hong Kong to the newly settled lands of California, creating in the process a historical novel that portrays "the broad living basis of historical events in their intricacy and complexity," as the Hungarian Georg Lukács has theorized in his writings on the historical novel.[5] Just as the historical novel contains a "struggle . . . between history and fiction, between information and creation,"[6] Allende also attempts to maintain a balance between legendary figures and events and those of her own imagination. This fusion of fiction and history, of imaginative scenarios and journalistic accounts, of romantic passion and serious reflection on the shaping of the West makes *Daughter of Fortune* a novel that is not only an example of historical fiction, but also an adventure story, a historical romance, and a female bildungsroman that permits its protagonist to integrate *bildung,* or growth and development, with mature love. It is also a novel in which Eliza Sommers's process of self-definition and independence in California is mirrored in the author's telling account of the creation of the state of California, thus uniting, in typical Allende fashion, the "collective heartbeat" of the times and the individual destinies of her characters (Allende, 1995, 457). To this degree, the central protagonists whose identities shape and motivate the novel are not only the fictional Eliza and Tao Chi'en, but the vast expanse of California itself, as well as Joaquín Murieta, the legendary bandit who roamed its terrain and whose enigmatic and elusive presence in Allende's novel adds a further mythical dimension to her blend of history and fiction.

Allende uses a well-seasoned narrative technique for uniting these central components of her novel that is divided into three parts and that progresses in linear fashion from 1843 to 1853, although references are continually made to events that occur before and after this ten-year period. *Daughter of Fortune* begins with the story of an orphan who is left in a soap crate at the doorstep of the Sommers's household in Valparaíso. Adopted and named Eliza by the 20-year-old British woman, Rose Sommers, and her brother Jeremy, Eliza spends the first 16 years of her life in the Sommers's home. Her upbringing is characterized by conflicting versions of her origins, some more embellished than others; a strict Victorian code of behavior overseen by Miss Rose and replete with piano lessons and skills designed to make her marriageable; and the rich aromas and herbs cultivated by Mama Fresia, the family's housekeeper and cook and Eliza's nana, who insists on letting Eliza know that she is as much Indian in blood as she is British in upbringing. A bilingual Eliza, fluent in both English and Spanish and with a smattering of Mama Fresia's native Mapuche tongue, inhabits the worlds of the sewing room and the kitchen until she falls madly in love at age 16 with one of her uncle Jeremy's employees, Joaquín Andieta, an 18-year-old seeker of social justice from a lower social class. They engage in a clandestine romance that leads to Eliza's pregnancy and subsequent desire to follow Joaquín to California, where he hopes to make his fortune and return home rich enough to marry her.

The person who helps Eliza seek refuge as a stowaway on a Chilean ship bound for California is Tao Chi'en, the cook on her uncle John's ship. Brought up as Fourth Son in a family of healers in his native province of Canton until he was eventually sold to an eminent acupuncturist and healer who served as his mentor for many years and gave him a proper name, Tao Chi'en is shanghaied in Hong Kong and forced to work as a cook in the Chilean ship captained by John Sommers. Tao Chi'en meets Eliza in Valparaíso in part 2 of the novel and is so taken with her courage and determination to follow her lover to America that he arranges to have her hidden on the ship *Emilia* bound for California without knowing that she is pregnant. His skill as a physician, or *zhong yi,* and his infinite compassion save her life when she miscarriages during the voyage and the two arrive in California unified by a tenuous bond that becomes stronger as they share a common destiny of healing the infirm and rescuing Chinese prostitutes from servitude. The rich cultural background that each one brings to the West—a terrain inhabited by throngs of Chileans, Mexicans, Peruvians, Chinese, Australians, and other immigrant groups—is simultaneously erased and affirmed in multiple ways throughout the novel as Allende ultimately celebrates the blending of difference that is a trademark of her fiction. Yet this very blending of difference is one fraught with countless problems of an ideological, historical, and psychological nature precisely because it is situated in the time of the California gold rush. Alternately extolled and condemned for being "either a triumph of American enterprise and determination, or the final proof of an American insanity of greed and restlessness," the gold rush has inspired thinkers, writers, and participants themselves to reflect on its significance.[7] As a literary topic, it has been revisited by twentieth-century writers in search of the stories and experiences of marginalized groups who participated in this epic venture but whose lives have been erased from historical and fictional accounts of the period. On still another level, the gold rush continues to stimulate the contemporary imagination because "as a collective experience it call[s] into question values about wealth, family, independence, gender, [and] cultural diversity" (Kowalewski, xxvii). *Daughter of Fortune* gives complex texture to this statement as Allende uses Eliza Sommers's adventures to interrogate and rewrite prescribed conventions of gender and the culture of romance and to highlight the relationship between the creation of personal identity and the identity of statehood.

Eliza Sommers is a quintessential Allende character, possessing all the personal attributes that define many of her female protagonists: independence, imagination, curiosity, sensuality, compassion, resourcefulness, lack of pretense, boldness, a willingness to defy social conventions, a propensity for action rather than philosophical contemplation, and an open spirit and mind. Although she succumbs to the tumultuous passion of first love, she simultaneously shows signs of an incipient feminism. When Miss Rose advises her to allow the man to feel superior to her, Eliza retorts, "That is very difficult" (*DF,* 75). Unlike the close bonds that Alba Trueba and Eva Luna enjoy with their mothers, Allende utilizes the story of Eliza's dubious origins to create both mystery and humor in her novel. It is not until the second half of the novel that Allende clarifies what the reader has come to suspect: that Eliza's biological father is Miss Rose's womanizing brother John Sommers, whose one-night fling on the port with a young Chilean woman leads to Eliza's birth and Rose's decision to adopt the child without ever telling her the truth.

This potentially sad story of dispossession is converted into humor when the source of milk for the young baby comes from a she-goat whose raucous bleating in the patio makes Eliza's sensitive nose go wild for her comforting teat.[8] Eliza's greatest legacy, her sensory ability, is so well developed, in fact, throughout the entire novel that she would rather smell Joaquín Andieta than listen to his impassioned discourses on social justice, thus revealing in an unusual way her gravitation toward practice over theory. In a deeper sense, the story of Eliza's mysterious origin gives special meaning to the title of the novel. Eliza is, ultimately, the daughter of fortune. The birth of her independence and autonomy as a woman may simultaneously be attributed to the good luck she has been blessed with; the sense of destiny that directs human life, as Tao Chi'en maintains; Eliza's own belief that deeds rather than birthright shape a life; the opportunities provided her by the fortune of the gold rush; and the broader concept of life as a journey, suggested by the name of the steamship, *Fortuna,* that transports produce from Chile to California.

Eliza does not arrive easily at this sense of self-possession. Even before she arrives in San Francisco, tremendously weakened by her miscarriage and two months of enclosure on the *Emilia,* Allende launches her on a contradictory trajectory where images of submission and control and servitude and authority collide. Affirming herself as the desiring subject instead of the object desired as is often the scenario in nineteenth-century fiction,[9] Eliza summons her sense of adventure and moral strength—as well as her tremendous fear of repercussion for her dishonor and pregnancy—to leave the protected environment of her Valparaíso home and seek Joaquín. Her strong sense of self is mitigated, however, by her overwhelming desire "to serve him wholeheartedly for the rest of her life, to sacrifice herself and suffer to prove her selflessness, to die for him if necessary" (*DF,* 115). Significantly, the part of her that must be sacrificed to achieve this goal is the very aspect that ties her to servitude and impedes her full realization as a human being: her femininity. First disguised as the mute Chinese half-brother of Tao Chi'en and later as the Chilean Elías Andieta or Chile Boy, brother of Joaquín, Eliza liberates herself externally from the strictures of gender norms—and corsets—while at the same time living internally the passion of a first love destined to convert her into the perfect female, slave to her lover. The process by which the external masquerade penetrates and transforms the internal spirit is one of the most interesting aspects of the novel and one that raises multiple questions about how gender is constituted and sustained in patriarchal society.

Researchers have documented that the paucity of women in California during the early years of the gold rush created a heightened interest in the female sex. Mark Twain himself wrote that "miners would flock in crowds to catch a glimpse of that rare and blessed spectacle, a woman!"[10] Within this context, dressing as a man—a disguise used by many gold rush women—provides Eliza with the invisibility necessary to participate in the mining venture where she hopes to find Joaquín. Although Eliza's delicate appearance raises the speculation that is effeminate, she is affectionately known as Chile Boy and never experiences sexual harassment of any nature during her years of travel. While Allende avoids the topic of homosexuality on the California frontier, she suggests that gender identity is not immutable but rather a product of historical circumstances and the individual's response to such a circumstance. Much as

Linda Alcoff has theorized that "being a 'woman' is to take up a position within a moving historical context and to be able to choose what we make of this position and how we alter this context,"[11] Eliza utilizes her female skills—piano playing and cooking—to survive economically as a male while recognizing that all gender roles rigorously enforced and codified stifle individual growth. As she writes to Tao during her travels through the mother lode in search of Joaquín: "I don't have a friend in all this lonely country and in my role as a man I have to watch everything I say. I go about with a scowl so people will think I'm tough. It is tedious to be a man, but being a woman is worse still" (*DF,* 277). The degree to which words such as *man* and *woman* are mere social constructs codified by use and abuse is highlighted most clearly when Eliza performs the difficult task of amputating two fingers from the hand of the bandit Jack. Praised for her bravery, she receives the supreme compliment from one of her companions who had previously doubted her masculinity. "You're a real man," he proclaims (*DF,* 308), thus underlining the status men enjoy in society and the stultifying associations between gender expectations and personality traits.

Eliza's most problematic experience with gender trouble arises when she joins up for a short stint with a group of itinerant actors and plays the role of the ingenue in their performances. "Everyone was amazed by how well I played the part of a woman," she writes Tao. "I couldn't stay with them, though, because the confusion was driving me crazy; I didn't know whether I was a woman dressed as a man, a man dressed as a woman, or an aberration of nature" (*DF,* 274). This confusion gradually leads to the creation of a self that integrates certain aspects of gendered male and female identity while eliminating others, as Eliza recognizes that California represents for her, and many others, a "blank page" on which to inscribe the person she wants to become (*DF,* 280). As Allende narrates: "She had grown up clad in the impenetrable armor of good manners and conventions, trained from girlhood to please and serve, bound by corset, routines, social norms and fear. Fear had been her companion: fear of God and his unpredictable justice, of authority, of her adoptive parents, of illness and evil tongues, of anything unknown or different; fear of leaving the protection of her home and facing the dangers outside; fear of her own fragility as a woman, of dishonor and truth" (*DF,* 275).

Although Eliza experiences an extraordinary sense of freedom as a man, she, nonetheless, salvages her femininity and sensuality. Reclaiming that lost part of her self at the novel's close when she abandons her masculine garb, refashions herself again as a woman, and explores her body with pleasure, her new concept of womanhood excludes, however, the desire to be possessed by her lost lover. While subscribing to female gender codes in appearance as well as in the touches of domesticity she adds to the home she shares with Tao Chi'en on the outskirts of Chinatown, her sense of self and her relationship to the culture of romance have undergone a dramatic transformation. The sense of freedom she experiences at the end of the novel has a significance that not only encompasses gender norms, but also conventions governing women's writings, a complex notion considering the fact that *Daughter of Fortune* is situated in the nineteenth century but written with a twentieth-century literary sensitivity.

Narrative codes pertinent to nineteenth-century women's fiction dictate that the dichotomy between love and quest be resolved through the erasure of female quest or *bildung* and the predominance of marriage or death at the novel's close.[12] If, however, "it is the project of twentieth-century women writers to solve the contradiction between love and quest and to replace the alternate endings in marriage and death that are their cultural legacy . . . by offering a different set of choices" (DuPlessis, 4), Allende's contribution to this endeavor of "writing beyond the ending" of nineteenth-century fiction is her celebration of freedom and independence accompanied by romance. Eliza's frenzied adolescent passion has been replaced by her growing awareness of the love she feels for Tao Chi'en that can only be expressed once she has freed herself of Joaquín Andieta. To this degree, Allende does not renounce love or marriage as a possibility for her protagonist but enables these options to coexist with Eliza's development and growth as a woman and human being. While Eliza's romantic desires and sexual passion are thus transferred from Joaquín Andieta to Tao Chi'en, this very act of transference involves much more than a displacement of feeling from one man to another, since Joaquín Andieta's role in the novel and his confusion with the legendary bandit, Joaquín Murieta, introduce the further notion of the mythification of love and heroism on both a personal and collective level.

Joaquín Andieta is, at best, a sketchy figure in the novel. He appears in the early pages as a thoughtful revolutionary with flashing eyes intent on eradicating a rigid class structure that discriminates against the poor and shuns his mother for having given birth to him out of wedlock. More inflamed by his passion for revolutionary rhetoric than by actual love, he is unable to satisfy Eliza sexually and is only capable of revealing the depth of his soul in letters he writes to her in between their clandestine trysts in hidden corners of her house. When the news of the discovery of gold reaches the port of Valparaiso, the busiest port in the Pacific, Joaquín, together with thousands of Chileans, seizes the opportunity to strike it rich and be part of a landscape where class differences are seemingly erased.[13] His disappearance from the novel following his departure from Chile and his gradual confusion with the legendary bandit, Joaquín Murieta, is foreseen in part 1 of the novel when Eliza continually refers to her lover as an illusion, a ghost, and tries to ascertain the reality of the real Joaquín. Unwilling to recognize that he is perhaps not the perfect lover, she mythifies him to such a degree that it will take four years of searching before she is prepared to psychologically let him go. While the reader may well surmise that Andieta becomes one more statistic in the countless number of immigrants who perished in California (Kowalewski, xx), Allende's genius in *Daughter of Fortune* is the ambiguity she sustains regarding this character and her introduction of Joaquín Murieta in the third part of the novel.

The legend of Joaquín Murieta is a complicated one involving conflicting versions and numerous works of prose published by nineteenth- and twentieth-century writers seeking to inscribe their own political ideology or agenda on the palimpsest of the California bandit. The very creation of Murieta himself is a product of the racial tension that characterized the gold rush and the hatred that existed between Americans and Mexicans, in particular. Researchers have noted that many Mexicans, driven from their mining claims by Anglos exalting in their victory in the Mexican War that ended in 1848, resorted to thievery as a means of surviving on the California frontier.[14] According to one account, whenever a robbery was committed, it was attributed to one Joaquín or another and thus grew the legend of Joaquín Murieta, considered one among the possible Joaquíns (Monaghan, 215). The need for a scapegoat on which to blame the robberies that became commonplace events in the California of the early 1850s reached such a point that the state constitution approved in 1853 the formation of a search party under the leadership of Captain Henry Love for the purpose of capturing "the party of robbers commanded by the five Joaquíns."[15] Eventually, Love's party apprehended and killed in July 1853 several Mexicans, one of whom they initially called Joaquín only to subsequently add the surname Murieta in order to collect the $1,000 reward. No identification was provided or requested attesting to the actual name of the beheaded bandit, whose head, preserved in alcohol, was displayed in various museums throughout California, and who undoubtably would have been a footnote in the annals of history were it not for the publication in 1854 of the book *The Life and Adventures of Joaquín Murieta: The Celebrated California Bandit* by John Rollin Ridge, who was half Cherokee and half white.[16]

Ridge, also known by his Cherokee name, Yellow Bird, fictionalizes the life of Joaquín Murieta as a means of highlighting racial discord in California. In Ridge's novel, the first to be written by a Native American, the Mexican bandit is a gentle man of noble background and disposition forced to engage in a life of thievery and murder by the brutal Americans who first rob his gold, beat him, and rape his mistress, then kick him off the fertile valley where he had begun a new life, accuse him of horse theft, whip him in public tied to a tree, and finally kill his half brother without a jury when they determine that he, and not Joaquín, has stolen the horse. In addition to his portrait of Joaquín, Ridge creates as a character foil to the genteel Murieta his cohort, the bloodthirsty Three-Fingered Jack, who loses one of his fingers in the Mexican War, rejoices in the suffering of his victims, and has a particular hatred for the Chinese. Ridge's narrative, which as one critic has noted, must have been viewed as a "tall tale" by the readers of his time (Jackson, xxxi) or as a "narrative masquerading as fact" (Jackson, xxvii), serves as a catalyst in later years for the refashioning of the Murieta myth and the claiming of his nationality by Chilean writers, most notably among them Nobel Prize Laureate Pablo Neruda.

Neruda's 1966 work, *Fulgor y muerte de Joaquín Murieta: Bandido chileno injusticiado en California el 23 de julio de 1853 (Splendor and Death of Joaquín Murieta,* 1972),[17] which he has called a "melodrama, an opera, and a pantomime" (Neruda, ix) in six scenes, clearly has a contemporary political agenda. Situating itself in the zone of what may be called an "anticolonist mythopoesis" designed to use "revisionary myths" to "attack cultural hegemony" (DuPlessis, 107), Neruda resurrects the legendary Joaquín Murieta as the anti-Yankee par excellence and claims that attempts to erase his memory or subsume him in a group of many Joaquíns is "one way of quashing a rebellion" (Neruda, vi). In Neruda's alternately dramatic and poetic play, Murieta emerges as the Chilean "avenger in search of our birthright, our country, our race" (Neruda, 123) who calls upon Pablo Neruda himself to "interpret [his] story or sing it in truth, in the end" (Neruda, 171), an endeavor the poet completes with a final evocation of the oppression suffered by Vietnamese and blacks at the hands of white America.

Allende's debt to both Ridge and Neruda is apparent in countless pages of *Daughter of Fortune,* but whereas both Ridge and Neruda take care

to document the chronology of Murieta's life and his nationality, Allende's
Murieta exists in all his ambiguity and elusiveness, a creation of those who
respond to him according to their own personal or ideological needs.[18] In
fact, in his very elusiveness, he comes to symbolize what Nobel Prize Laureate Czeslaw Milosz has called "the truth of that bygone California, of all
America" that is "ambiguous . . . pointless to seek . . . in myths devised to
keep us from being overly troubled by the disorder of the world."[19] If the
fabrication of the myth of Joaquín Murieta actually reveals the multiple
levels of disorder during the California gold rush, it also provides a mirror
reflection of the entire construction of Allende's novel and the erasure of
the boundaries between reality and fiction, fact and imagination, and different spheres of fiction itself. Much as Allende the novelist and journalist
creates *Daughter of Fortune* from the rich wealth of her imagination as well
as from the testimonies, letters, and other writings she read as background
research for her book (Allende, 2000a, 10), she presents in her novel a
character who fulfills a similar function with regard to the creation of
Joaquín Murieta: the British journalist Jacob Freemont.

Although somewhat of a secondary character, Freemont is one of
Allende's most interesting creations in this novel. A self-proclaimed pro-
ponent of an egalitarian and communal society, he travels from England
to Chile to sell the Bible under his real name, Jacob Todd, and is immediately taken with both Miss Rose and the fiery Joaquín Andieta, whose
passion for social justice he shares. When his evangelizing mission is
revealed as a fraud, Todd returns to England only to surface several years
later in San Francisco with his new name, Jacob Freemont, a symbolic
baptism designed to enable him to begin anew and erase the shame of
his past. Unlike Eliza, who initially seems able to forget her past and
fashion a new identity for herself—only to experience at the end of the
novel nostalgia for both her family and her lost femininity—Freemont is
acutely aware of the fact that "people come west to escape the past and
begin anew, but our obsessions pursue us, like the wind" (*DF,* 357). This
telling observation not only refers to Freemont and countless immigrants, but also to the new state of California itself and its xenophobic
inhabitants who "thought that a stroke of a pen could erase a long history of Indians, Mexicans, and Californians" (*DF,* 339). Allende skillfully
reveals the fallacy in this belief on both a personal and political level.
The myth of Joaquín Murieta, Hispanic bandit, refuses to be erased
from the history of California, and the propensity for fabrication and
fraud that marked Jacob Todd's existence shapes the journalistic
accounts that Jacob Freemont writes about Murieta.

Unlike Ridge and Neruda, who make claims for the reality of Joaquín Murieta, Allende makes it abundantly clear in her novel that Joaquín Murieta is merely a fictional creation born from the social reality of the times and the pen of her character, Jacob Freemont. As she notes, Freemont's "sensationalist articles" on the romanticized Robin Hood of California, which she apparently lifted from Ridge's novel except for the information about his country of origin, "created a hero for Hispanics and a devil for Americans" (*DF,* 338) and gave Mexicans and Chileans alike the opportunity to claim him as one of their own. Despite Freemont's own suspicion that there is not just one Murieta, but several, and despite his sense of chagrin at the "mountain of lies" (*DF,* 341) he resorts to as he literally pulls from his sleeve the life and legend of Murieta, he is unable to stop. And here, once again, the political and the literary intersect, as Allende suggests on multiple levels the racism of Americans only too eager to attribute wrongdoings to the rebel Murieta, the need for a countermythology or symbol of rebellion on the part of Hispanics, the impunity of journalists in California who were never asked to supply names, dates, or places to verify their reports (Milosz, 443), and the creative passion of Freemont himself.

Not surprisingly, given Allende's comment that journalism, as she practiced it, "was a kind of fiction" and that she had "no problem inventing a story or exaggerating" (Allende, 2000b), her description of Freemont might well be viewed as a portrait of the artist as journalist: "He was becoming enamoured of the character, and in the end was convinced that he knew him, that the secret meetings in caves were real, and that the fugitive himself had commissioned him to write about his feats because he thought of himself as the avenger of oppressed Spanish peoples and someone had to assume the responsibility of according him and his cause a proper place in the developing history of California. There was little journalism involved, but more than enough fiction for the novel Jacob Freemont was planning to write that winter" (*DF,* 342–43).

At the same time that Allende uses Freemont and Murieta to suggest that history or legend is created, much as narrative itself, in order to serve the needs and interests of those who write and propagate it, she adds a further dazzling effect to this contemporary theme by involving Eliza in the previously mentioned amputation of the fingers of Three-Fingered Jack. Although Eliza is never able to find Joaquín Andieta and actually begins to think that the deeds attributed to Murieta could well be the work of her lover, she is called upon to assist Murieta's cohort,

Jack, in the most unlikely of situations that far surpasses the scenarios that even Freemont was capable of imagining. While working in a traveling brothel as both cook and piano player and while disguised as Chile Boy, Eliza meets up with the dangerous Jack, who requires immediate hand surgery. Summoning the scant knowledge she gained while assisting Tao Chi'en in surgery and recalling the magical orations of her nana, Mama Fresia, Eliza successfully performs the surgery, and Jack is able to return to his evil deeds, among which are mentioned the brutal torture of two Americans and the throat slashing of six Chinese, all previously described in lurid detail in Ridge's novel.

If the encounter between Eliza and Jack seems unnecessarily arbitrary in a novel that skillfully combines the historical and the fictional, the confusion between Joaquín Murieta and Joaquín Andieta is a very useful one and provides a telling comment about the role of myth in love and popular folklore. It also enables Allende to open her novel to the ambiguous ending she has cultivated in such works as *Eva Luna* and several of *The Stories of Eva Luna*. At the novel's close, she recreates the capture and death of Joaquín Murieta and Three-Fingered Jack by Captain Love's search party and the announcement of the exhibition of Murieta's head and Jack's hand in San Francisco. She further narrates that Eliza and Tao Chi'en go to see what may be the remains of the lover Eliza has pursued for four years. While a passage from part 1 of the novel foreshadowed this event, thus preparing the reader for the image of "a human head preserved in a jar of gin" (*DF,* 80), Allende does not actually tell the reader whether or not Eliza identifies the head as that of Murieta. When Tao Chi'en asks Eliza the question that no doubt the reader is thinking—"Was it him?"—Eliza merely replies, "I am free," and thus concludes Allende's novel (*DF,* 399).

While Allende has indicated in public speaking engagements and during an Oprah Winfrey book discussion that her novel's conclusion responds to her realization that Eliza's quest was not about love, but about freedom (Allende 2000a, 8), the reader in search of a more definitive conclusion may have to do some careful legwork to understand that the novel does offer a conclusion. I would argue that the head cannot possibly be Joaquín Andieta's because Jacob Freemont, who knew Andieta well, also goes to see it and registers no sign of recognition. If this detail combined with Joaquín's lack of correspondence with his mother suggest that he is one of the many casualties of the gold rush, Murieta's legacy is obviously more lasting and one that loans itself to still further political meaning in the context of Allende's fiction. Allende reinforces in *Daughter of Fortune* a message she makes very clear at the end of *The House of the Spirits* when Alba stresses the need to break the cycle of violence that has shaped much of her family history. In the same vein, Eliza tells Tom No-Tribe, the Indian boy she befriends in the traveling brothel, to become a lawyer in order to seek justice for the brutal murder of his family and his people. To this degree, while Murieta lives in the imagination of those who need a symbol of vengeance for injustice, both he and Andieta are replaced in Eliza's spirit by the belief that justice can be obtained through nonviolent social action and that the mythification of love can be altered in the course of one's journey through life.

The person who shares Eliza's psychological evolution is one of Allende's most delightful literary creations, Tao Chi'en, a character who, like many others in Allende's novels, is based on an actual person, the acupuncturist Dr. Miki Shima. Dr. Shima initially appears in *Paula* as a consulting doctor for her daughter and is described by the author as "a colorful Japanese acupuncturist whom I am saving to be a character in a novel, that is, if I ever write fiction again" (*P*, 236). When Allende mentions him again in *Aphrodite*, it is with many of the characteristics that she will transfer years later to Tao Chi'en: wisdom, a delightful childlike laugh, a knowledge of herbs, familiarity with the erotic pillow books of the East, and a belief in the ancient Chinese system of divination, the *I Ching*. In *Daughter of Fortune*, Allende fashions Tao Chi'en as a character endowed with multiple levels of complexity, beginning with his rite of passage from Fourth Son to Tao Chi'en. If the process of naming is always bequeathed with symbolic meaning in Allende's writings, the name that Fourth Son is given by his master is one that marks his presence in the novel. Signifying "way," "direction," "sense," "harmony" and "the journey of life" (*DF*, 157–58), Tao, one of the key words of the *I Ching*, "offers a way or path to each thing in this world . . . [and] . . . brings joy, connection, freedom, compassion, creativity, and love."[20]

Tao's journey through life, characterized by the freedom, compassion, creativity, and love suggested by his name, is complicated, rich and marked by the feminist agenda of Allende who enables him to learn about respect for women—and the size of their feet—from his wife, Lin, and from Eliza. By the time he meets Eliza in Valparaíso, he has already lived several lives. He acquires his passion for healing from his family, senses the injustice of life when he is sold at age 11 to merchants, is reborn to knowledge and joy through the wisdom and caring of his acupuncturist master, feels passion and love when he weds the gentle

Lin, experiences tremendous desperation when she dies, knows the folly of excess when his drunken stupor leads to his kidnapping aboard a British ship, and learns to defend himself in a western world where the Chinese are devalued by the *fan wey,* or whites. Always willing to rectify his mistakes, he wisely and humorously has the word "NO" tattooed on the back of his right hand after he loses all his money gambling and continually seeks to integrate in his life the respect for knowledge, wisdom, spirituality, compassion, and service that his master teaches him. His ability to open himself to new experiences leads to his fascination with western medicine and the egalitarian relationship between husbands and wives that he observes in California, both of which are antithetical to the values of his Chinese heritage.

The chapters Allende devotes to Tao Chi'en in the second part of her novel have the same narrative freshness as those devoted to Eliza in the first section. Significantly, despite the enormous cultural differences that separate them, Tao Chi'en, nine years Eliza's senior, provides a mirror reflection of her beliefs and experiences. Both come from worlds steeped in tradition and rules of behavior for each social class and gender; both initially ascribe to such codes, as when Eliza wants to sacrifice herself for Joaquín and when Tao Chi'en is obsessed with marrying a woman with the bound feet he poetically calls "golden lilies" (*DF,* 170). Both experience the painful consequences of such codes; Eliza recognizes the fear that has been ingrained in her as a woman and Tao curses the tiny feet that cause Lin great suffering. Both are attracted to other cultures; Eliza carefully assimilates all the teachings of her Mapuche nana, Mama Fresia, and Tao Chi'en studies English and learns about western medicine from Dr. Ebanizer Hobbs.

On still another level, both Eliza and Tao Chi'en alter their physical appearance in order to achieve freedom; Eliza dresses as a man, and Tao Chi'en decides to keep his hair short after his queue is violently cut off and to attire himself in western dress, an act of defiance of tradition and an acknowledgment of the cultural symbols that designate power in California.[21] Both are labeled as the quintessential *other* in a racial climate that labels Tao Chi'en as "a revolting Chinese pagan" and Eliza as a "greaser" (*DF,* 363), and both struggle to find a place for themselves in a society that still seems better than their stultifying native lands. Both learn to relinquish the emotional hold the past has for them in order to experience the beginning of love for one another. And both share a rich reserve of resiliency in the face of life's problems, a sense of humor and play, and a desire to contribute to others less fortunate. More than a reflection of yin and yang, the traditional division of female and male energy in terms of passive and active, Eliza and Tao are able to reach harmony precisely because "their similarities . . . erased differences of race" (*DF,* 363) and because they know and respect one another. When Eliza poignantly tells Tao Chi'en at the novel's close that she wants to stop hiding her femininity and be herself, he wisely replies that she has always been herself, thus suggesting that gender roles constitute only one factor in the definition of self.

If Allende presents through Tao Chi'en and Eliza the blending of difference that is so crucial in all of her fiction, she also suggests on a more philosophical level that everything in life has a purpose, that "nothing is in vain" (*DF,* 395), and that the meaning of one's existence is found in the path one takes rather than the destination. She also makes it very clear that individual journeys have an intimate connection with the broader social sphere. As both Eliza and Tao Chi'en come to recognize that their life is in California and with each other, an integral part of their relationship is the rescue of Chinese prostitutes from servitude, illness, and death, a concern that is predominant in part 3 of the novel. Allende's presentation of the complex topic of prostitution during the California gold rush is one that reveals once more the extraordinary amount of research she did in preparation for her novel, which documents in precise fashion the different social settings that Mexican, Latin American, North American, and Chinese prostitutes inhabited during the late 1840s and early 1850s. Her descriptions range from slightly romanticized to patently realistic and initially focus on the seven prostitutes—five Chileans and two Peruvians—who board the *Emilia,* together with 87 men and Eliza, to make it rich in the new world. Reflecting the social reality of the times, she relates how the first prostitutes to arrive in California in 1849 came from Mexico and Latin America, enjoying a male to female ratio of 50 to 1 and hoping to earn in cantinas and fandango parlors the money to pay for their boat passage.[22]

While researchers have documented the lower-class status of Latin American and Chinese prostitutes in San Francisco within the social hierarchy, their isolation in the red-light districts of Little Chile and Chinatown, their position as indentured servants, and the abuse Latin American women often experienced by day at the hands of the men who used their services at night, Allende somewhat bypasses this harsh reality in her portrayal of Chilean prostitutes.[23] Briefly following the odyssey of Azucena Placeres, the round-faced Indian who cares for Eliza aboard the *Emilia,* she concentrates, instead, on how Azucena fantasizes—much like

Joaquín Andieta—about making it rich in California and returning to Chile decked out like a queen. Endowing her with a practical sense of self, Allende notes that Azucena refuses to "become an unpaid servant" (*DF,* 216) to the many men eager for her services during the journey, relishes the hearty applause she is given when she disembarks in San Francisco in full battle dress, and is last seen by Captain John Sommers in a dance hall in the red-light district wearing an "expression of genuine happiness" (*DF,* 325).

If this latter description, as well as her concern for protecting Eliza's reputation, evokes the clichéd image of the prostitute with a heart of gold so prevalent in gold rush literature (Kowalewski, xxi), Allende similarly gives a positive spin to the lives of the prostitutes in the traveling brothel where Eliza cooks and plays the piano and that is run by the big-hearted madam, Joe Bonecrusher, and safeguarded by Babalú the Bad. While clearly indicating the numerous infections the "soiled doves" (*DF,* 280) suffered, and their abortions, addictions, and difficult family situations that led to their prostitution, she also demonstrates that marriage was a very real option for prostitutes in California, as when the Quaker blacksmith, James Morton, falls in love with the 18-year-old Esther and marries her in grand style to the hearty congratulations of many of her former clients. It would be difficult for Allende to write such an ending for the Chinese prostitutes or so-called singsong girls who inhabit her novel, although here, too, her belief in social action and human compassion intervene in her graphic rendition of their dismal fate.[24]

Interestingly, in contrast to the agile narrative style that Allende uses in her chapters devoted to Eliza and Tao, the section devoted to describing the lives of Chinese prostitutes reads much like a sociological account based on the rigorous research of such social historians as Benson Tong, Jacqueline Baker Barnhart, Judy Yung, and Lucie Cheng Hirata. What emerges from their research seemingly transferred to Allende's novel is a complex portrait of a prostitution industry built on the pernicious foundation of the devaluation of women in China; the poverty of the Chinese families who sold their daughters to traffickers often for a mere $50; the young women's belief that they were going to the Gold Mountain to marry and prosper; the sexual abuse they often suffered during the journey at the hands of the sailors; the humiliation they experienced upon arriving in California, where they were forced to strip naked for public auctions, and sign contracts they couldn't understand; and the lonely deaths they had in so-called hospitals designed to expedite their rapid demise if their bodies still clung to life. While historians have made it abundantly clear that the prostitution industry served the economic interests of multiple sectors of the Chinese community in California at the same time that it helped to preserve and stabilize the Chinese family by guaranteeing that Chinese men would not have to resort to "permanent relationships with foreign women" for sexual pleasure, it clearly constitutes one of the most ignoble chapters of the California gold rush.[25]

Allende's interest in this topic seems to spring from her great concern for the issue of human rights, her particular passion for denouncing the abuse of women, and her desire to give her characters a mission greater than themselves that endows their life with special meaning. Allende's characters do not merely watch history; they help create it, acting from their most noble instincts and from the phantoms of their past. Tao Chi'en's obsession with the image of his seven-year-old sister sold by their father intersects with his concern for the prostitutes whose cause of death he is asked to falsify by the San Francisco tong, or brotherhood, that controls the industry. The inhuman sight of young girls chained by an ankle to a bed with a cup of water and a burned-out oil lamp at their side creates such anguish in his soul that he summons the spirits of Lin and his master to help him find the path to save them. While they provide him with the inspiration to buy the girls before they die and thus to attempt to save them from the ignominious hospital, Eliza provides a broader channel of social action when she suggests that they seek the aid of churches and missionaries and specifically enlists the Quaker James Morton in this effort.[26]

While chronologically, Allende's portrayal of the mechanisms of rescue is off by some 20 years given that the novel ends in 1853 and the rescue efforts on the part of Protestant missionaries, the Methodist Episcopalian Church, and the Presbyterian Mission Home was not in full force until the 1870s (Yung, 34–35), it anticipates the outcry on the part of concerned folk who, years later, would read the brutal exposé of the San Francisco "hospitals" in the *San Francisco Chronicle* of 5 December 1869 (Yung, 316). As Allende herself notes, she used "poetic license" in this part of the novel and limited the rescue efforts to isolated individuals to maintain historical truth (Allende, 2000b). While Allende curiously does not provide in *Daughter of Fortune* an individual drama or story to give her journalistic account a more human or poignant face,[27] she does introduce into the novel a historical figure much associated with the trafficking of women, the Chinese madam Ah Toy. Alternately presented as an exotic symbol of eroticism and a shrewd businesswoman who rises from prostitute to entrepreneur and whose participation in the prostitution industry demonstrates the role women had in the enslavement of other women, Ah Toy calls upon Tao Chi'en to treat her hacking cough. Initially moved by her tiny feet and soft voice that remind him of Lin, he is ultimately repulsed by the reality of her trafficking enterprise and is sorely tempted to give her a small pinch of poison, which undoubtably would have prevented her from reaching her ninety-ninth birthday as researchers have noted (Yung, 34).

While Allende seems as fascinated with historical and legendary figures in *Daughter of Fortune* as with her own fictional characters, even introducing in the last pages of the novel the famous nineteenth-century European courtesan Lola Montez, who appears in San Francisco in 1853 and who is also mentioned in *Aphrodite* (*A,* 57), I would suggest that part of this fascination stems from a desire to present lives that deviate from the traditional path, even if tinged with corruption or greed. Certainly, Eliza experiences a sense of awe as she gazes upon the "mocking and defiant . . . idol of perversity" (*DF,* 391), Lola Montez, who triumphantly parades through the San Francisco streets, conjuring images of lust in her spectators. If Eliza mentally compares Montez's fearless and open posture with the careful and discreet tactical maneuvers that Miss Rose advised for woman's survival and autonomy, Allende's novel reveals that deviation from gender codes has, in fact, various forms. While one suggestive model is provided by Paulina del Valle, whose brilliant idea to export to California produce packed in ice aboard her steamship, *Fortuna,* brings in more money than her husband's extensive gold mining ventures, the character Allende nurtures with special care in this regard is Rose Sommers. In fact, the chapter describing her past could well be viewed as a separate short story within the novel replete with humor, passion, a feminist undercurrent, and the sublimation of eroticism into narrative.

Brought up in a rigid British family during the Victorian era, the 16-year-old Rose exhibits a great disregard for convention and a desire to realize the full force of love with a Viennese tenor many years her senior. Carefully combining instinct, recollections of the furtive erotic books she read in her father's bookstore, and her innate imagination and sensuality, Rose delivers herself hand, foot, and mouth to the corpulent tenor and experiences both enormous pleasure and laughter as she compares the "frankly optimistic proportions" of the male organ portrayed in racy fiction and Japanese postcards with "the rosy, perky gherkin" of her beloved Karl Bretzner (*DF,* 93). When her brother Jeremy, acting as the family patriarch, discovers their relationship and the fact that Karl has a wife and children, Rose is promptly returned to her solitary and proper world in London, where only the continual memory of her amorous adventure and its sublimation into erotic fiction saves her from infinite boredom or, worse still, perpetual despair.

Accompanying her brother Jeremy, to Valparaíso when he is given the directorship of the British Import and Export Company, Ltd, in Chile, Rose develops the personality that defines her throughout her years of raising Eliza as her protégée: an external compliance with gender norms and rules of etiquette coupled with an internal rebellion manifested by her intense dislike of marriage, which she views as a form of female servitude, and by her extensive literary production. The prolific author of erotic fiction sold initially in London by her brother John, and subsequently in California, Rose Sommers, or her pseudonym, An Anonymous Lady, makes a small fortune from her one experience with love and rivals the Marquis de Sade in sexual imagination, although Allende never gives the reader the opportunity to sample her prose.

If Jacob Freemont is a mask for Allende the journalist, I would venture to say that Rose Sommers, whose pseudonym actually corresponds to a nineteenth-century writer of pornographic fiction (Allende, 2000b), is none less than the erotic fiction writer that Allende has lurking inside, judging from her frequent and humorous comments to this effect.[28] Rose's pornographic novels even have a plot, as Eliza herself notes while reading them aloud to the prostitutes in the traveling brothel, without realizing that they were penned by Miss Rose. Like Jacob Freemont, Rose is also marked by her past; her affair with Karl Bretzner "had shaped her destiny and the woman she had become" (*DF,* 250). But here, too, Allende demonstrates that the concept of destiny is not permanently fixed and that human beings have the potential to choose a different path that enables them to find another part of themselves. At the novel's close, Rose releases the secrets that have shaped her existence; she reveals to her brother Jeremy the complicity she has shared with her brother John concerning Eliza's birth, and she decides to follow Eliza to California after receiving the joyful news that she is alive. While the novel ends before the two reunite, Allende foreshadows, for a future novel, perhaps, the relationship the two women will share because each has already come to understand the bond that unites them.

This suggestion of an ending beyond the ending is typical of the narrative style Allende employs throughout *Daughter of Fortune*. In fact, it is not difficult to imagine a sequel to this novel, where all the suggestions for the future alluded to throughout—the marriage of Eliza and Tao, the French restaurant that Eliza wants to open in San Francisco, the medical license Tao Chi'en plans to obtain, the rejection of Jacob Freemont's hand in marriage by the independent Rose—are somehow recreated in a new adventure story. Indeed, Allende's claim that her novel's open ending is an "invitation to the second part"[29] should be taken quite seriously. Her subsequent novel, *Retrato en sepia* (2000) (*Portrait in Sepia*, 2001), completes, in fact, the lives of many of the characters of *Daughter of Fortune* at the same time that it introduces Severo and Nívea del Valle from *The House of the Spirits* and places them smack in the middle of nineteenth-century Chilean history.

If the integration of the fictitious and the historical or sociological is a constant element in all of Allende's fiction, it is interesting to note that, at times, the balance between the two disappears in *Daughter of Fortune,* particularly in the third part of the novel, which reads more like the social history of the California gold rush than like fiction. The letters that Eliza writes to Tao Chi'en from different mining sites and towns— letters that imitate in style and tone actual letters gold rushers wrote to loved ones, but with a heightened sensitivity toward minority groups— often reveal more about the period than about Eliza herself, although she continually questions her own identity in light of her different experiences. At other times, the tall tale predominates in the novel, stretching the imagination of the reader to believe in the strange intersections of Eliza and Three-Fingered Jack and of Karl Bretzner's first lover and mentor and the Marquis de Sade. Yet, if part of the inspiration for Allende's novel comes from the tall tales that emerge from the creation of California as a state, it seems fitting that she add her own personal seal to this founding moment and invent new legends perhaps no less bizarre or improbable than the ones that helped shape the nineteenth-century popular imagination in America. Above all, Allende's third-person narrative, which in her characteristic style contains very little dialogue and a continual foreshadowing of events, provides the space where the poetic and the humorous are gently interwoven, adding a wide range of tones to *Daughter of Fortune.* Whether the humor is associated with the Sommers's anxiety about sacrificing Eliza's so-called mother, the she-goat that nursed her; or Rose's observation, in the throes of amorous passion, that since the massive Karl Bretzner looked much better naked than dressed, he must need a good tailor; or Tao Chi'en's clever maneuvers for self-improvement; it provides delightful moments of narrative repose and reveals Allende's extraordinary bent for the comical, often found in the most unlikely places. In contrast, her poetic prose is reserved primarily for portraying the inner journey of Tao Chi'en and his sense of spiritual communication with both Lin and his acupuncture master. Here, Allende is particularly adept in evoking images of Chinese culture and religion to reflect the character's inner state, as when she describes Tao Chi'en's dream of buying a wife, a dream as "misty and tenuous" as "a beautiful landscape painted on silk" (*DF,* 179) or the sense of "his body dissolving into nothingness" and experiencing "perfect harmony, like a fine instrument resonating with the heavens and the earth" (*DF,* 361).

The many narrative styles that Allende brings together in *Daughter of Fortune* is ample proof that she, much like Eliza Sommers, is indeed the daughter of fortune or a benevolent muse that continues to find inspiration in the vast California terrain and in historical moments, past and present. If Allende initially began her novel as a story of love, in the intense nine months she spent writing it, love slowly became transformed into the very fiber of freedom, the most salient theme of the book.[30] Although Allende enables her courageous female protagonist to experience release from the strictures of social convention and enforced gender roles, she makes no attempt, however, to idealize or mythify an emerging society that imposes continual boundaries on its immigrants. Tao Chi'en himself voices the contemporary theme of identity displacement when he confesses to Lin's spirit that he doesn't belong anywhere. But since Allende's fiction is ultimately one that never gives in to despair without redemption and that always opposes the force of individual will to strong social and political currents, the reader concludes *Daughter of Fortune* with the sense that belonging is a cultural and psychological construct that can be reconfigured. Suggesting through the wisdom of Tao Chi'en that the "knots of karma" can indeed be untangled (*DF,* 81) so that human beings are freed from repeating the same mistakes, Allende allows her characters to travel multiple paths in life and find in the process their own definition of fortune.[31]

Chapter Nine
Portrait in Sepia

The theme of memory and the need to salvage the past from the erosion of time is a constant presence in all of Allende's fiction. Her characters engage in difficult journeys through regions both familiar and unknown in search of missing or incomplete pieces of their past. At times, their search is accompanied by letters, photos, and notebooks, as Alba records in *The House of the Spirits;* it is triggered by the encounter with someone who evokes a memory of the past, as Rolf Carlé experiences when he begins to photograph the dying Azucena in *The Stories of Eva Luna;* it is facilitated by a relationship with a woman eager to understand the complexities of her lover's life, as Gregory Reeves demonstrates in the recounting of his story to the narrator of *The Infinite Plan;* or it is fueled by the urgency to fix time in words and bequeath a past to a dying daughter, as Allende poignantly relates in *Paula.* At times, there is no way of reconstructing one's roots, as Eliza Sommers realizes growing up in a household where the story of her birth is cast in contrasting versions, none of which is determined to be the truth. In certain instances, the past is strictly invented to fill a cavernous void, as when Eva Luna invents a past for a warrior and transfers part of her own life to his. In other scenarios, imagination and reality fuse together to alter the contours of a life, presenting a past that is either enhanced or created through the narration itself, as Allende reveals in the story "Simple María," and in her memoir, *Paula.* On occasion, memory is transformed into art as when Miss Rose invents pornographic fiction out of her only love affair; at other moments, it gnaws away at those ashamed of their past, as in the story "Our Secret." Because memory in Allende's world is not only personal, but communal as well, the erasure of the past by repressive political regimes also appears in such novels as *The House of the Spirits* and *Of Love and Shadows.* Regardless of the circumstance, memory in Allende's fiction is always revealed as fragile.

Within this context, it is not surprising that Allende's sixth novel, *Retrato en sepia* (2000) (*Portrait in Sepia,* 2001), not only provides a further elaboration of this theme, but also configures it as the driving force behind the narrator's rendition of her life.[1] As Aurora del Valle confesses in the novel, "memory . . . after all is, the reason I'm writing these pages" (*PS*, 279). Memory for Aurora is more than the desire to preserve the past; it is the pressing need to identify the landscape of a past that is characterized by "the empty streets of an unfamiliar and exotic city" (*PS*, 94) and "shadowy caverns" (*PS*, 279). To this degree, her quest is more difficult than the one undertaken by Allende's other characters because she can rely neither on invention or objective materials to fill in the gaps. Like Eliza Sommers, Aurora's roots have been erased, but unlike Eliza, who was adopted as a baby, Aurora is five years old when her maternal legacy is obliterated by her paternal grandmother, Paulina del Valle. Thus, Aurora's memory—much more textured than Eliza's—is filled with shadowy images that reappear in her dreams and night-mares, asking to be deciphered.

If Aurora's roots initially appear truncated, the novel in which her life is inserted, *Portrait in Sepia,* is significantly situated in a broad literary family and is integrally related to Allende's previous fiction and most particularly, the novel that precedes it. That is, while the open ending of *Daughter of Fortune* gave Allende's readers ample opportunity to specu-late about the fate of her protagonists, Eliza Sommers and Tao Chi'en, it also provided the author herself with the possibility of completing their lives in another work. By her own account, that was not at all what she had in mind when she finished *Daughter of Fortune:* "I had in mind the idea of writing a book about a young woman photographer at the turn of the century because I was fascinated with the evolution of photogra-phy and image. But then when people started asking . . . 'What hap-pened to Tao and Eliza? Did they ever have children? What happened to their descendants?' . . . I said, 'Well, my photographer could be the granddaughter of Tao Chi'en and Eliza.' And then it all came together" (Allende, 2000b). The word *all* not only refers to the continuation of *Daughter of Fortune* in a new work of fiction, but more significantly to the bridge Allende constructs between her first novel, *The House of the Spirits,* her fifth novel, *Daughter of Fortune,* and her first novel of the new millen-nium, *Portrait in Sepia.* If Tao Chi'en suggests in *Portrait in Sepia* that "in every incarnation we must resolve what we left unfinished" (PS 16), Allende's latest novel may be viewed as her most recent literary incarna-tion, albeit one that can be read independently of her other two novels. Weaving together with multitextured strands the lives of Severo and Nívea del Valle—the grandparents of Alba in *The House of the Spirits*—and the story of the grandchild of Eliza and Tao Chi'en, Aurora del Valle, she creates a trilogy of epic proportions that spans from 1843 to 1853 in

Daughter of Fortune, from 1862 to 1910 in *Portrait in Sepia,* and from 1920 to 1973 in *The House of the Spirits,* offering in the process a complex view of Chilean history in the nineteenth and twentieth centuries.

Perhaps inadvertently, Allende foreshadowed the writing of this novel in a 1991 interview, when she discussed the tone of *The House of the Spirits* and noted that "the first part is like a mist, like an old sepia photograph where things are disfigured by time, by the haze of oblivion" (Allende, 1991c, 193). *Portrait in Sepia* gives special meaning to this description as Aurora endeavors to discover the roots of her past, a past disfigured by time and by the misty haze of carefully constructed oblivion. Aurora herself comments that while she wishes that she could tell the story of her life in tones as clear as a platinum print, the tone that more accurately captures the dark shades of her life is that of a "portrait in sepia" (*PS,* 304). The suggestion of a luminous dawn implicitly contained in the protagonist's name, Aurora, or its Chinese version, Lai Ming, continually collides with the shadows that envelop her nightmares. In this sense, it is no mere coincidence that Aurora del Valle is a photographer. Her photos—much like Rolf Carlé's in *The Stories of Eva Luna*—are simultaneously a means of freezing images in a frame "immune to the fading of memory" (*SEL,* 5), a form of encasing in black and white the contours of life, a vehicle for capturing complete landscapes that compensate for the empty spaces of her internal topography, and a way of alternately distancing herself from life and penetrating with depth and understanding the subjects of her art.

Yet the camera alone is not sufficient to apprehend time before it vanishes or to photograph Aurora's inner demons and in this way, "drive them away" (*PS,* 97). Aurora also resorts to writing as a means "to create [her] own legend" (*PS,* 304), an act that mirrors Allende's autobiographical endeavor in *Paula.* But whereas Allende's attempt to capture the complexities of her life is limited to words, her character avails herself of both the lens and the pen. Simultaneously spectator and actor, Aurora's writing recounts her past, whereas her photos prevent the present from disappearing. Her odyssey is best expressed through the verses of the poem "Wind" by the Chilean poet Pablo Neruda, which grace the novel's epigraph and suggest that the search for self and the past paradoxically involves the return to future places, also.

As Allende places before the reader the past, present, and future sites of Aurora's development, she summons a fascinating cast of characters, some figuratively and literally bigger than life itself, who add both depth and levity as well as countless opportunities for social commentary to this intriguing novel. Divided into three parts, each with its corresponding chronological time frame, the first section of the novel will no doubt either delight or disappoint those who have read *Daughter of Fortune* and who feel a special fondness for Eliza, Tao Chi'en, Rose Sommers, Jacob Freemont, and the outrageous Paulina del Valle, whose minor role in *Daughter of Fortune* is expanded to central stage in *Portrait in Sepia.* It is in this section that we find out what we always suspected—that Eliza acknowledges that the head of the man preserved in a jar was not the head of her former lover, Joaquín Andieta; that she and Tao are finally free to express the love and passion they feel for one another, although their marriage in a Buddhist ceremony is not recognized by American law; that they live together for more than three decades in a house in Chinatown, while Tao Chi'en, a U.S. citizen, devotes himself to his medical practice and to rescuing the singsong girls, or Chinese prostitutes, and Eliza owns not a French restaurant—as was foreshadowed in *Daughter of Fortune*—but a tea room near Union Square; that they eventually have two children, Lucky and Lynn, the latter named after Tao Chi'en's first wife, Lin; and that their love for one another does not diminish with time but continues to sustain them as they struggle in a racist society that obliges them to sit separately in the theater and walk apart in the street.

It is also in the first part of the novel that the life of Severo del Valle intersects with the paths of Eliza and Tao as this distinguished and highly ethical nephew of Paulina del Valle comes to San Francisco to escape from the strictures of Chilean society. During the years he spends in California, he becomes his aunt's right-hand man and lawyer in her business dealings and simultaneously falls in love with the beautiful daughter of Eliza and Tao Chi'en. His love for Lynn Sommers is so strong that he asks for her hand in marriage, well aware that she does not love him but his cousin, Matías, Paulina's son, who impregnated her and initially refused to acknowledge his paternity. Hence, the birth of Aurora del Valle, also named Lai Ming by her maternal grandparents, who raise her with great love following Lynn's death and Severo's departure to Chile and in opposition to Paulina's desire to raise the child herself.

While part 1 of the novel is situated in San Francisco, the remaining two sections take place primarily in Chile. Spanning a time frame of 30 years, they trace Severo's experiences in the battlefield of the War of the Pacific that waged Chile against Peru and Bolivia; his relationship with his indomitable and singularly original cousin, Nívea, whom he eventually marries; the Chilean Civil War or congressional revolt of 1891 and the various political forces that intervene in this conflict; and, most significantly, Aurora's upbringing in Chile by Paulina following Tao Chi'en's death when she is five years old and Eliza's decision to take his body back to China and entrust their granddaughter to her paternal grandmother. Paulina, scandalously defiant of gender norms, but remarkably conservative in issues of class, promptly attempts to eradicate all traces of her granddaughter's modest social class as well as her Chinese heritage, insisting that she be called Aurora and not Lai Ming.

It is precisely this displacement from the sheltered environment of the home of her grandfather Tao to the opulence of the home of her grandmother Paulina and the lack of explanation she receives for her move that explain Aurora's continual nightmares, timidity, and sense of emptiness regarding her past. Her narration is consistently driven by her attempt to decipher her family secrets, clarify her paralyzing nightmares of threatening children or demons dressed in black pajamas who surround her, give a name to the gentle spirit whom she feels as a presence in her life, and ultimately understand who she is and where she came from. Frequent allusions to Tao's death by a so-called accident and the relationship between this event and Aurora's nightmares are continually suggested throughout the last two parts of the novel, although they are not clarified until the very last pages.

On still another level, Allende suggests a strong relationship between nineteenth- and twentieth-century Chilean history. While carefully describing the War of the Pacific from 1879 to 1883; the Civil War that pitted President Balmaceda, the military, and members of his liberal party against Congress, the Navy, conservatives, and dissident liberals alike; the acts of detention, pillage, and torture that characterized the struggle; and the suicide of President Balmaceda that followed his defeat, Allende also offers her readers a bridge between events of the past and those of Chile's recent history. As she herself has noted regarding research for her novel:

> Chile at that time was a fascinating place because it was a time of war; we had six wars in the nineteenth century. There was revolution and war, cruelty, repression. All the things that happened afterwards in the 1970s with the military coup happened in the nineteenth century, also. There was a great deal of background that our history books totally deny or ignore or change. It was a fascinating thing to research because I could talk about the nineteenth century and the nineteenth-century revolution, for example, and suggest a parallel to the twentieth century, without actually saying this is what happened in the 1970s. (Allende 2000b)

To this degree, if Allende continually endeavored in her early fiction to recover "memories . . . blown . . . by the wind of exile,"[2] in *Portrait in Sepia* she attempts to recover the complexities of a century whose legacy is particularly clear 100 years later. Her graphic description of Civil War atrocities committed by conservatives and liberals alike, and her particular emphasis on the torture of the Catalan bookseller, Don Pedro Tey, and the army's calculated massacre of a group of young revolutionaries clearly replicates her portrayal of military brutality in *The House of the Spirits*. To this degree, *Portrait in Sepia* provides an important historical precedent for the understanding of Chilean politics in *The House of the Spirits* as well as a reconfiguration of historians' view of Chile as the Switzerland of South America. Significantly, the personal and the political are entwined in countless ways in the novel. Aurora begins to menstruate the day the Civil War begins, thus uniting her personal shedding of blood with the "orgy of blood" (*PS*, 180) that characterizes the revolution. Similarly, much as Paulina attempts to erase Aurora's maternal legacy, the government tries to eradicate the Chilean legacy of workers' strikes. In fact, Aurora's photographs constitute "the only irrefutable documents" (*PS*, 279) that the massacre of Iquique in 1907—only briefly alluded to in the novel—actually occurred despite the government's attempt to deny its existence.[3] While Allende further foreshadows the 1973 military coup through Nívea's description of Chile as a "bloodthirsty country" (*PS*, 176), she also suggests a hope for social change through the valiant acts of idealists and dissidents who oppose tyranny.

Allende's insights about Chilean culture and social norms, a significant aspect of the novel, are most clearly highlighted in Aurora's narration of coming of age in a social class that associates female sexuality with sin and that considers husband and children, rather than work and creativity, the natural destiny of the female sex. As Aurora struggles to articulate her own voice, she is assisted by many mentors of different ideologies, social classes, and genders who shape her development and reveal the possibilities for change in a stratified society. They include her private tutor, the agnostic feminist and socialist Matilde Pineda, who teaches her to question everything including gender, class, and religious hierarchies; her photography teacher, Don Juan Ribero, who helps her see what others cannot, who urges her to understand her subjects rather than to dominate them, and who imparts to her his philosophy of photography as a "personal testimony" (*PS*, 194); her friend, Nívea del Valle, who shares with her forbidden books and invaluable advice about sex; and even in absentia, Eliza's aunt, Miss Rose, whose pornographic novels inspire her great niece when she is most in need of good instruction.

Inevitably, good mentoring is never enough in Allende's world to ward off the overwhelming passion of first love, and Aurora succumbs in typical fashion to a young man incapable of returning her love. While her failed marriage and deep sense of rejection, together with her abandonment of her husband, convert her into a social outcast belonging to neither the category of married or single, they ultimately serve to harness her inner resources and propel her into an independent life. Rejecting the "domestic paradise" (PS, 239) ordained for women of her class, she defies social customs by sharing her life with her lover, Iván, and by traveling throughout Chile to photograph its land, its people, and political events, earning in the process a number of prizes for her work. Slowly, she comes to understand the first five years of her life with help from her dying father, Matías; her aging grandmother, Paulina, who mellows with the years; her maternal grandmother, Eliza, who visits her in Chile following Paulina's death; and a trip to San Francisco or—as the epigraph from Neruda suggests—a return "to so many places in the future," where she meets her uncle Lucky who celebrated her birth years before by blowing his good luck into her face. It is in the telling pages that conclude the novel where Allende not only completes Aurora's past, but also the story of Tao Chi'en, linking his tragic fate to the historical rescue of the singsong girls that took place in San Francisco in the 1870s and 1880s.

Utilizing in small measure the same narrative technique that was particularly effective in *Daughter of Fortune*—the integration of historical and fictional characters—Allende introduces into *Portrait in Sepia* the indomitable missionary Donaldina Cameron, "singled out as the bravest and cleverest savior of Chinese families,"[4] and portrays her soliciting the help of Tao Chi'en to rescue the singsong girls from the brothels and dingy cells in Chinatown. Acutely aware of the potential for repercussion from the Chinese brotherhood, or tong, and the powerful madam, Ah Toy, "who had become the major importer of new flesh into the country" (PS, 293), Tao Chi'en gladly loans his assistance to a collaborative rescue effort involving the police authorities and rejoices that the moment he had waited for during three decades had finally arrived. The interference of the *fan-güey*, or whites, in Chinese affairs and a particularly lucrative slave trade provokes the inevitable result: Tao Chi'en is brutally assaulted, while in the company of Lai Ming, by several men dressed in black commissioned by Ah Toy and is left an invalid. Unwilling to live in that state, he asks for Eliza's assistance in committing suicide. This conclusion to his noble life, consistent within the context of the power structure in Chinatown, is, nonetheless, an unusual twist in Allende's generally predictable manner of bestowing natural deaths on her characters. Given Tao Chi'en's ability to find meaning in life, regardless of the stage, his decision to end his life is somewhat surprising. However, given his total loss of all bodily movements and his sense that the spiritual world is a very real realm of being, his death marks his absence from the physical world only. His spirit remains alive in Eliza and is a continual presence for Aurora, who goes through life accompanied by her grandfather's gentle smell of the sea and the memory of his compassionate eyes.

While this missing piece completes Aurora's attempt to decipher her past and unravel her nightmares and marks as well Allende's homage to the character whose spirituality, wisdom, and concern for justice provide much of the narrative charm of *Daughter of Fortune,* it also suggests a philosophical approach to life that has become increasingly present in Allende's fiction throughout the years. If Aurora's art enables her to see that "everything is related, is part of a tightly woven design. What at first view seems to be a tangle of coincidences is in the precise eye of the camera revealed in all its perfect symmetry" (*PS,* 237); Allende's novelistic lens similarly creates meaning and symmetry out of the multitude of characters and events that fill her novel. She is, indeed, a master of weaving disparate events and characters together and of revealing the internal logic that underlines each of her character's lives. Tao Chi'en completes his path in life as healer, lover, and activist and can comfortably exit this world knowing that he has fulfilled his mission. Even when her characters engage in more contradictory modes of behavior, Allende still ties the pieces together in the end in a manner that is not only profoundly human and laden with social commentary, but frequently humorous.

Consider the case of the irreverent and amazonian Paulina del Valle, whose insatiable appetite for sweets is only matched by her appetite for making money, and whose gigantic bulk topped with several wigs and countless jewels literally sucks the air out of any room she enters. Thrilled at the thought of defying Chilean society by returning to Chile with her second husband, Frederick Williams, a man 10 years younger and 65 pounds lighter than herself, she caves in at the end of her life and tries to buy salvation much as she had bought land and material success during her life. Donating much of her prized possessions to the Catholic

Church, she asks to be buried in a simple Carmelite habit. Yet, lest she leave this world without the flourish that marked her scandalous presence in it, Allende casts a mischievous nod at Aurora and Nívea, who strategically place underneath her religious robe Paulina's finest French lingerie, thus crystallizing her underlying resistance to institutionalized Catholicism.

Countless other stories similarly emerge in *Portrait in Sepia* as Allende completes the tapestry of certain lives left inconclusive in *Daughter of Fortune:* Eliza Sommers, accompanied by the spirit of her husband, Tao, rediscovers her passion for travel and for adventure following his death and journeys to the far corners of the world; Rose Sommers never travels to California as was foreshadowed in *Daughter of Fortune* but moves instead to London where she is named Dame Sommers by Queen Victoria, who delights in reading her novels of romance without suspecting that she is actually the famous Anonymous Lady who penned pornographic fiction in her youth; and Jacob Freemont finally achieves posthumous fame following the scandalous rebuke he received for his fabrication of the legend of Joaquín Murieta when he covers with dignity and accuracy the raids on the Chinese brothels by Presbyterian missionaries and memorializes Tao Chi'en's accomplishments in his obituary.

Other stories are simply initiated, waiting perhaps for a future novel to reach completion. Particularly compelling in this regard is the story of one of Allende's most delightful literary characters, Frederick Williams, who quietly takes care of everyone's needs throughout the entire novel, even placing gloves on Paulina's cold hands before she dies. Self-portrayed as an ex-convict locked up in an Australian jail for horse theft until he escapes and makes his way to America following enslavement on a Chinese pirate ship, he winds up as the loyal butler turned devoted second husband of Paulina del Valle and manages to convince everyone in Chile that he is pure British aristocracy. It is he who ultimately persuades Aurora to leave her husband and who suggests to her that they buy a house together following Paulina's death because he loves her like a granddaughter. At the novel's close, while Aurora cultivates her photography and her relationship with her lover, Iván, Williams plays croquet and breeds pedigree dogs and horses, carefully concealing the scars on his back that mark his constant beatings in jail. His hidden scars are in some way symbolic of Allende's narrative magic; her characters are never immobilized by their past but possess endless resiliency that enables them to create themselves anew with humor, grace, and an occasional subversive flair.

In the same way that *Portrait in Sepia* completes the lives of the characters of *Daughter of Fortune* and introduces others, it also anticipates aspects of *The House of the Spirits*. Severo del Valle's involvement with the liberal party and Nívea's efforts on behalf of female suffrage, major components of their political activism in *The House of the Spirits,* are already initiated in *Portrait in Sepia*. Further, Nívea is seen as possessing a form of the clairvoyance that will characterize her daughter, Clara, whose future birth is mentioned in the novel. She is, in fact, so clairvoyant that she knows that her cousin Severo will return home safely from the Civil War and that they would die together in an accident.[5] While not providing the details of this couple's future decapitation in a car accident in *The House of the Spirits,* Allende cannot resist a playful self-referential nod at her first novel. When Paulina tells Nívea that she has lost her head defending female suffrage, Nívea seriously but perhaps prophetically replies, "Not yet, Aunt, not yet—" (*PS,* 185). If on another level, few of Nívea's 15 children are mentioned in *Portrait in Sepia,* the beautiful five-year-old Rosa who seemingly floats through the air with her angelic face and green hair, is given special attention, thus foreshadowing the importance she will have in the first chapter of *The House of the Spirits*.

Allende's continual allusions to her former body of fiction and the tribute she pays in *Portrait in Sepia* to various kinds of writing—Miss Rose's early pornographic novels and her later romantic novels, Jacob Freemont's professional journalistic accounts, and Aurora's memoir—is also accompanied by a further twist when she reveals that Eliza Sommers has actually penned some of Miss Rose's romantic novels when her aunt was too ill to continue writing them herself simply by repeating her narrative formula, a technique one imagines Allende herself would categorically reject for her own writing. Allende, however, is at her most playful in this novel when she unites Nívea and Miss Rose in a bond of complicity that transcends countries and decades and portrays the young Chilean woman pouring over the pornographic novels of An Anonymous Lady to further her sexual prowess.

It is inevitable that some readers and critics will take exception to Allende's endeavor to complete the lives of her characters in her new novel and to clarify the ambiguities and suggestive possibilities of *Daughter of Fortune.* They may feel that Allende's creation of a trilogy— to be read in chronological order in the future—detracts from the individual power of each novel and evokes a form of serialized art. Others, no doubt, will evoke such literary models as the nineteenth-century writers Benito Pérez Galdós, Émile Balzac, or Marcel Proust, or even the more contemporary writer Mario Vargas Llosa, who similarly introduce their characters into more than one novel, taking care to reconfigure their reality in each new book. Still others will comment that since all three novels are independent of one another, the completion of certain characters' lives and the beginning of others, as in the case of Severo and Nívea, do not detract from the new narrative scenario Allende offers in *Portrait in Sepia* or from the experience the reader had upon finishing either *The House of the Spirits* or *Daughter of Fortune*. In response to—and anticipating—both positions, I would argue that while my personal preference is for the suggestion of ambiguity rather than the certainty of conclusion, Allende's interweaving of characters and events in *Portrait in Sepia* strikes me as a highly effective vehicle for providing a coherent view of Chilean history and for offering political and sociological insights about North and South America that are particularly interesting because they are encased in lives already familiar to the reader.

While *Portrait in Sepia* springs directly from *Daughter of Fortune*, it evokes aspects of other Allende works as well. Curiously, Aurora's recurring nightmare of threatening figures dressed in black pajamas echoes Gregory Reeves's haunting image of Vietnam in *The Infinite Plan*, when he finds himself firing "against dark silhouettes in black pajamas" (*IP*, 1). If Aurora is able to exorcise her nightmare by allowing Iván's love to compensate for her sense of abandonment and by understanding the source of her trauma with the help of her grandmother Eliza, Reeves is able to lay his nightmares to rest after years of therapy and confrontation with his own inner demons. Significantly, as Aurora gives a name to her memories, transcribes them in her writing, and uses her photos to understand the contours of her adult life, she comes to the same conclusion that Allende herself has articulated in both *Paula* and her many interviews. In the novel's epilogue, Aurora writes, "Memory is fiction. We select the brightest and the darkest, ignoring what we are ashamed of, and so embroider the broad tapestry of our lives" (*PS*, 303). To this degree, Aurora's photos in black and white as well as her inscription of black ink on the white page graphically capture the sense of this fluctuation between two intense tones and moods at the same time that they highlight Allende's recurring theme of the transformation of life by the lens of art.

Portrait in Sepia not only invites comparisons with Allende's previous fiction, but also bears a certain resemblance to the novel *Tinísima* (1992) by the Mexican writer Elena Poniatowska. This novel is centered on the life of the Italian-born photographer and militant, Tina Modotti, whose photos of Mexican life in the 1920s reveal her passion for social justice and her desire to use her art to implicitly denounce the inequities in Mexican society. While Poniatowska includes in her novel actual photos taken by Modotti that bestow a sense of immortality on the deceased people and past events she describes, Allende's text, composed exclusively of words, is propelled instead by photographic metaphors and images that take shape in the reader's imagination. Indeed, it is not difficult to picture the rich contours of Aurora's photos of striking workers, ragged children, immigrants, brothels, and indigenous peoples, images of a disturbing social reality that members of her husband's wealthy family prefer not to see. In her quest to use "truth and beauty" to capture "the vital essence of some object" (*PS*, 98) and to give a face to the dispossessed people of her country, Aurora mirrors Modotti's political endeavor and her feeling that her art enabled her to seek "the essence of life, her own essence."[6]

Yet beyond this identification of Tina Modotti and Aurora del Valle, it is clear that there is a more intimate relationship between the protagonist of *Portrait in Sepia* and Allende herself. In fact, the intense sense of awe that Aurora experiences when contemplating the vast Chilean landscape evokes some of the most lyrical passages of Allende's writings that similarly bear tribute to her native country. Similarly, if the fugacity of life and the concern for social justice are themes that permeate Allende's fiction, *Portrait in Sepia* portrays both writing and photography, two different forms of artistic expression, as passionate endeavors designed to address each of these issues in different ways. As the writer Susan Sontag has so eloquently theorized, "photography is an elegiac art, a twilight art. . . . To take a photograph is to participate in another person's (or thing's) mortality, vulnerability, mutability. Precisely by slicing out this moment and freezing it, all photographs attest to time's relentless melt."[7] While both Aurora del Valle and Allende would inevitably agree with Sontag's assessment, their respective work does not remain frozen on the page or the print but comes alive through the shared experience of the viewer or reader. To this degree, while the tone of Aurora's narrative is the subdued shade of sepia, Allende's novel radiates a platinum sheen that illuminates and recovers the complexity of social codes, political struggles, and intricate lives in nineteenth-century Chile.

Conclusion

Almost two decades have passed since Isabel Allende wrote her first novel, *The House of the Spirits*. Since that time, her literary and personal odyssey has affected innumerable readers; more than 15 million copies of her books have been sold throughout the world. It has been suggested that she is not only the best-selling Latin American woman writer, but also one of the most successful women writers of serious fiction. There is no doubt that her contribution to contemporary literature far surpasses national boundaries and has broad universal significance. There is, indeed, something almost magical about Allende's ability to create in countless novels, short stories, and works of nonfiction a literary world that becomes powerfully alive and real for her many readers. Her magic is conveyed from the very first sentence of her books, where she invites the reader into a world of suggestive possibilities that become delightfully and powerfully complex as the work unfolds. Her fiction is about the raw material that life is made of—love, hatred, despair, hope, political commitment, social change, daring, and adventure. It never avoids difficult issues of dominance and oppression but configures them in such a way that her readers are ultimately empowered from the experience of reading her work.

Allende has not deviated from this distinctive endeavor since her first novel. She has continually traversed both ends of the Pacific in her life and her writings and has provided her readers with compelling renditions of Latin American history and the shaping of North American individualism. Her most recent novels, *Daughter of Fortune* and *Portrait in Sepia*, are situated, in fact, in both North and South America, a tribute to her ability to navigate with ease ideological and national divides. This breaking down of barriers is a constant presence in all of Allende's writing where the boundaries separating the real and the magical, the historical and the imaginative, the wealthy and the dispossessed, the serious and the comical, the male and the female, and different nationalities are continually eroded as new realities are born from the fusion of opposites. The creation of a hybrid and utopian realm, where entrapment is replaced by freedom, is Allende's gift to her readers. It not only gladdens our hearts but offers us a powerful antidote to fossilized discourses of power that permeate public life. If by her own account, "Art is an act of alchemy. It is an effort to take the evil of the world and, by internalizing it, transform it into its opposite: hope, love, friendship, solidarity, generosity,"[1] Isabel Allende might rightly be called a master alchemist whose writings transform the dark side of humanity and illuminate the potential for goodness in the world. Her profound sense of optimism and spirituality infuses her countless protagonists—female and male—who have such a sense of vitality and passion that they are rarely defeated by overwhelming social and political realities. They subvert cultural norms, they fashion their own identity, and they celebrate sensuality and love. In this way, they make us believe that we, too, can do the same and that oppressive notions of gender, class, race, and ethnicity are not fixed in stone but can be transformed through individual acts of will and communal support.

While this endeavor encompasses all of humanity, Allende has made a special contribution to contemporary Latin American literature through her portrayal of pressing historical concerns and her refashioning of such genres as the historical novel and the bildungsroman. Infusing her fiction with her underlying feminist convictions, she situates her female characters smack in the middle of difficult historical moments and enables them to skirt the minefields of convention and tradition. While many Latin American women writers, including Elena Garro, Diamela Eltit, Marta Trueba, and Luisa Valenzuela, combine political concerns and complex portrayals of female characters, Allende's highly accessible narrative style has enabled her to reach a vast public that far surpasses the reading audience of any other Latin American woman writer. In this way, she has familiarized readers throughout the world with Chilean history in the nineteenth and twentieth centuries, the struggles of the guerrilla movement in Venezuela, and the vast landscape of Latin America. Her extraordinary ability to seamlessly blend together history and fiction enables her to create a literature that has tremendous educational value for her readers at the same time that it entertains them. If readers have similarly gained insights into the complexity of contemporary Latin America through the writings of Gabriel García Márquez or Mario Vargas Llosa, they have yet to understand the potential for individual and collective acts of feminism until they read Isabel Allende.

But it is not only her uplifting message that accounts for her appeal. It is also her extraordinary talent as a storyteller, her gift of weaving a narrative of epic proportions that encompasses historical moments, past and present, but that never loses sight of the individuals who populate it and make it real. Allende's fiction, however, is not designed for passive readers. In the tradition of the best oral storytellers who actively engage their public in the experience of listening, Allende's tales demand an active reader, willing to participate in her narrative adventure and to complete her stories or accept their very inconclusiveness as emblematic of life itself. Her readers, in fact, have often been so intrigued by the open ending of some of her works that they have written her letters inquiring about the fate of her characters. As she herself recounts, that is one of the reasons why she wrote *Portrait in Sepia,* thus demonstrating how authors not only influence readers, but how readers similarly propel and fuel their favorite author's imagination. Although there is nothing in Isabel Allende's fiction comparable to part 2 of *Don Quixote,* where Sancho Panza relishes the public fame he has acquired as a result of the enormous popularity of part 1, Allende does offer her faithful readers playful nods of recognition as familiar characters and places reappear in several of her works, most notably in *The Stories of Eva Luna* and *Portrait in Sepia,* in addition to her memoir, *Paula,* which reads like a creative blend of Allende's life and her fiction.

Despite the relationship that exists among Allende's different works and most notably, *The House of the Spirits, Daughter of Fortune,* and *Portrait in Sepia,* Allende is not intent on creating a self-contained narrative world that reproduces itself. Much as she challenges her readers to think about difficult questions fraught with political meaning, she challenges herself to expand the limits of her art. In a 1991 interview, Allende explained that "every writer of fiction should confront these three challenges: write short stories, an erotic novel, and children's literature" (Allende, 1991c, 198). Nearly a decade later, Allende has indeed written a collection of short stories, numerous erotic passages interspersed throughout her body of fiction, and a tantalizing cookbook complete with countless tidbits on aphrodisiacs that may have satisfied in some measure her desire to write an erotic novel. Now she reports in a recent interview with this author that her next literary project is young adult literature for children ten years old and above (Allende, 2000b).[2] It is tempting to say, Harry Potter and J.K. Rowling, beware, but for now, both can rest easy.

A final word must be said about Allende's personal involvement with her reading public, for that, too, is part of the Allende mystique. She answers every letter her readers write to her on textured paper engraved with a forget-me-not. She creates a tremendous sense of intimacy in her public speaking engagements by sharing with her audience details of her personal life, real or imagined, that alternately make them laugh and cry. She recounts with great humor family anecdotes that make their way into her fiction, among them the popular story of her Great Aunt Rosa, who appears with green hair in *The House of the Spirits* because she was considered as beautiful as a mermaid. If the erasure of boundaries is a driving force in her narrative, she achieves that same end in her life by breaking down the barrier between author and reader. Allende's readers not only love her fiction, they also love her, and they allow her personal journey through despair and death to unleash similar moments in their own lives. Many, in fact, consider her memoir, *Paula,* her finest piece of writing as well as her most spiritual work.

Allende has stated on countless occasions that it is too early to judge the impact of her work, that only time will tell if she endures as a writer of note. I would argue that her extensive body of writing produced over nearly two decades gives the critic ample criteria to evaluate the long-range significance of her work. Her distinctive voice will continue to occupy a prominent place throughout her native Latin America, throughout her adopted country, the United States, and throughout Europe and Australia as she transmits her hope for a "society where those who have too much will learn to have less."[3] The author and journalist, Pete Hamill, pointedly noted when he presented Allende with the Dorothy and Lillian Gish Award in 1998, "Fine literature can also find a wide popular audience."[4] This, indeed, explains the magic and the legacy of Isabel Allende.

Interview: 8 August 2000

LGL: *You've commented many times that your novels are all born from strong emotions—nostalgia in* The House of the Spirits, *anger in* Of Love and Shadows, *acceptance of yourself as a woman and a writer in* Eva Luna, *love for your husband in* The Infinite Plan, *and grief in* Paula. *What is the emotion that gave rise to* Daughter of Fortune?

IA: I think that it is the realization that all my life has been about freedom, the search for freedom, and that the most important thing in my life has been to be independent, and not depend on anyone. I think that the story of *Daughter of Fortune* is about freedom; it's not a love story, really. It's a journey of the soul, and a journey in time and space of a young woman towards freedom. Eliza Sommers symbolizes in many ways what the journey of feminism has been in my life. The novel begins with the corsets and the restrictions that were imposed on women and it explores how they find their way in a masculine world, having to invent everything, discover everything, with no skills, no weapons, no help. That has been my life story.

LGL: *Although* Daughter of Fortune *is situated in the nineteenth century, it seems to be written with a twentieth-century sensitivity toward issues of gender and cultural diversity. Does it appear that way to you?*

IA: To a certain extent, but what we think is a twentieth-century sensitivity was there in the nineteenth century as well. When you read the texts of the suffragettes, or of many photographers, women photographers of the time, or women who by their own needs and merits were able to escape patriarchy, you see that their aspirations and their language are very similar to the language of the feminists in the 1950s.

LGL: *It's apparent that you did a tremendous amount of research for* Daughter of Fortune. *I can imagine that you poured over journals, memoirs, letters, and photos. You have said many times that your favorite kind of research involves the information you get from first-hand accounts and personal interviews. Obviously that was impossible in this situation. Were you able to get the real-life flavor of the period from your research? Did the photos and the letters make the nineteenth century come alive for you?*

IA: Yes, in a way, they did. Let me give you an example. There were things that I did not even imagine, but learned through research. I had the idea that the story was going to be told from a first-person perspective by a young woman who was an immigrant from Chile, a person of color. But I didn't know what a young woman from Chile would do in the gold rush to survive, if she wasn't a prostitute. Because the first women who came, and the only women who came at the beginning, were prostitutes. But I didn't want that. So when I started doing research, I realized that there were women who dressed like men; everyone knew that they were women but they were treated as men because they acted like men, dressed like men, and they did jobs that only men did—like being a cowboy, for example, or distributing the mail. And then there were other women who dressed like men and had men's names and no one discovered that they were women until they were dressing their bodies for the funeral. I found this out in my research, in newspaper reports or accounts, and sometimes in history books. So there was a blend of many things I used in order to compensate for the direct account that I would have had if I had interviewed the real people.

LGL: *The interesting thing for me is that I feel like I've been on your trail, trying to read what I think you read!*

IA: I can give you several piles of books that I still have. But there was also a lot of information that I found here in California in 1999, because it was the 150th anniversary of the gold rush. The whole year before that, there were exhibits in museums, documentaries on TV, and books of photography that weren't published. The research was there; it was just an incredible coincidence.

LGL: *Did that inspire the topic, or did you already have the topic in mind and then the universe kind of aligned itself with your plans, as has happened in the past?*

IA: I had a very vague idea when I started writing. And then things started to happen; the characters evolved and just did what they had to do, in spite of me sometimes! Then there were all this information available that I had never thought I would find.

LGL: *Daughter of Fortune is a wonderful example of historical fiction. How would you describe the relationship between history and fiction in your novels?*

IA: Most are a blend of historical facts and fiction. The historical facts make the fiction believable. It's the solid ground on which the story stands. When the reader realizes that the historical facts are all accurate, they surrender to the fiction.

LGL: *I was particularly fascinated by the portrayal of the Chinese prostitution industry in Daughter of Fortune and how carefully you document the*

details of the trafficking in women. Some of the books I read stated that
the rescue efforts didn't begin until the 1870s, whereas you have your
characters involved in the rescue effort of the singsong girls back in the
1850s. Is this an example of poetic license?

IA: Yes. It is poetic license, but I do it in such a way that it is a very
private rescue; it's not an organized rescue. In 1870, the Presbyterian missionaries started the real rescue of the Chinese girls.
But you can have that effort before in a sort of private and quiet
way, and it's not wrong—because it may have happened.

LGL: *It doesn't defy the facts.*

IA: Yes. Similarly, Joaquín Murieta was a legend, a mythical character. And it was never proven that the head that was exhibited
in a jar was really from a man called Joaquín Murieta and
there's no proof that a man called Joaquín Murieta—the
famous bandit—really existed. What is most probable is that
there were several bandits committing several crimes, and they
sort of created this mythological figure that embodied all the
crimes committed by the Hispanics. Because it was impossible
that a crime committed in Sacramento in the morning could be
committed by the same person who would commit another
crime in Los Angeles, because there was no way that he could
get there in the afternoon.

LGL: *One of my favorite parts of the novel is the confusion you create between*
Joaquín Murieta and Joaquín Andieta. There seems to be a parallel
between the mythification of love on a personal level, that is, what
Eliza does with Andieta, and what different nationalities have done
with Murieta as a legendary bandit. In other words, the need to create
myths and heroes occurs on both a personal level and on a collective
level. Is that something that you were thinking of when you created
Joaquín Andieta and your version of Joaquín Murieta?

IA: I was not thinking about that, but you are absolutely right;
that's a very strong parallel. But, of course, and any writer can
tell you this, one writes in a very unconscious way and then
later, when people analyze your work, they find all these things
that are probably there and that the writer never imagined.

LGL: *I'll pursue this topic a little more. I love the presence of two writers in*
Daughter of Fortune *who seem to be alter egos of Isabel Allende.*
There's Jacob Fremont, the creative, inventive journalist who's not
adverse to lying to get a good story or to create a good story. And there's
Rose Sommers, the author of erotic fiction, whose novels even have a
plot, as Eliza pointedly observes. Can you comment on the presence of
these two writers in your novel, both of whom reflect different aspects of
your own creativity?

IA: I don't know how they appear in the book or why they appear. When I first started writing about Miss Rose, I realized that she was a very flat character. What I had in mind was this typical Victorian spinster. And then she rebelled, and she was beautiful, and she had a past. Then I started thinking, "What if she compensates for all this boredom by writing things, and by writing something that'll be totally forbidden—let's say pornography. But where would she get the information?" So I started thinking of the love affair that she had with Karl Bretzner. And then the character became very complicated. But, of course, you're right; one always writes about oneself. The only thing I can write about are things I know, from a personal experience. I've been a journalist, so I could be Fremont and be the wrong kind of journalist because that's the kind of journalist I was! I had no problem inventing a story or exaggerating, or taking sides and being totally subjective and emotional about something. I never had a problem with that; I always thought that journalism was a kind of fiction. Then as a writer, when I wrote *Aphrodite*, I realized that I had in me that trend towards a sort of funny eroticism. I cannot take eroticism seriously; I think it's always funny and playful, and there's nothing serious that you can say about it. I realized that this is very much present in the person I am. So that's why the character of Miss Rose was so easily developed in that direction.

LGL: *I think that actually one of the funniest parts in the novel is the part that describes Rose's affair with Karl, from the way she watches him devour desserts to her thought that since he looked better naked than dressed, he obviously needed a good tailor, to her hysterical description of his "perky gherkin." When I read that, I thought, "That's a short story. That can be lifted whole from the novel and be read as a wonderful short story."*

IA: When I did the book tour and I had to do readings from the novel, I read that part because it stands alone. It's so hard to find in a novel something that you can read and that people will relate to because it's thoroughly detached from the context.

LGL: *Yes. It easily travels on its own. After you finished* Eva Luna, *everyone asked, "Where are her stories?" And then you published* The Stories of Eva Luna. *I'm wondering if anyone's asked you where Rose Sommers's erotic novels are and if that's going to be next!*

IA: They haven't, but you know, in the nineteenth century, there was a collection of pornography written by a person called An Anonymous Lady. Nobody believed it was a woman; they thought it was a man. But those novels existed. I never read them, but when I was doing research for *Aphrodite*, I found out about that and thought, "This is fascinating. I can give any of my characters these pornographic novels because nobody knows who the author was." So that's why she's called An Anonymous Lady after the author of those novels. But I have written another book that I just finished, and it will be published in October in Spanish.

LGL: Is it a novel?

IA: Yes, it's a novel that is totally independent from *Daughter of Fortune*, but I take some of the characters from that novel and bring them back in this new one. Because people ask so often, "What happened to Tao Chi'en and Eliza? Did they ever have children? What happened to their descendants?" I get a letter every day about this. So I started writing another book that you can read without having read any of the others, but this book is a bridge between *Daughter of Fortune* and *The House of the Spirits*. Because characters from both books appear there and the novel takes place at the turn of the century. I was able to pick up on the grandchild of Eliza and Tao Chi'en, and the parents of Clara del Valle from *The House of the Spirits*. I connected the three books, and the publishers already have the idea that they can publish them as a trilogy in a couple of years. This new novel is called *Portrait in Sepia*.

LGL: *That is a perfect title because you have mentioned this color so often. In one of your interviews, you describe the tone of the first part of* The House of the Spirits *as the tone of sepia that is transformed into a brilliant whiteness at the end of the novel. Was it fun writing the novel?*

IA: I had a lot of fun because I brought all my characters back to Chile after the first few chapters. Chile at the time was a fascinating place because it was a time of war; we had six wars in the nineteenth century. There was revolution and war, cruelty, repression. All the things that happened afterwards in the 1970s with the military coup happened in the nineteenth century, also. There was a great deal of background that our history books totally deny or ignore or change. It was a fascinating thing to research because I could talk about the nineteenth century and the nineteenth-century revolution and suggest a parallel to the twentieth century, without saying this is what happened in the 1970s.

LGL: *I remember that back in 1994 you mentioned that you were working on something having to do with the Chilean coup. And then I never saw any reference to that again. Is* Portrait in Sepia *at all related to that earlier project?*

IA: I tried to write that and it didn't work because I was, and I still am, too close. You know, fiction requires distance—emotional distance—and I don't have it. It was such a poor text that I never published it.

LGL: *Did you have the idea of another novel in mind when you gave* Daughter of Fortune *its open ending or did the idea just sit for awhile?*

IA: I did not have it in mind. I had in mind the idea of writing a book about a young woman photographer in the turn of the century because I was fascinated with the evolution of photography and image. But when people started asking, "What happened with Tao and Eliza?," I said, "Well, my photographer could be the granddaughter of Tao and Eliza." And then it all came together.

LGL: *Is what happens to Tao and Eliza in* Portrait in Sepia *also of interest to you?*

IA: No, it is interesting to me only in relation to the character of the new book. When *Daughter of Fortune* was finished, my mother and several other people said, "This is a bad ending. What happened to Tao and Eliza? Did they stay together? Was it the head of Joaquín Murieta or not? You can't leave it like that." However, when I wrote the sentence, "I am free now," I realized that was the end of the book and there was nothing that I could add. I tried to write another chapter that I more or less had in mind and it didn't work, because it was phony; the whole thing was phony. So I left it there without it. But then the pressure was so awful—[laughter]

LGL: *I love that! {laughter} But you've said in interviews that you don't want to create a self-contained world. When someone asked you some time ago if you weren't tempted to bring your characters back, you said that you didn't want to create a literary world where you're the god and you just keep writing about the same characters. But this sounds different; it's as if you are just extending the family of your characters.*

IA: Yes. I realized that this family saga begins in 1832 when Eliza was born and it extends all the way to the twentieth century with *The House of the Spirits.* But I have taken 20 years to write these three books in different order. So they're not even in chronological order. You don't plan these things; they just sort of evolve in a very organic way.

LGL: *Are you getting faster in your writing?*

IA: I'm getting better with the research!

LGL: *Are you amazed at the speed at which you work?*

IA: Yes. With the last book, I was amazed at the speed because it took me seven years to research *Daughter of Fortune.* And then I wrote it very fast, because the research gave me so much. But with *Portrait in Sepia,* I already had the research from *Daughter of Fortune,* which helped me a lot. But I also needed to do other research about Chile. I could do it very quickly because I had learned how to do it. When I did the research for *Daughter of Fortune,* I just plunged into the information without any criteria and couldn't remember where I had seen a certain fact. I had piles and piles of books marked and I didn't know what the marks meant, or how to find what I wanted to find. I knew that I had read it somewhere but I couldn't find it again. So I had to go through the whole book to find whatever I was looking for. This time I was much better because I had a huge blackboard in the room, and I had columns with the dates and the characters and everything, and I had stickers on each date and on each event and where to find the book and the information. So it was a matter of just bringing the sticker out and looking for the book.

LGL: *I'm more in your first style! In other words, the writing part was never the slow part; it was really the research part. So now you have both of them at the same level.*

IA: Yes. It was always the research that was difficult. And also before it was harder for me, and writing was a much slower process because I was not able to clear my calendar; I was doing too many things. Now I have this policy that I don't do anything. When I'm writing, I don't do interviews, I don't travel, I don't do lectures, reading, nothing. I just write. And that creates a sort of emotional space, which is extremely important because you can be very productive if you are in total silence and solitude.

LGL: *From now until January 8th, are you in a different mode?*

IA: Yes. Now I'm free and I'm filling up the reservoirs because I'm totally empty!

LGL: *Do you have a sense of anticlimax when you finish a book?*

IA: It depends. When I finished *Paula,* for example, I was so depressed, so depressed that I thought that I was never going to be able to write again. But when I finished *Aphrodite,* I felt so stimulated that I couldn't wait for January 8th to start *Daughter of Fortune,* because I was running to get there. And when I finished *Daughter of Fortune, Portrait in Sepia* just came naturally. I didn't have to think much about it.

LGL: *Was there a specific emotion that triggered the writing of* Portrait in
      Sepia, *apart from your desire to write a novel about a female photogra-*
      pher in the nineteenth century, to suggest a parallel between nineteenth-
      and twentieth-century Chilean history, and to complete the lives of the
      characters from Daughter of Fortune?

IA: Yes, a desire to explore memory. The theme of the novel is
      memory.

LGL: *Do you have a new book in mind for January 8, 2001?*

IA: I have in mind something that I'm not sure is going to work. I
      want to write a young adult book, for children of 10 and
      above. I have grandchildren that age now and I tell them sto-
      ries and I have been thinking about this for a very long time
      without really trying. So this is what I want to try now.

LGL: *Have you read the* Harry Potter *series?*

IA: Yes they are very good. I love *Harry Potter*, but there are things
      that are better than that.

LGL: *So this is a tremendous challenge for you.*

IA: Yes. I don't know if I'm going to be able to do it, but I will try.

LGL: *You once mentioned that any serious writer needs to face three chal-*
      lenges: write a short story collection, erotic fiction, and children's liter-
      ature. You've written a collection of short stories, your next project is to
      write children's literature, and eroticism is sprinkled throughout your
      work even if you haven't written a novel that matches those of An
      Anonymous Woman. *I'm particularly intrigued by the relationship*
      between eroticism and storytelling in your writing. I'm specifically
      thinking about how Hermelinda in your short story, "Toad's Mouth,"
      creates desire in her public through her erotic games, in the same way
      that Belisa Crepusculario creates longing through her two words.
      Erotic art and narrative art have so much in common in your fiction
      and are united by the desire they create in the recipient of the action. Is
      that something that you've thought about much?

IA: I don't think that I've thought about it, but that has been my
      life experience. The only thing that really turns me on is a good
      story. I mean, if I watch one of those porno movies, I get so
      bored that I fall asleep! I just can't find anything arousing in
      that stuff. But if a man murmurs in my ear, oh my God! So
      what really turns me on is a story. It's words; it's always the
      beauty of words. It's the text. So in my erotic fantasies, there's
      always a story going on.

LGL: *And in these many stories that you write, it seems that you have very*
      few characters who are really anguished. I would say that Gregory
      Reeves from The Infinite Plan *is your only truly anguished character.*

I don't know if you would agree with that at all. Are you not inter-ested in naked, tortured souls? Your characters are so resilient and independent and resourceful; they struggle and they pursue their quest. But they're not consumed with the kind of angst that Gregory Reeves has. He seems an anomaly in your fiction.

IA: Well, maybe because he's based on a real character and he's real life. And I was fascinated by the anguish and by the fact that he had had so many ordeals and had been on his knees so many times, and was always able to get back on his feet. I found that fascinating, and I think that I fell in love with the man because of that.

LGL: *I know that Reeves was inspired by your husband and his story. Can we assume that without that inspiration you wouldn't have come up with a character who's as tortured as Reeves is?*

IA: You know, I'm not really very interested in people who whine all the time! I mean it. I don't like whiners. I want people to just confront whatever comes, and to get beaten up and fall and pick themselves up again. This American idea that the world owes you something, that this is a safe place where you can walk with an insurance for everything, is very strange to me.

LGL: *Is that why you say you write for those who are not pessimists and who believe in their own strength? You're not interested in nihilists as read-ers. Is that correct?*

IA: I'm not interested in them as characters. Maybe they can find strength in my books and in other books, and maybe they can find a way out of their misery. But, you know, the professional whiner never changes! And this is very much in the American culture, where they think they've been betrayed by the Ameri-can dream and they start whining. And I'm not interested in those kind of people, because I feel that they are very spoiled; they don't know what the world is about and how hard it is for most people. I have many of these readers, as well, but my hope is that they will see how hard it is for other people and just get a life!

LGL: *Easier said than done. Continuing with this topic of your readers, you've often said two different things about writing that are not neces-sarily contradictory, but have always made me wonder. You've spoken about art as an act of alchemy that can transform the evil of the world into its opposite, hope and love. And you've also said that you don't think your books have had much impact on the world because fiction can not really transform people's attitudes. Which feeling is most true for you—art as transformation or art as words without power? Or are both equally true?*

IA: Well, I think that art has the capacity to transform, to explain, to put a mirror in front of society's face so that an individual or the society can look at itself. Art has the possibility of doing that and it can be photography, a work of literature, whatever. On the other hand, I am very aware that literature has a very limited capacity to reach a limited number of people, the readers. If you talk about art, for example, in the cinema or on television, the impact is so powerful that it reaches millions of people in eight seconds. But literature, more and more, has become elitist in a way. And who reads? Not only people who can afford books, but people who have the habit of reading. And those people are with you anyhow; I mean, you seldom acquire new readers. The authors who are able to reach people who are not readers are very few. Very, very few.

LGL: *But you have such a wide public.*

IA: I have a very wide public, but I'm very aware, for example, that a person like Oprah is ten million times more powerful than the most powerful book in the world.

LGL: *Are you at all tempted by television? You've said that you could never write a* telenovela *or soap opera, because you couldn't follow the formula. You've mentioned that you would like to write a screenplay some day. You've mentioned going into other genres. Do you think about this much?*

IA: Now, I don't; I did before because I had all the training as a journalist. And journalists, when they are good, can get feedback immediately and they are very aware of how much impact their writing has. While with writers, it sometimes takes years to know if your books are read or not.

LGL: *Yes, you have often said that the test will be time.*

IA: Time. But on the other hand, as I get older, I am more aware of my limitations. One of my limitations, for example, is that I live in another language. I have a very heavy accent; I live in an English-speaking country, and I write in Spanish and I think in Spanish.

LGL: *You don't have a heavy accent.*

IA: Well, heavy enough that I couldn't do television. I know that this is maybe very fortunate for me, because it creates a no-man's land that is like a buffer between me and all the temptations of the world! Because I am separated by the language barrier. And that is very important for a writer, because it forces me to be quiet and alone, and realize what my limitations are and not be tempted.

LGL: *In other words, you would really let loose if you could. {laughter}*

IA: Right! Of course! I'm so vain! [laughter]

LGL: *What are you struggling with these days? Are you struggling with being less of a perfectionist, being less goal oriented? Or have you made peace with who you are and with your demons?*

IA: I'm in therapy. I'm dealing with *all* the demons!

LGL: *You have always said therapy doesn't work!*

IA: I am sorry I said that. It's not true. Therapy works very well! [laughter] I just started again! I started because I am entering into another stage of my life, and I don't seem to be well prepared. I still think of myself as the person I was 20 years ago, and my reality has changed tremendously. I'm 58; I was 58 on August 2, and I know that I'm entering into the older age. And I want to be prepared for that. I don't want to be hooked on impossible youth. One thing is to feel young and another is to try to look young, no matter what. I don't want to be caught up in the Hollywood youth culture.

LGL: *You seem very aware of everything you are feeling.*

IA: Yes. I am aware intellectually, and I try to live accordingly. But the truth is that when I confront myself in the mirror, I realize that I'm 58 and no matter what, I will keep on aging. And then there are many things happening in our family right now that are hard for me to deal with. I have a couple of stepchildren who are drug addicts. This is affecting the family very much. I just can't cope sometimes. I am trying to get some advice because this is so alien to me. I try to apply a formula that I think is infallible, boundaries plus love; it doesn't always work. When you have messed-up people, it doesn't . . .

LGL: *When you were grieving over your daughter, Paula's death, you said that therapy didn't help, that only writing helped in that case.*

IA: Writing only helps in cases that concern me. But what if your reality is collapsing all around? Then you need a person who is a professional and who is not emotionally involved, to tell you, "Well, this is what you can expect; this is how you handle this."

LGL: *With regard to Paula, I have one question about the book's title that is a little confusing. I read in one place that the original title of the book was "Para Paula," {For Paula} and in other places that it was "Escucha, Paula" {Listen, Paula}.*

IA: It was "Escucha, Paula," because the first sentence of the book is: "Listen, Paula, I'm going to tell you a story." So the natural title was "Listen, Paula." But many of the publishers in other languages said that it sounded harsh. In German, it was like an order. In Spanish, it would be fine; maybe in English, too. But in German or in any Scandinavian language—even in Italian, it was too much like a military order.

LGL: *Can you tell me something about the Isabel Allende Foundation that I know is related to the writing of* Paula?

IA: There is some information about that in my Web site.[1] When Paula died and I wrote that book, I decided that all the income that I would get from *Paula* would go to a foundation. So I created a foundation that helps programs that support education and well being, mainly of women and girls. However, it's not limited to women and girls. But without even saying it, that's what we're trying to do because I feel that if, for example, you help the women in a village in Bangladesh, then the whole community rises. If you help the men, they spend the money on bicycles or whatever. So we support programs in the United States and in other countries like Chile, Guatemala, or Bangladesh, and it's always for programs that already exist. The foundation cannot give money to individuals. However, we do have a program for scholarships. But the scholarships are directed through other institutions, for example, a university. Because I don't have an infrastructure to provide, I have to trust that other people will use the money in the right way. I have no capacity for supervision; our foundation has absolutely zero overhead. Everybody that works for the foundation is there as a volunteer. And my office pays the accountant, the secretary, the building, the telephone.

LGL: *What a wonderful tribute to your daughter's memory. Before we finish, I want to ask you a few more questions about the critical reception of your work and the backlash against it in the United States. Your short story, "Toad's Mouth," one of my favorites among* The Stories of Eva Luna, *has been blacklisted by conservatives. It's quite incredible to contemplate that. Are there any others that are blacklisted?*

IA: Well, there are books that are blacklisted. I know that *The House of the Spirits* was blacklisted in Utah in some Mormon schools and they also tried to blacklist it in Virginia because the parents objected to the rape in the book, the language. And I don't remember what else. They didn't object to the torture, or to the abuse of the poor, or to the concentration camps, or the military coup. They objected to the sex scenes, which tells you something about their mentality.

LGL: *The hypocrisy is quite incredible. And it's indicative of the very strong reactions your books have received. I know that you have an acute sense of being a writer very much in the public eye. You have even said that in recent years, you feel as if you're passing an exam every day, and that there's a lot of pressure on you to jump higher and higher.*

IA: That's true.

LGL: *Do you experience that feeling often and how do you cope with it?*

IA: I try to ignore the critics, because the readers are much more generous and supportive than the critics. When you write a good first novel or a successful first novel, the critics all bestow their praises on the author and it's wonderful. The second novel, they will tear apart. And if you start writing books that sell, then automatically you become a commercial writer and therefore a bad writer in their eyes. Because they underestimate the readers; they think that readers will only read something that is bad. What a criteria—it's very strange. So the critics are very hard, and they get harder and harder as I write more and more. But Oprah selected *Daughter of Fortune* for her book club.

LGL: *Do you know how many copies of your books have been published throughout the world?*

IA: No, I really don't know because it's impossible to keep track. My books have been translated into 27 languages; there are many pirate editions in addition to special editions. If you add in pocket book editions, there are probably 15 million, but the number changes daily. All of my books are in print. I have been very lucky!

Notes and References

Chapter One

1. Betty Fussell, "Isabel Allende's Fantasy Life," *Lear's,* May 1993, 52; hereafter cited in the text as Allende, 1993a.

2. The description of Allende as "story-giver" is offered by her friend the writer Amy Tan in Allende, 1993a, 81. "Story junkie" is from Isabel Allende, foreword to *Conversations with Isabel Allende,* ed. John Rodden (Austin: University of Texas Press, 1999), xi; hereafter cited in the text as Allende, 1999.

3. Isabel Allende, "If I Didn't Write, I Would Die," interview by Marie-Lise Gazarian Gautier (1989), in *Conversations with Isabel Allende,* ed. John Rodden (Austin: University of Texas Press, 1999), 139; hereafter cited in the text as Allende, 1989.

4. Isabel Allende, *Paula,* trans. Margaret Sayers Peden (New York: Harper Perennial, 1996), 27; hereafter cited in the text as *P.*

5. Isabel Allende, "Chile's Troubadour," interview by Magdalena García Pinto (1991), trans. Trudy Balch and Magdalena García Pinto, in *Conversations with Isabel Allende,* ed. John Rodden (Austin: University of Texas Press, 1999), 71; hereafter cited in the text as Allende, 1991a.

6. Isabel Allende, *Aphrodite: A Memoir of the Senses,* trans. Margaret Sayers Peden (New York: HarperFlamingo, 1998), 62; hereafter cited in the text as *A.*

7. Isabel Allende, "An Orgy of the Senses," interview by Pilar Alvarez-Rubio (1994), trans. Virginia Invernizzi, in *Conversations with Isabel Allende,* ed. John Rodden (Austin: University of Texas Press, 1999), 366; hereafter cited in the text as Allende, 1994a.

8. Sara Castro-Klarén, "Women, Self, and Writing," in *Women's Writing in Latin America: An Anthology,* ed. Sara Castro-Klarén, Sylvia Molloy, and Beatriz Sarlo (Boulder, Colo.: Westview Press, 1991), 4.

9. For a detailed description of the history of military intervention in Chilean politics and the suspension of civil liberties in the 1920s and 1940s, see Thomas E. Skidmore and Peter H. Smith, "Chile, Democracy, Socialism, and Repression" in their book *Modern Latin America* (New York: Oxford University Press, 1984), 124–27; hereafter cited in the text.

10. Eduardo Galeano, *Memory of Fire. III. Century of the Wind,* trans. Cedric Belfrage (New York: Pantheon Books, 1988), 209; hereafter cited in the text.

11. There has been some controversy over whether Salvador Allende committed suicide or was killed by the military during the coup. Isabel Allende

states in her article "Pinochet without Hatred" that "Salvador Allende took his life in the burning presidential palace" on 11 September 1973. Isabel Allende, "Pinochet without Hatred," *New York Times Magazine,* 17 January 1999, 26.

12. Isabel Allende, "Writing from the Belly," interview by Michael Toms (1994), in *Conversations with Isabel Allende,* ed. John Rodden (Austin: University of Texas Press, 1999), 336; hereafter cited in the text as Allende, 1994b.

13. Isabel Allende, "From Silence and Anger to Love and Vision," interview by David Montenegro (1991), in *Conversations with Isabel Allende,* ed. John Rodden (Austin: University of Texas Press, 1999), 248; hereafter cited in the text as Allende, 1991b.

14. Isabel Allende, "A Sacred Journey Inward," interview by Alberto Manguel (1992), in *Conversations with Isabel Allende,* ed. John Rodden (Austin: University of Texas Press, 1999), 270; hereafter cited in the text as Allende, 1992a.

15. Isabel Allende, "The 'Uncontrollable Rebel,' " interview by Juan Andrés Piña (1991), trans. Virginia Invernizzi, in *Conversations with Isabel Allende,* ed. John Rodden (Austin: University of Texas Press, 1999), 177; hereafter cited in the text as Allende, 1991c.

16. Isabel Allende, "On Shadows and Love," interview by Michael Moody (1986), trans. Virginia Invernizzi, in *Conversations with Isabel Allende,* ed. John Rodden (Austin: University of Texas Press, 1999), 55; hereafter cited in the text as Allende, 1986.

17. Isabel Allende, "Pirate, Conjurer, Feminist," interview by Marjorie Agosín (1984), trans. Cola Franzen, in *Conversations with Isabel Allende,* ed. John Rodden (Austin: University of Texas Press, 1999), 39; hereafter cited in the text as Allende, 1984.

18. Celia Correas Zapata, *Isabel Allende: Vida y espíritus* (Barcelona: Plaza & Janés Editores, 1998), 218; hereafter cited in the text.

19. Carmen J. Galarce, *La novela chilena del exilio (1973–1987): El caso de Isabel Allende* (Santiago: Universidad de Chile, 1994), 51; hereafter cited in the text.

20. Isabel Allende, Faculty Lecture Series address, Jersey City State College, Jersey City, N.J., 14 April 1997.

21. See Isabel Allende, "Pinochet without Hatred," *New York Times Magazine,* 17 January 1999, 27. Also see note 11 and chapter 2 for additional references to this article. The background information concerning this story is as follows: Augusto Pinochet was arrested in Britain on 16 October 1998 while recovering from back surgery. He was charged by Judge Baltasar Garzón of Spain of crimes against humanity and was held responsible in the death, disappearance, and torture of more than 3,000 people following the 1973 coup, among them Spanish citizens. The intent of Judge Garzón's decision was to have General Pinochet extradited to Spain to face charges for those crimes. Britain ruled that the 84-year-old Pinochet was too ill to stand trial in Spain. Pinochet returned to Chile on 3 March 2000; on 8 August 2000, the Chilean

Supreme Court divested him of his senatorial immunity, paving the way for his possible trial in Chile. On 29 January 2001, Judge Juan Guzmán of Chile charged Pinochet with the execution and disappearance of more than 70 political opponents. These acts were allegedly committed in October 1973 by the so-called caravan of death, a special army squadron. Chilean courts subsequently reduced these charges to abetting and aiding. On 9 July 2001, the Santiago appeals court ruled that Pinochet suffered from moderate dementia and ordered the case closed. On 21 August 2001, the Second Bench of the Chilean Supreme Court agreed to consider an appeal to the 9 July ruling. In order to overturn this ruling, the prosecuting attorney must prove that Pinochet does not suffer from dementia and is fit to stand trial for human rights violations relating to the 1973 caravan of death.

22. Isabel Allende, Abramovitz Guest Lecture, Massachusetts Institute of Technology, Cambridge, Mass., 15 March 1993; hereafter cited in the text as Allende, 1993b.

23. Isabel Allende, "Unas palabras sobre América Latina," Montclair State University, Upper Montclair, N.J., 18 April 1985.

24. Isabel Allende, telephone interview by author, 8 August 2000; hereafter cited in the text as Allende, 2000b. The complete interview is included in this volume.

25. Jean Franco, "Afterword: From Romance to Refractory Aesthetic," in *Latin American Women's Writings: Feminist Readings in Theory and Crisis,* ed. Anny Brooksbank Jones and Catherine Davies (New York: Oxford University Press, 1996), 228; hereafter cited in the text as Franco, 1996.

26. See Susan Frenk, "The Wandering Text: Situating the Narratives of Isabel Allende," in *Latin American Women's Writings: Feminist Readings in Theory and Crisis,* ed. Anny Brooksbank Jones and Catherine Davies (New York: Oxford University Press, 1996), 66–84.

27. Isabel Allende, address to the American Library Association, San Antonio, Tex., 20 January 1996.

28. Roland Barthes, cited in Thomas LeClair, "Postmodern Mastery," in *Postmodern Fiction: A Bio-Bibliographical Guide,* ed. Larry McCaffery (Westport, Conn.: Greenwood Press, 1986), 118.

29. Annie Leclerc, "Woman's Word," trans. Gillian C. Gill, in *New French Feminisms: An Anthology,* ed. Elaine Marks and Isabelle de Courtivron (New York: Schocken Books, 1981), 79.

30. Isabel Allende, *Civilice a su troglodita: Los impertinentes de Isabel Allende* (Santiago, Chile: Editorial Lord Cochrane, 1974), 5.

31. The mention to John Wayne Bobbit refers to the 1993 case of a man whose battered wife cut off his penis in anger; it was retrieved by police and sewed back on by doctors.

32. Jean Franco, *Plotting Women: Gender and Representation in Mexico* (New York: Columbia University Press, 1989), 187.

188 NOTES AND REFERENCES

33. Amy K. Kaminsky, *Reading the Body Politic: Feminist Criticism and Latin American Women Writers* (Minneapolis: University of Minnesota Press, 1993), xiii.

34. Alexander Coleman, "Reconciliation among the Ruins," review of *The House of the Spirits*, by Isabel Allende, *New York Times*, 12 May 1985, Book Review section, 1.

35. For an analysis of post-Boom aesthetics and its relationship to Allende, see Juan Manuel Marcos, "El género popular como meta-estructura textual del post-boom latinoamericano," *Monographic Review/Revista Monográfica* 3, no. 1–2 (1987): 268–78; and Elzbieta Sklodowska, "*Ardiente paciencia* y *La casa de los espíritus*: Traición y tradición en el discurso del post-boom," *Discurso Literario* 9, no. 1 (1991): 33–40. For an analysis of the relationship between the Chilean novel of exile and the fiction of Isabel Allende, see Carmen J. Galarce, *La novela chilena del exilio (1973–1987): El caso de Isabel Allende* (Santiago: Universidad de Chile, 1994).

36. Isabel Allende, acceptance speech of the Dorothy and Lillian Gish Prize, New York, N.Y., 13 October 1998.

Chapter Two

1. Isabel Allende, "La magia de las palabras," *Revista Iberoamericana* 51, no. 132–33 (1985): 449–50; hereafter cited in the text as Allende, 1985. Also see Allende, 1991a, 89.

2. Peter G. Earle, "Literature as Survival: Allende's *The House of the Spirits*," *Contemporary Literature* 28 (1987): 545; hereafter cited in the text.

3. Carmen J. Galarce, *La novela chilena del exilio (1973–1987): El caso de Isabel Allende* (Santiago: Universidad de Chile, 1994), 136.

4. Gerald Martin, *Journeys through the Labyrinth: Latin American Fiction in the Twentieth Century* (London: Verso, 1989), 351; hereafter cited in the text.

5. Isabel Allende, *The House of the Spirits*, trans. Magda Bogin (New York: Alfred A. Knopf, 1985), 72; hereafter cited in the text as *HS*.

6. Alejo Carpentier, "Introducción," *El reino de este mundo* (1949; reprint, Buenos Aires: Edhasa, 1978), 53.

7. Lois Parkinson Zamora and Wendy B. Faris, "Introduction: Daiquiri Birds and Flaubertian Parrot(ie)s," in *Magical Realism: Theory, History, Community*, ed. Lois Parkinson Zamora and Wendy B. Faris (Durham, N.C.: Duke University Press, 1995): 2; hereafter cited in the text.

8. Isabel Allende, "The Shaman and the Infidel," Interview by Marilyn Berlin Snell (1991), in *Conversations with Isabel Allende*, ed. John Rodden (Austin: University of Texas Press, 1999), 238.

9. Patricia Hart, *Narrative Magic in the Fiction of Isabel Allende* (Cranbury, N.J.: Associated University Presses, 1989), 27; hereafter cited in the text.

10. Robert Antoni, "Parody or Piracy: The Relationship of *The House of the Spirits* to *One Hundred Years of Solitude*," *Latin American Literary Review* 16, no. 32 (1988): 24; hereafter cited in the text.

11. For a discussion of the term "double-voiced discourse," see Mikhail M. Bakhtin, *The Dialogic Imagination: Four Essays,* ed. Michael Holquist, trans. Caryl Emerson and Michael Holquist (Austin: University of Texas Press, 1981), 324. For a feminist interpretation of this concept as applied to Isabel Allende, see Linda Gould Levine, "A Passage to Androgyny: Isabel Allende's *La casa de los espíritus,*" in *In the Feminine Mode: Essays on Hispanic Women Writers,* ed. Noël Valis and Carol Maier (Cranbury, N.J.: Associated University Presses, 1990), 169–70, 173. Elaine Showalter discusses the "muted" and "dominant" aspects of women's writings in "Feminist Criticism in the Wilderness," an essay in *The New Feminist Criticism: Essays on Women, Literature and Theory,* ed. Elaine Showalter (New York: Pantheon Books, 1985), 263.

12. Pamela Moore, "Testing the Terms: 'Woman' in *The House of Spirits* and *One Hundred Years of Solitude,*" *The Comparatist* 18 (1994): 96.

13. The phrase "luminous dimension in ascending gradation" is from Marcelo Coddou, "Dimensión del feminismo en Isabel Allende," in *Los libros tienen sus propios espíritus: Estudios sobre Isabel Allende,* ed. Marcelo Coddou (Mexico: Universidad Veracruzana, 1986), 30. The phrase "corresponds to the Marxist unfolding of history" is from Richard McCallistar, "Nomenklatura in *La casa de los espíritus,*" in *Critical Approaches to Isabel Allende's Novels,* ed. Sonia Riquelme Rojas and Edna Aguirre Rehbein (New York: Peter Lang, 1991), 24.

14. P. Gabrielle Foreman, "Past-On Stories: History and the Magically Real, Morrison and Allende on Call," in *Magical Realism: Theory, History, Community,* ed. Lois Parkinson Zamora and Wendy B. Faris, (Durham, N.C.: Duke University Press, 1995), 286; hereafter cited in the text.

15. Rodrigo Cánovas, "Los espíritus literarios y políticos de Isabel Allende," in *Critical Approaches to Isabel Allende's Novels,* ed. Sonia Riquelme Rojas and Edna Aguirre Rehbein (New York: Peter Lang, 1991), 41.

16. Isabel Allende, Interview by author, New York, 3 February 1988; hereafter cited in the text as Allende, 1988.

17. Ruth Y. Jenkins, "Authorizing Female Voice and Experience: Ghosts and Spirits in Kingston's *The Woman Warrior* and Allende's *The House of the Spirits,*" *MELUS: The Journal of the Society for the Study of the Multi-Ethnic Literature of the United States* 19, no. 3 (1994): 64.

18. Kavita Panjabi, "*The House of the Spirits,* Tránsito Soto: From Periphery to Power," in *Critical Approaches to Isabel Allende's Novels,* ed. Sonia Riquelme Rojas and Edna Aguirre Rehbein (New York: Peter Lang, 1991), 12; hereafter cited in the text.

19. Susan Frenk, "The Wandering Text: Situating the Narratives of Isabel Allende," in *Latin American Women's Writing: Feminist Readings in Theory and Crisis,* ed. Anny Brooksbank Jones and Catherine Davies (New York: Oxford University Press, 1996), 68.

20. Mario Rojas, " '*La casa de los espíritus*', de Isabel Allende: un caleidoscopio de espejos desordenados," *Revista Iberoamericana* 51, no. 132–33 (1985): 919.

21.   I am indebted to my colleague JoAnne Engelbert for sharing with me a paper she read at the Modern Language Association Convention in 1984 entitled "The Anatomy of Dominance: Isabel Allende's *The House of the Spirits.*"

22.   Mario Rodríguez Fernández, "García Márquez/Isabel Allende: Relación textual," in *Los libros tienen sus propios espíritus: Estudios sobre Isabel Allende,* ed. Marcelo Coddou (Mexico: Universidad Veracruzana, 1986), 79.

23.   Doris Meyer, " 'Parenting the Text': Female Creativity and Dialogic Relationships in Isabel Allende's *La casa de los espíritus,*" *Hispania* 73 (1990): 363; hereafter cited in the text. Meyer borrows from Elaine Showalter in her discussion of parenting a text.

24.   Debra A. Castillo, *Talking Back: Toward a Latin American Feminist Literary Criticism* (Ithaca, N.Y.: Cornell University Press, 1992), 300. Castillo does not refer here specifically to Allende but to the "poetics of gender" in general.

25.   Isabel Allende, "Of Love and Truth," interview by Inés Dölz-Blackburn, George McMurray, Paul Rea, and Alfonso Rodríguez (1990), in *Conversations with Isabel Allende,* ed. John Rodden (Austin: University of Texas Press, 1999), 155–56.

26.   Raúl Zurita, "Chile: Literatura, lenguaje y sociedad," in *Fascismo y experiencia literaria: Reflexiones para una recanonización,* ed. Hernán Vidal (Minneapolis: Institute for the Study of Ideologies and Literature, 1985), 326. Zurita cites from José Joaquín Brunner.

27.   Isabel Allende, "Magical Feminist," interview by Jennifer Benjamin and Sally Engelfried (1994), in *Conversations with Isabel Allende,* ed. John Rodden (Austin: University of Texas Press, 1999), 386; hereafter cited in the text as Allende, 1994c.

28.   Gerald Martin cites from Eduardo Galeano's "Notes Towards a Self-Portrait."

29.   Nina Molinaro, *Foucault, Feminism and Power: Reading Esther Tusquets* (Cranbury, N.J.: Associated University Presses, 1991), 23.

30.   Isabel Allende, "The World is Full of Stories," interview by Linda Gould Levine and JoAnne Engelbert (1985), in *Conversations with Isabel Allende,* ed. John Rodden, 44. Allende states: "In Latin America we've seen that in situations of extreme danger the people who take the greatest risks are women. They are capable of total selflessness, of total courage."

31.   Jean Franco, "Going Public: Reinhabiting the Private," in *On Edge: The Crisis of Contemporary Latin American Culture,* ed. George Yúdice, Jean Franco, and Juan Flores (Minneapolis: University of Minnesota Press, 1992), 80.

32.   Elizabeth J. Ordóñez, *Voices of Their Own: Contemporary Spanish Narrative by Women* (Cranbury, N.J.: Associated University Presses, 1991), 20. I apply Ordóñez's theories on Spanish women writers to Allende's fiction.

33. Marketta Laurila, "Isabel Allende and the Discourse of Exile," in *International Women's Writings: New Landscapes of Identity*, ed. Anne E. Brown and Marjanne E. Goozé (Westport, Conn.: Greenwood Press, 1995), 183; hereafter cited in the text.

34. Gabriela Mora, "Las novelas de Isabel Allende y el papel de la mujer como cuidadana," *Ideologies and Literature* 2, no. 1 (1987): 55.

35. Barbara Mujica, "Isabel Allende: La fuerza vital del lenguaje," *Américas* 47, no. 6 (1995): 43; hereafter cited in the text.

36. I am indebted to my deceased colleague at Montclair State University, Kenneth J. Aman, for showing me a copy of his unpublished paper "Amnesty vs. Punishment: Latin America's Continuing Ethical Dilemma" from which my comments are taken.

37. Adrienne Rich, "Re-forming the Crystal," in *Poems: Selected and New, 1950–1974* (New York: W. W. Norton, 1975), 228.

38. Isabel Allende, letter-interview by Odile Travnicek, in *La narrativa de Isabel Allende: Claves de una marginalidad*, ed. Adriana Castillo de Berchenko (Perpignan, France: Université de Perpignan, 1990), 141.

39. Isabel Allende, "Isabel Allende Unveiled," interview by Douglas Foster (1988), in *Conversations with Isabel Allende*, ed. John Rodden, 107.

40. Hayden White, *The Content of the Form: Narrative Discourse and Historical Representation* (Baltimore: The Johns Hopkins University Press, 1987), 1.

41. Isabel Allende, "Pinochet without Hatred," *New York Times Magazine*, 17 January 1999, 27.

42. Philip Swanson, "Tyrants and Trash: Sex, Class and Culture in *La casa de los espíritus*," *Bulletin of Hispanic Studies* 71, no. 2 (1994): 225.

Chapter Three

1. This information is taken from *P*, 280–85. It also draws from Michael Moody, "Isabel Allende and the Testimonial Novel," *Confluencia* 2, no. 1 (1986): 40–42; hereafter cited in the text.

2. Isabel Allende, *Of Love and Shadows*, trans. Margaret Sayers Peden (New York: Bantam Books, 1988), 272; hereafter cited in the text as *OLS*.

3. René Jara, "Testimonio y literatura: Prólogo," in *Testimonio y literatura*, ed. René Jara and Hernán Vidal (Minneapolis: Institute for the Study of Ideologies and Literature, 1986), 1.

4. Jean Franco, "Going Public: Reinhabiting the Private," in *On Edge: The Crisis of Contemporary Latin American Culture*, ed. George Yúdice, Jean Franco, and Juan Flores (Minneapolis: University of Minnesota Press, 1992), 70.

5. Hayden White, *The Content of the Form: Narrative Discourse and Historical Representation* (Baltimore: The Johns Hopkins University Press, 1987), 5.

6. Raúl Zurita, "Chile: Literatura, lenguaje y sociedad (1973–1983)," In *Fascismo y experiencia literaria: reflexiones para una recanonización,* ed. Hernán Vidal (Minneapolis: Institute for the Study of Ideologies and Literature, 1985), 306; hereafter cited in the text.

7. Doris Meyer, "Exile and the Female Condition in Isabel Allende's *De amor y de sombra,*" *The International Fiction Review* 15, no. 2 (1988):156.

8. Kirkwood is cited in Patricia M. Chuchryk, "From Dictatorship to Democracy: The Women's Movement in Chile," in *The Women's Movement in Latin America: Participation and Democracy,* ed. Jane S. Jacquette (Boulder, Colo.: Westview Press, 1994), 81.

9. Ambrose Gordon, "Isabel Allende on Love and Shadow," *Contemporary Literature* 28, (1987): 538.

10. Isabel Allende has commented that she read in a newspaper about a convention of frogs that actually took place in Peking. She also indicates this in the novel. See Isabel Allende, letter-interview with Odile Travnicek, in *La narrativa de Isabel Allende: Claves de una marginalidad,* ed. Adriana Castillo de Berchenko (Perpignan, France: Université de Perpignan, 1990), 145.

11. See Monique J. Lemaitre, "Deseo, incesto y represión en *De amor y de sombra,*" in *Critical Approaches to Isabel Allende's Novels,* ed. Sonia Riquelme Rojas and Edna Aguirre Rehbein (New York: Peter Lang, 1991), 99–101.

12. Bernardo Subercaseaux, "Notas sobre autoritarismo y lectura en Chile," in *Fascismo y experiencia literaria: Reflexiones para una recanonización,* ed. Hernán Vidal (Minneapolis: Institute for the Study of Ideologies and Literature, 1985), 392. I am indebted to Professor Pamela Smorkaloff for her help with this translation.

13. Manuel Alcides Jofré, "La novela en Chile: 1973–1983," in *Fascismo y experiencia literaria: reflexiones para una recanonización,* ed. Hernán Vidal (Minneapolis: Institute for the Study of Ideologies and Literature, 1985), 336.

14. Isabel Allende, "The World is Full of Stories," interview by Linda Gould Levine and JoAnne Engelbert (1985), in *Conversations with Isabel Allende,* ed. John Rodden (Austin: University of Texas Press, 1999), 46.

15. Máximo Pacheco, *Lonquén* (Santiago: Editorial Aconcagua, 1980, 1983), 104–106; hereafter cited in the text.

16. The 1994 movie *Of Love and Shadows* was directed by Betty Kaplan.

17. Isabel Allende, "Something Magic in the Storytelling," interview by Jan Goggans (1994), in *Conversations with Isabel Allende,* ed. John Rodden, 327.

18. Maureen E. Shea, "Love, Eroticism, and Pornography in the Works of Isabel Allende," *Women's Studies* 18, no. 2–3 (1991), 228.

19. I am indebted to my deceased colleague at Montclair State University, Kenneth J. Aman, for sharing with me his paper, "Amnesty vs. Punishment: Latin America's Continuing Ethical Problem."

20. The theme of memory is suggested in other ways as well; Irene's mother runs a retirement home called The Will of God Manor where several of

the residents suffer from memory loss, a condition the general would like to see extended to the entire population.

Chapter Four

1. Isabel Allende, *Eva Luna*, trans. Margaret Sayers Peden (New York: Bantam Books, 1989), 1; hereafter cited in the text as *EL*.

2. Isabel Allende, "Conversando con Isabel Allende," interview by Sonia Riquelme Rojas and Edna Aguirre Rehbein, in *Critical Approaches to Isabel Allende's Novels,* ed. Sonia Riquelme Rojas and Edna Aguirre Rehbein (New York: Peter Lang, 1991), 195.

3. For a discussion of the fusion of opposites in *Eva Luna*, see Wolfgang Karrer, "Transformation and Transvestism in *Eva Luna*," in *Critical Approaches to Isabel Allende's Novels*, ed. Sonia Riquelme Rojas and Edna Aguirre Rehbein (New York: Peter Lang, 1991), 161; hereafter cited in the text.

4. For a discussion of the blending of various fictional modalities in *Eva Luna*, see Lynne Diamond-Nigh, "*Eva Luna:* Writing as History," *Studies in Twentieth Century Literature* 19, no. 1 (1995): 29–42; hereafter cited in the text.

5. Hayden White, *The Content of the Form: Narrative Discourse and Historical Representation* (Baltimore: The John Hopkins University Press, 1987), 41–42.

6. George Yúdice, "Postmodernity and Transnational Capitalism in Latin America," in *On Edge: The Crisis of Contemporary Latin American Culture*, ed. George Yúdice, Jean Franco, and Juan Flores (Minneapolis: University of Minnesota Press, 1992), 12.

7. For an ample description of thematic and stylistic aspects of the *Thousand and One Nights,* see Robert Irwin, *The Arabian Nights: A Companion* (New York: The Penguin Press, 1994).

8. For an interesting analysis of the complex play of textual mirrors in *Eva Luna*, see Vicente Cabrera, "Refracciones del cuerpo y la palabra de *Eva Luna*," *Revista Interamericana de Bibliografía/Review of Inter-American Bibliography* 42, no. 4 (1992): 591–615.

9. Isabel Allende, "Isabel Allende: 'Somos una generación marcada por el exilio,'" interview by Fernando Alegría, *Nuevo Texto Crítico* 4, no. 8 (1991): 80–81. In this interview, Allende describes the real people and events who inspired her creation of Professor Jones and the Yugoslavian *patrona*.

10. Jorge Luis Borges, *Seven Nights,* trans. Eliot Weinberger (New York: New Directions Books, 1984), 50.

11. Linda Hutcheon, *A Poetics of Postmodernism: History, Theory, Fiction* (New York: Routledge, 1988), 60. See also Isabel Allende, "A Sniper between Cultures," interview by Jacqueline Cruz, Jacqueline Mitchell, Silvia Pellarolo, and Javier Rangel (1991), trans. Virginia Invernizzi, in *Conversations with Isabel Allende,* ed. John Rodden (Austin: University of Texas Press, 1999), 221; hereafter cited in the text as Allende, 1991d. Allende mentions that the inspiration

for Mimí is the transsexual actress, Bibi Andersen, and comments that she "wanted to have a character that would be a parody, a character who would question many aspects of machismo."

12. For a discussion of the "green world," see Annis Pratt, *Archetypal Patterns in Women's Fictions* (Bloomington: Indiana University Press, 1981), 16–24.

13. Michel Perrin, *The Way of the Dead Indians: Guajiro Myths and Symbols,* trans. Michael Fineberg (Austin: University of Texas Press, 1987), 83; hereafter cited in the text.

14. M. Esther Harding, *Woman's Mysteries: Ancient and Modern* (New York: G. P. Putnam's Sons, 1971), 53; hereafter cited in the text.

15. Ester Gimbernat de González, "Entre principio y final: La madre/materia de la escritura en *Eva Luna,*" in *Critical Approaches to Isabel Allende's Novels,* ed. Sonia Riquelme Rojas and Edna Aguirre Rehbein (New York: Peter Lang, 1991), 122.

16. Allende mentions in the Allende (1988) interview that she read about the two-headed baby with one black head and one white head in a Venezuelan newspaper from the year 1947. Also see Allende, 1986, 61.

17. Susana Reisz, "¿Una Scheherazada hispanoamericana?: Sobre Isabel Allende y *Eva Luna,*" *Mester* 20, no. 2 (1991): 118.

18. Also see Pilar V. Rotella, "Allende's *Eva Luna* and the Picaresque Tradition," in *Critical Approaches to Isabel Allende's Novels,* ed. Sonia Riquelme Rojas and Edna Aguirre Rehbein (New York: Peter Lang, 1991), 132–33.

19. Allende discusses in several interviews the inspiration for Rolf Carlé and the uncanny coincidence between the fictional name she gives her character and the name of the real father on whom her character is based. See Isabel Allende, "Something Magic in Storytelling" interview by Jan Goggans (1994), in *Conversations with Isabel Allende,* ed. John Rodden (Austin: University of Texas Press, 1999), 326; and Allende, 1994c, 396.

20. Richard Cott, *Guerrilla Movements in Latin America* (Garden City, N.Y.: Doubleday and Company, 1971), 137; hereafter cited in the text.

21. José Otero, "La historia como ficción en *Eva Luna* de Isabel Allende," *Confluencia* 4, no. 1 (1988): 61.

22. Daniel H. Levine, *Conflict and Political Change in Venezuela* (Princeton, N.J.: Princeton University Press, 1973), 60.

23. Eliana S. Rivero, "Scheherazade Liberated: *Eva Luna* and Women Storytellers," in *Splintering Darkness: Latin American Women Writers in Search of Themselves,* ed. Lucía Guerra-Cunningham (Pittsburgh, Pa.: Latin American Literary Review Press, 1991), 156. Rivero cites Allende as commenting that *Eva Luna* was originally entitled "Bolero" until a novel with the same title was published by the Cuban author Lisandro Otero.

24. William Rowe and Vivian Schelling, *Memory and Modernity: Popular Culture in Latin America* (London: Verso, 1991), 232; hereafter cited in the text.

25. Linda J. Craft, *"Testinovela/Telenovela:* Latin American Popular Culture and Women's Narrative," *Indiana Journal of Hispanic Literatures* 8 (1996): 202.

26. For the relationship between popular music and collective memory, see Luis Rafael Sánchez, "Que viva la música popular," in *Proyecciones sobre la novela: Actas del XIV Congreso de Literatura Latinoamericana,* ed. Linda Gould Levine and Ellen Engelson Marson (Hanover, N.H.: Ediciones del Norte, 1997), 24.

27. Allende has indicated that she would love to write a soap opera, but would not want to be limited by the "formula." See Allende, 1991d, 221.

Chapter Five

1. Walter Benjamin, *Illuminations: Essays and Reflections,* ed. Hannah Arendt (New York: Harcourt, Brace and World, 1968), 87; hereafter cited in the text.

2. Isabel Allende, "An Overwhelming Passion to Tell the Story," interview by Elsye Crystall, Jill Kuhnheim, and Mary Layoun (1992), in *Conversations with Isabel Allende,* ed. John Rodden (Austin: University of Texas Press, 1999), 288; hereafter cited in the text as Allende, 1992b.

3. Isabel Allende, "An Interview with Isabel Allende: Love, Life and Art in a Time of Turmoil," interview by Margaret Munro-Clark, *Antípodas* 6–7 (1994–1995): 17.

4. Robert Alter, *Partial Magic: The Novel as a Self-Conscious Genre* (Berkeley: University of California Press, 1975), 79; hereafter cited in the text. Alter paraphrases Diderot on storytelling.

5. Isabel Allende, foreword to *Short Stories by Latin American Women: The Magic and the Real,* ed. Celia Correas de Zapata (Houston: Arte Público Press, 1990), 5; hereafter cited in the text as Allende, 1990.

6. Edgar Allan Poe, "On the Aim and Technique of the Short Story," in *What is the Short Story?,* ed. Eugene Current-García and Walton R. Patrick (Glenview, Ill.: Scott, Foresman and Company, 1968), 8. See also Allende, 1990, 5.

7. Isabel Allende, "Of Love and Truth," Interview by Inés Dölz-Blackburn, George McMurray, Paul Rea, and Alfonso Rodríguez (1990), in *Conversations with Isabel Allende,* ed. John Rodden (Austin: University of Texas Press, 1999), 152.

8. George R. McMurray, "The Spanish American Short Story from Borges to the Present," in *The Latin American Short Story: A Critical History,* ed. Margaret Sayers Peden (New York: Twayne, 1983), 97; hereafter cited in the text.

9. Robert Irwin, *The Arabian Nights: A Companion* (New York: Penguin Press, 1994), 283.

10.   Allende, 1985, 447–48; the translation is mine. See also *EL,* 72 and Isabel Allende, *The Stories of Eva Luna,* trans. Margaret Sayers Peden (New York: Bantam Books, 1992), 12; hereafter cited in the text as *SEL.*

11.   Allende has movingly commented in the following way on the relationship between her daughter, Paula, and Omaira Sánchez: "[W]hen I think of my daughter, I always think that maybe some place she walks hands in hand with Omaira Sánchez. Her story and the fact that her eyes haunted me for so many years was a premonition. Life was telling me that I was going to have to go through this, and that man holding Omaira Sánchez was me holding my daughter, years later. That man helping her into death is me helping my daughter into death." See Isabel Allende, "Something Magic in the Storytelling," interview by Jan Goggans (1994), in *Conversations with Isabel Allende,* ed. John Rodden (Austin: University of Texas Press, 1999), 329–30.

12.   For the origin of this story, see Isabel Allende, "Writing to Exorcise the Demons," interview by Farhat Iftekharuddin (1997), in *Conversations with Isabel Allende,* ed. John Rodden (Austin: University of Texas Press, 1999), 357.

13.   Julia Kristeva, "Oscillation between Power and Denial," trans. Marilyn A. August, in *New French Feminisms: An Anthology,* ed. Elaine Marks and Isabelle de Courtivron (New York: Schocken Books, 1981), 165–66.

14.   Luce Irigaray, *This Sex Which Is Not One,* trans. Catherine Porter (Ithaca, N.Y.: Cornell University Press, 1985), 187.

15.   Patricia Hart, "Magic Feminism in Isabel Allende's *The Stories of Eva Luna,*" in *Multicultural Literatures through Feminist/Poststructuralist Lenses,* ed. Barbara Frey Waxman (Knoxville: University of Tennessee Press, 1993), 109. Hart also discusses "Toad's Mouth" as a parody of the Cinderella myth (107).

16.   Jane Gallop, *The Daughter's Seduction: Feminism and Psychoanalysis* (Ithaca, N.Y.: Cornell University Press, 1982), 89; hereafter cited in the text.

17.   Jessica Benjamin, "A Desire of One's Own: Psychoanalytic Feminism and Intersubjective Space," in *Feminist Studies: Critical Studies,* ed. Teresa de Lauretis (Bloomington: University of Indiana Press, 1986), 84.

18.   Sylvia G. Carullo, "Fetishism, Love-Magic and Erotic Love in Two Stories by Isabel Allende," trans. James A. Dunlop, *Readerly/Writerly Texts* 3, no. 1 (1995): 195.

19.   Isabel Allende, *The Woman's Voice in Latin American Literature,* 56 min., Princeton, N.J., Films for the Humanities and Sciences, 1991, videocassette.

Chapter Six

1.   Also see Allende, 1994a, 371–72.

2.   Alice Walker, Isabel Allende, and Jean Shinoda Bolen, *Giving Birth, Giving Form,* audiotape of discussion held at Grace Cathedral, San Francisco, 23 January 1993.

3. Catherine R. Perricone, *"El plan infinito:* Isabel Allende's New World," *Secolas Annals* 25 (1994): 60; hereafter cited in the text as Perricone, 1994.

4. Isabel Allende, "Poets and Writers," Interview by Barbara Szerlip, *Poets & Writers Magazine,* Jan.-Feb. 1993, 54; hereafter cited in the text as Allende, 1993c.

5. Isabel Allende, *The Infinite Plan,* trans. Margaret Sayers Peden (New York: HarperCollins, 1993), 6; hereafter cited in the text as *IP.*

6. Adriana Castillo de Berchenko, "La inversión de los tópicos: *El plan infinito* de Isabel Allende," *Etats-Unis/Mexique: Fascinations et répulsions récipro- ques,* ed. Serge Ricard (Paris, France: Hermattan, 1996), 161; hereafter cited in the text.

7. Gloria Anzaldúa, *Borderlands/La Frontera: The New Mestiza* (San Francisco: Aunte Lute Books, 1987), preface; hereafter cited in the text..

8. James Diego Vigil, *Barrio Gangs: Street Life and Identity in Southern California* (Austin: University of Texas Press, 1988), 1; hereafter cited in the text.

9. Antonio Gramsci is cited in Kathleen Weiler, *Women Teaching for Change: Gender, Class and Power* (New York: Bergin and Garvey, 1988), 74. All other references to this book cited in the text are to Weiler.

10. Sandra Cisneros, *The House on Mango Street* (New York: Vintage Books, 1989), 88.

11. Susan Frenk, "The Wandering Text: Situating the Narratives of Isabel Allende," in *Latin American Women's Writing: Feminist Readings in Theory and Crisis,* ed. Anny Brooksbank Jones and Catherine Davies (New York: Oxford University Press, 1996), 78.

12. See W. J. Rorabaugh, *Berkeley at War: The 1960s* (New York: Oxford University Press, 1989), 113–14, 123.

13. Anne E. Brown and Marjanne E. Goozé, "Introduction: Placing Identity in Cross-Cultural Perspective," in *International Women's Writing: New Landscapes of Identity,* ed. Anne E. Brown and Marjanne E. Goozé (Westport, Conn.: Greenwood Press, 1995), xix.

14. Sandra M. Gilbert and Susan Gubar, *No Man's Land: The Place of the Woman Writer in the Twentieth Century,* vol. 1, *The War of the Words* (New Haven, Conn.: Yale University Press, 1988), 241.

15. Tim O'Brien, *The Things They Carried* (New York: Penguin Books, 1991), 123; hereafter cited in the text.

16. Rubén L. Gómez, "La maternidad en la obra de Allende: 'una histo- ria inacabable de dolor, de sangre y de amor,'" in *Narrativa hispanoamericana contemporánea: entre la vanguardia y el posboom,* ed. Ana María Hernández de López (Madrid: Editorial Pliegos, 1996), 288.

17. Robert Alter, *Partial Magic: The Novel as a Self-Conscious Genre* (Berkeley: University of California Press, 1975), 239.

18. Isabel Allende, "Writing as an Act of Hope," in *Paths of Resistance,* ed. William Zinsser (Boston: Houghton Mifflin, 1989), 45.

19. Allende has commented that there "really is a man who invented a religion called 'The Infinite Plan.'" See Isabel Allende, "The Writer as Exile, and Her Search for Home," interview by John Rodden, in *Conversations with Isabel Allende,* ed. John Rodden (Austin: University of Texas Press, 1999), 436.

Chapter Seven

1. Catherine R. Perricone, "Genre and Metarealism in Allende's *Paula,*" *Hispania* 42, no. 81 (1998): 42; hereafter cited in the text as Perricone, 1998.

2. Sidonie Smith, *A Poetics of Women's Autobiography: Marginality and the Fiction of Self-Representation* (Bloomington: Indiana University Press, 1987), 46; hereafter cited in the text. Smith cites here from Francis R. Hart.

3. Janet Varner Gunn, *Autobiography: Toward a Poetics of Experience* (Philadelphia: University of Pennsylvania Press, 1982), 8; hereafter cited in the text.

4. Janice Haaken, *Pilar of Salt: Gender, Memory, and the Perils of Looking Back* (New Brunswick, N.J.: Rutgers University Press, 1998), 14; hereafter cited in the text. This chapter borrows from Haaken's suggestive image of Lot's wife looking back.

5. Estelle C. Jelinek, *The Tradition of Women's Autobiography: From Antiquity to the Present* (Boston: Twayne, 1986), 3; hereafter cited in the text. Jelinek cites here from James Olney.

6. Isabel Allende, "Modern Politics, Modern Fables," interview by Alvin P. Sanoff (1988), in *Conversations with Isabel Allende,* ed. John Rodden (Austin: University of Texas Press, 1999), 104.

7. Sylvia Molloy, *At Face Value: Autobiographical Writing in Spanish America* (Cambridge: Cambridge University Press, 1991), 7; hereafter cited in the text.

8. Isabel Allende, "A Mother's Letter of Loss," interview by Rosa Pinol (1995), in *Conversations with Isabel Allende,* ed. John Rodden (Austin: University of Texas Press, 1999), 401.

9. Isabel Allende, "Listen, Paula," interview by Alfred Starkmann (1995), trans. John Rodden, in *Conversations with Isabel Allende,* ed. John Rodden (Austin: University of Texas Press, 1999), 407. Also see Rodden, xvii.

10. Maria DiBattista, *"Paula,"* *Review: Latin American Literature & Arts* 52 (Spring 1995): 105; hereafter cited the text.

11. Isabel Allende, "I Remember Emotions, I Remember Moments," interview by Virginia Invernizzi (1995), in *Conversations with Isabel Allende,* ed. John Rodden (Austin: University of Texas Press, 1999), 443; hereafter cited in the text as Allende, 1995.

12. Smith paraphrases here the theory of Domna Stanton.

13. For a discussion of this aspect, see Verónica Cortínez, *"Paula:* memorias en silencio," *Antípodas: Journal of Hispanic Studies of Australia and New Zealand* 6–7 (1994–1995): 63; hereafter cited in the text.

14. Isabel Allende, "An Interview with Isabel Allende: Love, Life and Art in a Time of Turmoil," interview by Margaret Munro-Clark, *Antípodas: Journal of Hispanic Studies of Australia and New Zealand* 6–7 (1994–1995): 23.

Chapter Eight

1. *Aphrodite: A Memoir of the Senses,* unlike other books by Allende, is the result of a collaborative effort. It includes drawings by Allende's friend Robert Shekter and recipes provided by her mother, Panchita Llona.

2. John Rodden, "Introduction: 'I Am Inventing Myself All the Time': Isabel Allende in Her Interviews," in *Conversations with Isabel Allende,* ed. John Rodden (Austin: University of Texas Press, 1999), 25; hereafter cited in the text.

3. Isabel Allende, *Daughter of Fortune,* trans. Margaret Sayers Peden (New York: HarperCollins, 1999); hereafter cited in the text as *DF.*

4. Isabel Allende, interview by Oprah Winfrey, *Oprah Winfrey Show,* "Book Club, *Daughter of Fortune,*" 28 March 2000 (Chicago: Harpo Productions), 10; hereafter cited in the text as Allende, 2000a.

5. Georg Lukács, *The Historical Novel,* trans. Hannah and Stanley Mitchell (New York: Humanities Press, 1965), 43.

6. Noé Jitrik, "De la historia a la escritura: predominios, disimetrías, acuerdos en la novela histórica latinoamericana," in *The Historical Novel in Latin America: A Symposium,* ed. Daniel Balderston (Gaithersburg, Md.: Ediciones Hispamérica, 1986), 22. Jitrik summarizes the ideas of the Latin American writer José María Heredia.

7. Michael Kowalewski, "Introduction," in *Gold Rush: A Literary Exploration,* ed. Michael Kowalewski (Berkeley: Heyday Books, 1997), xvii; hereafter cited in the text.

8. There is an interesting relationship between Eliza's nursing of the she-goat and a story by Bret Harte, "The Luck of Roaring Camp," situated in the time of the gold rush. A group of miners decides to adopt the son of a woman of ill repute who dies in childbirth. Lacking a wet nurse for the boy, they use Jinny the ass to nurse the child, who thrives from such good nursing. This story is included in Kowalewski, 351–60. Allende indicated to me in a telephone interview included in this volume that she read Harte's short story after she thought of the idea of a she-goat nursing Eliza (Allende, 2000b). The name Eliza also evokes the name of feminist-abolitionist Eliza Farnham, who arrived in San Francisco in 1849 and wrote about the gold rushers' lack of regard for women (see Kowalewski, 314–17).

9. Doris Sommer, "Not Just Any Narrative: How Love Can Romance Us to Death," in *The Historical Novel in Latin America: A Symposium,* ed. Daniel Balderston (Gaithersburg, Md.: Ediciones Hispamérica, 1986), 56.

10. Mark Twain, *Roughing It,* in *Gold Rush: A Literary Exploration,* ed. Michael Kowalewski (Berkeley: Heyday Books, 1997), 362.

11. Linda Alcoff, "Cultural Feminism versus Post-Structuralism: The Identity Crisis in Feminist Theory," in *Feminist Theory: A Reader,* ed. Wendy

Kolmar and Frances Bartkowski (Mountain View, Calif.: Mayfied Publishing, 2000), 413.

12. Rachel Blau DuPlessis, *Writing beyond the Ending: Narrative Strategies of Twentieth-Century Women Writers* (Bloomington: Indiana University Press, 1985), 3–4; hereafter cited in the text.

13. Statistics indicate that among the 5,677 male immigrants to California from April to June 1849, 1,360 of them were Chileans. See Steve Giacobbi, *Chile and Her Argonauts in the Gold Rush, 1848–1856* (San Francisco: R and E Research Associates, 1974), 18.

14. Jay Monaghan, *Chile, Peru, and the California Gold Rush of 1849* (Berkeley: University of California Press, 1973), 215; hereafter cited in the text.

15. Joseph Henry Jackson, introduction to *The Life and Adventures of Joaquín Murieta: The Celebrated California Bandit*, by John Rollin Ridge (Yellow Bird) (Norman: University of Oklahoma Press, 1955), xxii; hereafter cited in the text.

16. John Rollin Ridge, *The Life and Adventures of Joaquín Murieta: The Celebrated California Bandit* (Norman: University of Oklahoma Press, 1955). In his introduction to Ridge's novel, Jackson suggests that Ridge appropriated some of the material for his book from the *Shirley Letters* of Dame Shirley (xxxi).

17. Pablo Neruda, *Splendor and Death of Joaquín Murieta*, trans. Ben Belitt (New York: Farrar, Strauss and Giroux, 1972); hereafter cited in the text. Among other books by Chilean writers and historians who make a similar claim for the reality of Joaquín Murieta, Monaghan mentions *Forjadores de Chile*, by the historian Ramón Pérez Yáñez (218–19).

18. It is interesting to note that Joaquín Murieta's death is cited as 25 July 1853 in Ridge's novel, 24 July in Allende's, 23 July in the original Spanish version of Neruda's play, and 24 July on the back cover of the English translation of Neruda's work.

19. Czeslaw Milosz, "On the Western," in *Gold Rush: A Literary Exploration,* ed. Michael Kowalewski (Berkeley: Heyday Books, 1997), 445; hereafter cited in the text.

20. Stephen Karcher, *How to Use the I Ching: A Guide to the Ancient Oracle of Change* (Boston: Element Books, 1997), 5.

21. Tao Chi'en's decision to keep his hair short is especially significant because, as researchers have documented with regard to the Chinese immigrant in California, "The loss of his queue placed him in a dubious position in the eyes of his fellow countrymen; it would not be known without explanation whether it was evidence of his having served a prison term or of his having voluntarily adopted the American style of hairdressing." Pauline Minke, *Chinese in the Mother Lode, 1850–1870* (San Francisco: R and E Research Associates, 1974), 4.

22. Jacqueline Baker Barnhart, *The Fair but Frail: Prostitution in San Francisco, 1849–1900* (Reno: University of Nevada Press, 1986), 15.

23. Judy Yung, *Unbound Feet: A Social History of Chinese Women in San Francisco* (Berkeley: University of California Press, 1995), 31–32; hereafter cited in the text.

24.   Allende's "singsong girls" are at the bottom of the social hierarchy in the world of Chinese prostitution in California. The description of their harsh reality in *Daughter of Fortune* seems to correspond more to the fate of the prostitutes confined to narrow cribs or shacks and forced to repeat the cry of "Two bittee lookee, flo bittee feelee, six bittee doee" to passersby. Yung notes that the sing-song girls who sang, conversed, drank, and flattered were primarily in parlor houses, many of which were quite luxurious (28–29).

25.   Lucie Cheng Hirata, "Free, Indentured, Enslaved: Chinese Prostitutes in Nineteenth-Century America," *Signs: Journal of Women in Culture and Society* 5, no. 1 (1979), 7.

26.   The Quaker blacksmith James Morton may well be inspired by a good friend of Allende, whom she describes in *Aphrodite* as "a burly, bearded descendant of Quaker blacksmiths" (33).

27.   One novel based on the life of a real Chinese woman whose family sold her and sent her to California in the 1870s is *One Thousand Pieces of Gold*, by Ruthanne Lum McCunn (Boston: Beacon Press, 1981).

28.   Allende has commented in an interview, "I really would like to write erotic novels. Unfortunately I was raised as a Catholic, and my mother is still alive, so it's difficult." Isabel Allende, "Writing to Exorcise the Demons," interview by Farhat Iftekharuddin (1997), in *Conversations with Isabel Allende*, ed. John Rodden (Austin: University of Texas Press, 1999), 358.

29.   Isabel Allende, letter to the author, 24 June 1999. Allende wrote that "the open ending is an invitation to the second part."

30.   Isabel Allende, reading and discussion of *Daughter of Fortune*, New York, N.Y., 18 October 1999.

31.   Allende has indicated in various interviews that she does believe "that there is a destiny" or karma and that "you can do much to modify it." See Allende, 1994a, 374.

Chapter Nine

1.   Isabel Allende, *Portrait in Sepia*, trans. Margaret Sayers Peden (New York: HarperCollins, 2001). Allende's novel reached my hands as I was completing the manuscript for this book. Allende very kindly sent me a copy of the original Spanish version in galley proofs so that I could include it as a final chapter. Because of lack of time, the analysis I provide does not do full justice to the novel. The English translation of *Portrait in Sepia* was published when my manuscript was in its final stage; hence, all translations are from Peden.

2.   Isabel Allende, "Isabel Allende Unveiled," interview by Douglas Foster (1988), in *Conversations with Isabel Allende*, ed. John Rodden (Austin: University of Texas Press, 1999), 107.

3.   Iquique was the principal nitrate port of Chile at the beginning of the twentieth century. In 1907, thousands of striking nitrate workers and their families sought redress for their grievances and were attacked by the troops of

the local military commander. It is estimated that hundreds were killed. See Simon Collier and William F. Sater, *A History of Chile, 1808–1994* (Cambridge: Cambridge University Press, 1996), 196.

4. Lucy Cheng Hirata, "Free, Indentured, Enslaved: Chinese Prostitutes in Nineteenth-Century America," *Signs: Journal of Women in Culture and Society* 5, no. 1 (1979): 27.

5. Although Severo does indeed return home safely from the Civil War, he also returns minus one leg. After their marriage, Nívea's passionate and ingenious acrobatic lovemaking works miracles on Severo's weakened body and within months he is able to walk with the help of a crutch and an artificial leg. Allende's readers may well wonder why Severo appears intact with two legs in *The House of the Spirits.* Allende has humorously commented with regard to this one leg/two leg discrepancy that she should have reread *The House of the Spirits* before writing *Portrait in Sepia* and that she is not sure how she is "going to get out of that one." Isabel Allende, interview by Mirta Ojito, New York, 3 November 2001; hereafter cited in the text as Allende, 2001.

6. Elena Poniatowska, *Tinísima* (Mexico: Ediciones Era, 1991), 178. I am also indebted to Helene M. Anderson's penetrating analysis, "*Tinísima:* imagen y discurso en la obra de Elena Poniatowska," in *Proyecciones sobre la novela,* ed. Linda Gould Levine and Ellen Engelson Marson (Hanover, N.H.: Ediciones del Norte, 1997), 61–74.

7. Susan Sontag, *On Photography* (New York: Farrar, Strauss and Giroux, 1977), 15.

Conclusion

1. Isabel Allende, "The Shaman and the Infidel," interview by Marilyn Berlin Snell (1991), in *Conversations with Isabel Allende,* ed. John Rodden (Austin: University of Texas Press, 1999), 244.

2. In an appearance in New York (Allende, 2001), Allende stated that she had completed her new book of young adult fiction. It is entitled *La ciudad de las bestias* (The city of the beasts) and will be published in 2002 by Plaza & Janés Editores.

3. Isabel Allende, acceptance speech of Dorothy and Lillian Gish Prize, New York, N.Y., 13 October 1998.

4. Pete Hamill, introduction of Isabel Allende, Dorothy and Lillian Gish Prize awards ceremony, New York, N.Y., 13 October 1998.

Interview

1. Isabel Allende's Web site address is <www.isabelallende.com>.

Selected Bibliography

Primary Works

Novels

La casa de los espíritus. Barcelona: Plaza & Janés Editores, 1982.
De amor y de sombra. Barcelona: Plaza & Janés Editores, 1984.
Eva Luna. Barcelona: Plaza & Janés Editores, 1987.
Hija de la fortuna. Barcelona: Plaza & Janés Editores, 1999.
El plan infinito. Buenos Aires: Editorial Sudamericana; Barcelona: Plaza & Janés Editores, 1991.
Retrato en sepia. Santiago and Buenos Aires: Editorial Sudamericana; Barcelona: Plaza & Janés, 2000.

Memoir

Paula. Buenos Aires: Editorial Sudamericana; Barcelona: Plaza & Janés Editores, 1994.

Short Stories

Cuentos de Eva Luna. Buenos Aires: Editorial Sudamericana; Barcelona: Plaza & Janés Editores, 1989.
La gorda de porcelana. Madrid: Alfaguara, 1984.

Nonfiction

Afrodita: Cuentos, recetas y otros afrodisíacos. Barcelona: Plaza & Janés Editores, 1997. [Drawings by Robert Shekter. Recipes by Panchita Llona.]
Civilice a su troglodita: Los impertinentes de Isabel Allende. Santiago: Editorial Lord Cochrane, 1974.

Essays and Articles

"Los libros tienen sus propios espíritus." In *Los libros tienen sus propios espíritus: Estudios sobre Isabel Allende,* ed. Marcelo Coddou, 15–20. Mexico: Universidad Veracruzana, 1986.
"La magia de las palabras." *Revista Iberoamericana* 51, no. 132–33 (1985): 447–52.
"Pinochet Without Hatred." *New York Times Magazine,* 17 January 1999, 24–27.

"Writing as an Act of Hope." In *Paths of Resistance,* ed. William Zinsser, 41–63. Boston: Houghton Mifflin, 1989.

Forewords (Selected)

Foreword to *Short Stories by Latin American Women,* ed. Alberto Manguel, xiii. New York: Clarkson N. Potter, 1986.
Foreword to *Short Stories by Latin American Women: The Magic and the Real,* ed. Celia Correas Zapata, 5–6. Houston: Arte Público Press, 1990.
Foreword to *Conversations with Isabel Allende,* ed. John Rodden, ix–xi. Austin: University of Texas Press, 1999.
"Unas palabras a modo de explicación. . . ." In *Isabel Allende: vida y espíritus,* by Celia Correas Zapata, 9–16. Barcelona: Plaza & Janés Editores, 1998.

Other

The Woman's Voice in Latin American Literature. 56 min. Princeton, N.J., Films for the Humanities and Sciences, 1991, Videocassette.

English Translations

Aphrodite. A Memoir of the Senses. Trans. Margaret Sayers Peden. New York: HarperFlamingo, 1998. [Drawings by Robert Shekter. Recipes by Panchita Llona.]
Daughter of Fortune. Trans. Margaret Sayers Peden. New York: HarperCollins, 1999.
Eva Luna. Trans. Margaret Sayers Peden. New York: Alfred A. Knopf, 1988. New York: Bantam Books, 1989.
The House of the Spirits. Trans. Magda Bogin. New York: Alfred A. Knopf, 1985.
The Infinite Plan. Trans. Margaret Sayers Peden. New York: HarperCollins 1993. New York: HarperPerennial, 1994.
Of Love and Shadows. Trans. Margaret Sayers Peden. New York: Alfred A. Knopf, 1987. New York: Bantam Books, 1988.
Paula. Trans. Margaret Sayers Peden. New York: HarperCollins, 1995. New York: HarperPerennial, 1996.
Portrait in Sepia. Trans. Margaret Sayers Peden. New York: HarperCollins, 2001.
The Stories of Eva Luna. Trans. Margaret Sayers Peden. New York: Atheneum, 1991. New York: Bantam Books, 1992.

Secondary Works

Books

Anzaldúa, Gloria. *Borderlands/La Frontera: The New Mestiza.* San Francisco: Aunte Lute Books, 1987. Excellent and creative analysis of the experience of living between two cultures; very useful for understanding aspects of *The Infinite Plan.*

Castro-Klarén, Sara, Sylvia Molloy, and Beatriz Sarlo, eds. *Women's Writing in Latin American: An Anthology.* Boulder, Colo.: Westview Press, 1991. Valuable collection of writings by major Latin American authors with introductory essays by the three editors dealing with theoretical concerns in women's writing.

Castillo de Berchenko, Adriana, ed. *La narrativa de Isabel Allende: Claves de una marginalidad.* Perpignan, France: Université de Perpignan, 1990. Collection of essays that addresses Allende's first three novels and offers considerations about "the Allende phenomenon." Includes critical bibliography up to 1989.

Castillo, Debra A. *Talking Back: Toward a Latin American Feminist Literary Criticism.* Ithaca, N.Y.: Cornell University Press, 1992. A valuable source for understanding theoretical concerns of Latin American women writers and the various strategies they use to talk back. Although this volume does not deal specifically with Allende's work, many of the strategies and themes discussed are a springboard for analyzing her writings.

Coddou, Marcelo, ed. *Los libros tienen sus propios espíritus: Estudios sobre Isabel Allende.* Mexico: Universidad Veracruzana, 1986. The first collection of essays on Allende's *House of the Spirits,* including an essay by Allende herself and informative articles on a wide range of topics by noted scholars.

Correas Zapata, Celia. *Isabel Allende: Vida y espíritus.* Barcelona: Plaza & Janés Editores, 1998. An insightful and highly readable book that combines interviews with the author on her novels and her life together with observations of a personal and literary nature by Correas Zapata.

Galeano, Eduardo. *Memory of Fire. III. Century of the Wind.* Translated by Cedric Belfrage. New York: Pantheon Books, 1988. Includes incisive and highly political snapshots of major events in Chile from 1970 to 1973.

Galarce, Carmen J. *La novela chilena del exilio (1973–1987): El caso de Isabel Allende.* Santiago: Universidad de Chile, 1994. A very useful description of the different stages of the Chilean novel of exile and the importance of Allende's first three novels within this context.

Hart, Patricia. *Narrative Magic in the Fiction of Isabel Allende.* Cranbury, N.J.: Associated University Presses, 1989. One of the first books written about Allende. Hart adeptly coins the phrase "magical feminism" to describe the blending of magical realism and "feminocentric" concerns in Allende's fiction.

Jones, Anny Brooksbank, and Catherine Davies, eds. *Latin American Women's Writings: Feminist Readings in Theory and Crisis.* New York: Oxford University Press, 1996. Excellent introductory essay by the two co-editors provides a concise and readable review of major theories of Latin American feminist criticism. Particularly useful essays by Susan Frenk and Jean Franco address such issues as Allende's portrayal of family romance, female pleasure, and empowerment, as well as considerations about the relationship between Allende's writing and mass market appeal. Other essays of value about contemporary authors.

Kaminsky, Amy K. *Reading the Body Politic: Feminist Criticism and Latin American Women Writers*. Minneapolis: University of Minnesota Press, 1993. A perceptive and politicized reading of Latin American women's writings that highlights the need to consider the relationship among gender oppression, sexual repression, and issues of economic and political dependency in the construction and representation of women's lives in literature and literary criticism.

Kowalewski, Michael, ed. *Gold Rush: A Literary Exploration*. Berkeley: Heyday Books, 1997. Wide range of writings with excellent introductions by Kowalewski on the gold rush experience. Very valuable for understanding *Daughter of Fortune*.

Martin, Gerald. *Journeys through the Labyrinth: Latin American Fiction in the Twentieth Century*. London: Verso, 1989. Excellent background on the contemporary novel.

Molloy, Sylvia. *At Face Value: Autobiographical Writing in Spanish America*. Cambridge: Cambridge University Press, 1991. Excellent presentation of theoretical concerns in autobiographical writings of the nineteenth and twentieth centuries, with emphasis on the blend of the personal self and the communal self, and individual concerns and a testimonial imperative.

Pacheco, Máximo. *Lonquén*. Santiago: Editorial Aconcagua, 1980, 1983. Fascinating account, complete with documents, witness reports, church statements, and editorials concerning the events that inspired *Of Love and Shadows*.

Riquelme Rojas, Sonia, and Edna Aguirre Rehbein, eds. *Critical Approaches to Isabel Allende's Novels*. New York: Peter Lang, 1991. Excellent collection of essays of a varied nature dealing with diverse themes and narrative strategies in *The House of the Spirits*, *Of Love and Shadows*, and *Eva Luna*.

Rodden, John, ed. *Conversations with Isabel Allende*. Austin: University of Texas Press, 1999. Invaluable collection of more than 30 interviews with Isabel Allende spanning a 10-year period. It gathers together in one volume important interviews previously published in a wide variety of journals. Excellent introduction by Rodden, useful chronology, and selected bibliography.

Rowe, William, and Vivian Schelling. *Memory and Modernity: Popular Culture in Latin America*. London: Verso, 1991. An excellent and readable discussion of various forms of popular culture and the "culture industry" in Latin America.

Zamora, Lois Parkinson, and Wendy B. Faris, eds. *Magical Realism: Theory, History, Community*. Durham, N.C.: Duke University Press, 1995. Useful introductory essay by the two co-editors that defines magical realism and situates it in Latin American and international contexts. Interesting essays on a wide range of international writers. Perceptive analysis by P. Gabrielle Foreman on the relationship between the magical and the historical in *The House of the Spirits*. Valuable contribution by Faris on magical realism and postmodern fiction in general.

Book Chapters and Articles

Antoni, Robert. "Parody or Piracy: The Relationship of *The House of the Spirits* to *One Hundred Years of Solitude*." *Latin American Literary Review* 16, no. 32 (1988): 16–28. Interesting discussion of Allende's first novel as a parody, though not a conscious one, of García Márquez's novel, with a useful Bahktin-inspired analysis of the discursive practices of Allende's text.

Chuchryk, Patricia M. "From Dictatorship to Democracy: The Women's Movement in Chile." In *The Women's Movement in Latin America: Participation and Democracy*, ed. Jane S. Jacquette, 65–107. Boulder, Colo.: Westview Press, 1994. Excellent overview of women's groups and their theoretical and practical concerns and organizations from 1973 to 1992.

Franco, Jean. "Going Public: Reinhabiting the Private." In *On Edge: The Crisis of Contemporary Latin American Culture*, ed. George Yúdice, Jean Franco, and Juan Flores, 65–83. Minneapolis: University of Minnesota Press, 1992. Interesting reflections on Latin American women writers and the transformation of public space, the relationship between testimonial literature and the public sphere, the international marketing of Latin American literature, and Allende's role in this endeavor; suggests a critique of Allende's popularized writing.

Hart, Patricia. "Magic Feminism in Isabel Allende's *The Stories of Eva Luna*." In *Multicultural Literatures through Feminist/Poststructuralist Lenses*, ed. Barbara Frey Waxman, 103–36. Knoxville: University of Tennessee Press, 1993. Interesting analysis that discusses Allende's use of magic feminism to create unusual perspectives in her stories toward such pressing social issues as rape and prostitution.

Jenkins, Ruth Y. "Authorizing Female Voice and Experience: Ghosts and Spirits in Kingston's *The Woman Warrior* and Allende's *The House of the Spirits*." *MELUS: The Journal of the Society for the Study of the Multi-Ethnic Literature of the United States* 19, no. 3 (1994): 61–73. Comparative approach that highlights the subversive value of female silence.

Laurila, Marketta. "Isabel Allende and the Discourse of Exile." In *International Women's Writings: New Landscapes of Identity*, ed. Anne E. Brown and Marjanne E. Goozé, 177–86. Westport, Conn.: Greenwood Press, 1995. Analysis of the trajectory of exile in Allende's first three novels.

Levine, Linda Gould. "A Passage to Androgyny: Isabel Allende's *La casa de los espíritus*. In *In the Feminine Mode: Essays on Hispanic Women Writers*, edited by Noël Valis and Carol Maier, 164–73. Cranbury, N.J.: Associated University Presses, 1990. Analyzes Allende's subversion of monolithic categories of gender through her creative fusion of opposites, including books, authors, narrative strategies, double-voiced discourse, characters, and events.

Marcos, Juan Manuel. "El género popular como meta-estructura textual del post-boom latinoamericano." *Monographic Review/Revista Monográfica* 3, no. 1–2 (1987): 268–78. Useful analysis and vindication of aspects of popular culture in post-Boom literature.

Meyer, Doris. " 'Parenting the Text': Female Creativity and Dialogic Relationships in Isabel Allende's *La casa de los espíritus.*" *Hispania* 73 (1990): 360–65. Interesting examination of the novel as a "polyvocal feminist text" with different levels of female empowerment and rebirth.

Moody, Michael. "Isabel Allende and the Testimonial Novel." *Confluencia* 2, no. 1 (1986): 39–43. Very useful in providing the political background of *Of Love and Shadows.* No definition of testimonial literature is provided, although it is frequently mentioned.

Moore, Pamela. "Testing the Terms: 'Woman' in *The House of Spirits* and *One Hundred Years of Solitude.*" *The Comparatist* 18 (1994): 90–100. Useful discussion of the relationship between masculine and feminine history in the two novels.

Mora, Gabriela. "Las novelas de Isabel Allende y el papel de la mujer como cuidadana." *Ideologies and Literature* 2, no. 1 (1987): 53–61. Interesting and polemical analysis of Allende's first two novels. Mora evaluates their shortcomings in contributing to a progressive political and cultural agenda.

Rojas, Mario. " '*La casa de los espíritus*' de Isabel Allende: un caleidoscopio de espejos desordenados." *Revista Iberoamericana* 51, no. 132–33 (1985): 917–25. Useful examination of *The House of the Spirits* as a "feminocentric" novel and of the kaleidoscope as a central metaphor that unites different aspects of the novel.

Shea, Maureen E. "Love, Eroticism, and Pornography in the Works of Isabel Allende." *Women's Studies* 18, no. 2–3 (1991): 223–31. Analyzes the conflict between the forces of Eros and Thanatos in Allende's first three novels and the triumph of Eros, defined as the "life-force in the form of mothering" in opposition to Thanatos represented by patriarchy.

Skidmore, Thomas E., and Peter H. Smith. "Chile, Democracy, Socialism, and Repression." In *Modern Latin America,* ed. Thomas E. Skidmore and Peter H. Smith, 113–44. New York: Oxford University Press, 1984. Contains excellent background information on Chilean politics from the nineteenth century to the 1980s with special emphasis on Salvador Allende's government.

Subercaseaux, Bernardo. "Notas sobre autoritarismo y lectura en Chile." In *Fascismo y experiencia literaria: Reflexiones para una recanonización,* ed. Hernán Vidal, 384–403. Minneapolis: Institute for the Study of Ideologies and Literature, 1985. Excellent description of three stages in Chilean political and cultural life from the military coup to the 1980s and the relationship between political vigilance and cultural practices.

Swanson, Philip. "Tyrants and Trash: Sex, Class and Culture in *La casa de los espíritus.*" *Bulletin of Hispanic Studies* 71, no. 2 (1994): 217–37. Very interesting analysis of the relationship between issues of class and gender in *The House of the Spirits* and of the role of a political narrative earmarked for a broad reading public.

Index

The Author

Linda Gould Levine is Professor of Spanish at Montclair State University (New Jersey), where she has also directed the Women's Studies program. She received her Ph.D. from Harvard University and has also taught at Rutgers University and Dartmouth College. Her areas of specialization are contemporary Spanish literature and women writers from Spain and Latin America. She is the author of *Juan Goytisolo: la destrucción creadora* (1976) and a critical edition of Juan Goytisolo's novel *Reivindicación del Conde don Julián* (1986). She is coauthor with Gloria Feiman Waldman of *Feminismo ante el franquismo: entrevistas con feministas de España* (1980) and coeditor with Gloria Feiman Waldman and Ellen Engelson Marson of *Spanish Women Writers: A Bio-Bibliographical Source Book* (1993). She is also coeditor with Ellen Engelson Marson of *Proyecciones sobre la novela* (1997), a collection of essays on the contemporary Spanish and Latin American novel. She has published articles and essays on contemporary Spanish and Latin American literature. She serves as Program Chairperson and Chair of the Women's Colloquium for the International Institute in Spain.